MORALITY WARS

*How Empires, the Born-Again,
and the Politically Correct
Do Evil in the Name of Good*

CHARLES DERBER
WITH YALE R. MAGRASS

Paradigm Publishers
Boulder • London

Copyright © 2010 by Paradigm Publishers

Published in the United States by Paradigm Publishers, 3360 Mitchell Lane, Suite E, Boulder, Colorado 80301 USA.

Paradigm Publishers is the trade name of Birkenkamp & Company, LLC, Dean Birkenkamp, president and publisher.

Library of Congress Cataloging-in-Publication Data

Derber, Charles.
  Morality wars : how empires, the born again, and the politically correct do evil in the name of good / Charles Derber, with Yale R. Magrass.
    p. cm.
  Includes bibliographical references and index.
  ISBN 978-1-59451-512-5 (hardcover : alk. paper)
  ISBN 978-1-59451-513-2 (pbk. : alk. paper) 1. Political ethics—United States.
2. United States—Politics and government—Moral and ethical aspects. I. Magrass, Yale R. II. Title.
  JK468.E7D47 2008
  172.0973—dc22

                                                              2007050055

Printed and bound in the United States of America on acid-free paper that meets the standards of the American National Standard for Permanence of Paper for Printed Library Materials.

Designed and Typeset by Straight Creek Bookmakers.

14 13 12 11 10   1 2 3 4 5

MORALITY WARS

OTHER BOOKS BY CHARLES DERBER

The Wilding of America, 4th ed. (2006)
"*The Wilding of America* holds the glass up to our time, and one winces at the likeness."
　　　　　—JACK BEATTY, *Atlantic Monthly* and *On Point* political analyst at NPR

Hidden Power (2005)
"*Hidden Power* is the must-read book of the year. Buy three copies, at least, because you'll want to share a few with friends, and will never want to part with your own well-marked-up copy."
　　　　　—THOM HARTMANN, best-selling author and host of *Air America*

Hidden Power was selected as one of the top three current events books by the Independent Book Publishers Association.

Regime Change Begins at Home (2004)
"Derber provides a penetrating and compelling analysis of why this particular regime's days are numbered."
　　　　　—JULIET SCHOR, author of *The Overworked American* and *Born to Buy*

People before Profit (2003)
"Professor Derber's impressive analysis is an important contribution to the ongoing worldwide debate about globalization."
　　　　　—SENATOR EDWARD KENNEDY

The Pursuit of Attention (2000)
"Competition and individualism in America are fresh topics in his hands, and he works out a theory of great interest."
　　　　　—RICHARD SENNETT, author of *Hidden Injuries of Class*
　　　　　and *The Corrosion of Character*

Corporation Nation (2000)
"A work of generation imagination … and a sober plan of action for Americans committed to a truly just and equitable social order."
　　　　　—JONATHAN KOZOL, author of *Amazing Grace* and *Savage Inequalities*

Power in the Highest Degree (1990) coauthored with William Schwartz and Yale R. Magrass
"An excellent guide to understanding the system of Mandarin capitalism … and its wide-ranging human consequences."
　　　　　—NOAM CHOMSKY, author of *Perilous Power* (2006)

To Elena, my anchor and love (from Charles Derber)

To Anna, for her love and support (from Yale Magrass)

Contents

Acknowledgments

Charles Derber and Yale Magrass developed the ideas for this book together. The argument grew out of our many hours of conversation, mutual reflection, and shared research and analysis. Derber did the writing.

We want to thank, first, Dean Birkenkamp, the founder of Paradigm Publishing. We are fortunate to have a publisher who is intellectually engaged, willing to risk controversy, and generous with his time and spirit. Many thanks, Dean, for your support and for your humanity.

Derber wants to thank David Karp and John Williamson—colleagues and friends who keep me going with humor, intellectual stimulation, and generous attention.

Derber also wishes to thank most Elena Kolesnikova, who made a major contribution to this book. Elena edited and transformed the entire manuscript, creating a new flow and coherence. Her contributions have made her a full co-conspirator in this project. Elena, thank you for your inspired work on this project and for being my beautiful, feisty partner who warms hearth and heart.

Introduction: When Right Is Wrong
Why Immoral Morality Is Epidemic in America

In the summer of 2005, Jane McGonigal, a doctoral student in performance studies at the University of California, launched the "Ministry of Reshelving Project." Along with at least one hundred other "reshelving ministers," her goal was to reshelf George Orwell's classic novel *1984* from the fiction to the nonfiction sections of all bookstores in all fifty states. In the main Borders bookstore of Boston, our own city, a "minister" reshelved Orwell's book in the political science section, right next to a book called *Inside the Mind of Bush*.[1]

McGonigal had gotten the idea to reshelf *1984* when a friend had casually commented that the police state of Orwell's imagination—in which Big Brother used omnipresent telescreens to watch you, employed "thought police" from the Ministry of Truth to monitor your thinking, and invented Newspeak to control your very language so that you couldn't think heretical ideas—had now come to pass. Within a week of McGonigal coming up with the idea, more than fifty reshelving ministers filtered into bookstores from California to Kentucky to New York, took *1984* from the literature section, and moved it into the current events or political science sections.

Indeed, Orwell was telling us something important about our own society. Big Brother ruled through terror, but he ruled in the name of truth and morality. The Ministries of Truth and Love, and the high moral dogma they plastered on every telescreen, kept Big Brother in power. It was his unquestionable moral authority—and the unchallengeable goodness of Oceania, the Empire he ruled—that made *1984* so maddeningly persuasive and so relevant to us today.

In this book, we argue that America is increasingly ruled through a system of "immoral morality," something similar to—but with important differences from—the mass propaganda of Orwell's Oceania. American immoral morality wraps the increasingly unaccountable power of American leaders in a cloak of moral and spiritual truth. Political and religious leaders of both the Republican and Democratic parties propagate this immoral morality, a vision that accepts, on faith, the core values and special destiny of America. We have an American Ideological Apparatus—our own more informal version of the Ministries of Truth and Love—to enforce these beliefs. All of this allows ordinary Americans to question certain wars and politicians and to enjoy freedoms unknown in Oceania, but not to question the deeper goodness of America itself.

Our aim is to define immoral morality, show its three main forms in the United States, and explain how it keeps leaders in power and the gears of society churning smoothly. Immoral morality plays a key role in American culture and politics. While it is not new, a variety of historical circumstances have turned immoral morality into an American epidemic, touching every American and every feature of American life.

Americans started rereading Orwell's classic today because of the intransigence of the George W. Bush administration and its seeming slide toward a form of Big Brotherism in America. But the epidemic of immoral morality was growing before Bush arrived, and it has not disappeared now that he has left office. Immoral morality has a long history in America and is now entrenched throughout the nation, both in red and blue states. It goes well beyond politics itself, and it shapes the culture and identity of Americans in all aspects of their lives. Yet, there is also hope. As we show later, conditions for new values are emerging from catastrophes that now threaten to engulf America as well as the entire planet.

The George W. Bush administration—and its legacy already permeating the Obama administration—is just a starting point for the study of American immoral morality today. It illuminates what immoral morality is, how it is shaping American politics and culture, and how it could take us in the direction of Orwell's nightmarish dystopia. The Bush administration was one of the most moralistic in U.S. history, while carrying out many of the most harmful and unethical practices of any presidency, lying about the reasons to go to war in Iraq, approving torture, and coddling the rich at the expense of the poor. Moreover, Bush carried out his wars and pro-rich policies *in the very name of values and God.* The war was to spread "God's gift of liberty," the torture was to protect civilization from "barbarians," and pro-rich economics was to promote prosperity for all.[2] These are all examples of principles used explicitly in the service of immorality.

We define immoral morality as principles and beliefs that help justify socially harmful or unethical behavior or policies. Very often, immoral morality is used to gain or retain power. Sometimes it is used to get or keep wealth. Sometimes it is used to punish or humiliate others in the name of developing their character or moral fiber. Whenever principled arguments are made to disguise or justify any form of exploitation, oppression, abuse, intolerance, suppression of speech, dissent, or other unethical acts, it constitutes a form of immoral morality.

It is one thing to do evil, another to do evil in the name of good. Both are destructive. But immoral morality involves a special warping of the moral fabric. Since it uses values to advance evil, it undermines the credibility of all values. People who simply do selfish or bad things without moralizing them can end up strengthening the moral fabric because when society identifies and punishes the wrongdoer, the understanding of morality is reinforced. But people who successfully carry out immoral acts in the name of values blur the line between morality and immorality, undermining confidence in ethical codes and eroding the credibility of all principles. Unchallenged and unchecked immoral morality is the fastest ticket to moral breakdown.

With the rise of the Religious Right and the exploits of the highly moralistic Reagan-Bush Jr. regime, as well as the influence of politically correct dogmatists on both Left and Right, the alarm rings. The Religious Right and Republican political leaders say they are driven by values and God, but then they plunged the nation into illegal and unethical wars and social policies in the name of lofty principles. Politically correct moralists on the Left as well as the Right seek power or status in the name of truth. They have propagated a kind of moral doublethink that obscures the real nature of the crisis in American values. It is a moral breakdown orchestrated by those decrying the collapse in values that is now engulfing the nation.

The new crisis of immoral morality contaminates personal life as well as politics. The immoral moralists of everyday life are not just the leading preachers from the pulpits or the halls of government. They are the "everyman" or "everywoman" moralists—and you can recognize them by their paternalism. Many of them may take their moralism from the official preachers of truth and love, but many operate from their own personal pulpits. Many are not as closely connected to official power as the snoops and moral busybodies in Orwell's Oceania. They are the annoying friends, spouses, or parents who are always telling you what to do in the name of helping you. They control with the guise of concern or love. It is the kind of morality in personal life that can drive people literally mad, since the double message of control and love can quickly break down a person's clarity about what is real and what is good.

Such personal immoral morality has much in common—and can overlap—with the escalating epidemic of immoral morality in politics. Political leaders—and their allies in the church, media, schools, and the business world—are using moral justifications to gain power and pursue oppressive policies. Religious Right leaders pronounce a "decline in moral values" that justifies their own dangerous influences on politics and society. Corporate leaders—such as the CEO of Coca-Cola writing under the banner "Things go Better with Social Justice"[3]—are advertising their social responsibility while they lead us into an insecure and inequitable global economy. This is not at all new in politics. Far from it. But it has risen to a level of almost unbearable intensity.

The Bush Jr. administration created a new perfect storm of immoral morality, one still brewing with different characteristics than earlier cycles and peaks of the phenomenon. It involves three moral stories: one of Empire, a second of the Born-Again, and a third of the Politically Correct. The Empire story claims that the United States has a moral obligation to go to war in order to spread democracy and protect the world against a new breed of barbarians. The Born-Again story argues against new rights and equalities for women, gays, immigrants, and minorities in the name of restoring traditional values. The Politically Correct story seeks to silence debate in the name of truth and purity.

Each of these stories has a long history. But the simultaneous intensification of them all in America is the first of several reasons why we are now facing a new "category five" moral storm that is capable of blowing apart our moral fabric, just as Hurricane Katrina did with New Orleans. The Empire, Born-Again, and Politically Correct versions of immoral morality each carry their own dangers. But when they all rise together, they carry a tremendous wallop that's capable of undermining the whole American moral order.

A second factor contributing to the new crisis involves America's special place as the most powerful nation ever on earth. *American global power—or hegemony—is the root cause of its immoral morality.* While the United States has long been an empire, the collapse of European empires after World War II opened a new stage of American world dominance. This necessarily gave rise to evolving moral stories that would bathe that unaccountable power in a lofty moral and spiritual glow. Moreover, America's military, political, and technological prowess that arose after World War II allowed it to propagate its moral stories with a new and extreme force across the planet. The fact that these stories have taken a new form, more nuanced and sophisticated than in earlier eras, and the fact that they are shrouded in genuinely more progressive morals on race, gender, and other moral issues, only adds to the danger both to Americans and to the rest of the world.

A third factor involves the extent to which stories of immoral morality are now propagated by liberals and the Left as well as the Right. Historically, the Right and conservatives have owned and told the three stories described here, and they are still the main carriers. But today's liberals, including Democratic Party leaders such as Hillary Clinton and Barack Obama, support the core of the Empire story, albeit with different moral rhetoric and strategies. This includes most liberals who oppose the Iraq war but support U.S. "leadership" or hegemony. The Left, meanwhile, spews forth its own political correctness on gender and race. This means that immoral morality has spread like a virus across the American political spectrum, contaminating all forms of political morality. Our analysis challenges reigning American morals but does not offer complacency for liberal or Left dissenters who mirror some of the pathology of elites they critique. As discussed soon, our analysis is likely to surprise and distress many of our own compatriots in the Democratic Party and in Left social movements. But, as insiders, we have seen firsthand too many Left groups—from the student radicals of the 1960s to the identity politics movements of today—fall on the sword of their own moral purity. We write here not only from outrage at those who do not share our values, but also to caution and seriously critique many who do. Immoral morality has become an equal opportunity plague, although it has not touched all Americans and we see grounds for hope.

Some of this hope involves the relation of America to the rest of the world. America in no way monopolizes immoral morality, and part of the growing global moral crisis is that poisonous forms of immoral morality are spreading in non-Western civilizations. Many will, no doubt, see the rise of Islamic suicide bombing and broader Islamic extremism symbolized by Osama bin Laden and al-Qaeda as prime examples of immoral morality: murderous violence carried out in the name of liberation and God. Much of this behavior does signal the resurgence of horrifying forms of immoral morality throughout the world, and it is yet another reason for deep concern.

While we touch on these non-Western immoral moralities, our main analysis is centered on the United States. The United States is the world's sole superpower—and its moral stories carry far more force than those of any other nation. As Americans, we feel our first moral responsibility is to deal with the violence and immoral morality that America itself fuels in the name of goodness and God. Curing America's own crisis of immoral morality will not solve the moral crises of other civilizations, but it is the best place for Americans themselves to begin. Healing oneself—and doing no harm, especially in the name of good—is the first moral obligation not just in Hippocratic medicine but also in politics and life. Moreover, whatever capacity the United States has to abate the global storm can only be realized when it has quieted its own ill moral winds.

To speak of immoral morality immediately raises the question of how to distinguish it from more authentic values and principles. It is not difficult to see the doublethink of Orwell's Ministries of Truth and Love as a form of immoral morality. *It is morality with an official monopoly on the "values" of conversation: always right because it is controlled by the ruling elites and silences alternative or opposing principles.* And it is moral doublethink obviously created in the service of evil and official power, with social harm the clear end result.

Orwell's protagonist, Winston Smith, after years of toiling deep in the bowels of the Ministry of Truth, saw doublethink this way:

> His mind slid away into the labyrinthine world of doublethink. To know and not to know, to be conscious of complete truthfulness while telling carefully constructed lies, to hold simultaneously two opinions which cancelled out, knowing them to be contradictory and believing in both of them; to use logic against logic, to repudiate morality while laying claim to it, to believe that democracy was impossible and that the Party was the guardian of democracy; to forget whatever it was necessary to forget, then to draw it back at the moment when it was needed, and then promptly to forget it again.[4]

The most telling phrase is "to repudiate morality while laying claim to it." This captures the heart of immoral morality: doing socially harmful or unethical things in the name of values. In Oceania, Big Brother ran a terrorist empire as a form of moral inspiration—indeed, as a moral imperative.

Doublethink makes the moral justification of immorality possible by embracing contradictions: to be conscious of truth while telling lies and believing both. Doublethink is based on lies, but it is not only lies, and it is different than the deceit or manipulation of classic propaganda. The perpetrators believe fervently in their own morality and truth, even after they have constructed their lies; they view their lies as truth and their immorality as moral purity, even when they know they have prevaricated and manipulated. The whole doublethink process is so full of contradictions that "you had to become unconscious of the hypnosis you had just performed. Even to understand the word doublethink involved using doublethink."[5]

Immoral morality has similar contradictions. On the one hand, while immoral moralists lie, they can simultaneously believe in their own assertions and values. Most come to believe with great fervor, especially as contradictions between their professed principles and the harm or immorality of their conduct becomes more intense. The effect is to largely render unconscious the contradictions, so that immoral moralists will claim that there is no gap between their beliefs and their behavior. In this sense, immoral morality, while it is often intertwined with lies and the familiar manipulation or spin of Bush-world, can also be undertaken without any conscious deceit.

Perpetrators of immoral morality may persuade themselves that they are pursuing principled values. How, then, can we know whether their morality is immoral? Is it not a subjective matter of one person's morals versus someone else's? While, ultimately, there is an irreducible element of subjectivity, certain criteria offer a way to distinguish immoral morality, *the most important of which is that it always involves clear social harm done in the name of high principles or values.*

In saying this, we recognize that what you see as social harm is shaped by your values. For example, conservatives argue that liberal social welfare policies are socially harmful because they deny the poor the incentive to pull themselves up "by their own bootstraps." What liberals or the Left see as social good, conservatives view as a way of encouraging people to "wallow in their own misery," and to make bleeding heart liberals feel good about themselves. While conservatives do not use the term "immoral morality," they do see the whole enterprise of social welfare and the New Deal as doing evil in the name of good.

This example shows that personal values cannot be eliminated from a definition of immoral morality, which, as just noted, always has a subjective element. We would be succumbing to our own moral absolutism to say otherwise. That said, most people would agree that genocide, slavery, and imperial conquest are morally wrong and constitute social harm, even if these have been legalized—or sometimes made obligatory—in many societies. What we describe in this book as social harm, and which becomes a defining attribute of immoral morality, is not absolutely objective but has achieved enough consensus around the world to be embodied in the United Nations Declaration of Human Rights, the most widely signed political covenant expressing near-universal agreement on basic social values.

Other markers that identify immoral morality include:

- *Moral double standards.* Immoral moralists apply one set of principles and values to themselves and another to everyone else.
- Moral intolerance. Immoral moralists seek to silence or repress people who express principles or values different than their own.
- Moral absolutism and literalism. Immoral moralists believe that there is one set of eternal values, often inscribed in a religious text, that cannot be questioned or reinterpreted by anyone, even though they have to make their own interpretations.

- Power-driven morality. Immoral moralists use principles and values to gain and sustain their own power.

The last criterion points to the intimate and especially important relation between immoral morality and power—our main concern in this book. Immoral morality is a weapon or an instrument of personal or political power, although it can also be used to gain or justify wealth and status or to simply satisfy sadistic or abusive personal needs. In this book, we focus mainly on morality that justifies political power. This form of immoral morality—*which can be defined as the use of high principles and values to seek, wield, and justify overweening and harmful state power*—is what we call *hegemonic morality*.

Such hegemonic morality is at the heart of the American political and moral crisis. As the United States has increased its global power, it has created a brand of hegemonic morality that rivals Orwell's Oceania in its intensity and madness. While this book is focused on moral discourse, our attention to it cannot be separated from the military and political power that gives rise to it. To analyze America's moral stories outside the context of America's vast global influence would be like studying the evolving symptoms of a lethal cancer without ever looking at the underlying tumor and disease process.

Immoral morality—and especially its hegemonic form—always has structural roots. Virtually all empires promote hegemonic morality and could not survive long without it. The more hegemonic the power, and the more exploitative its character, the more deeply rooted and taken-for-granted the hegemonic morality. It is the same in personal life: the more evil the conduct, the greater the need to justify it by clothing it in inspirational principles. The most hegemonic and abusive states must not only moralize their power but also create language and thought control that makes it impossible for the masses to see the social order as illegitimate.

Hegemony always requires moralization because it is inherently exploitative and unaccountable. Naked force—the barrel of a gun—can secure such power but not sustain it: only moral and spiritual stories captivating hearts and minds can do that. As hegemonic power grows, so, inevitably must the moral stories we describe in this book.

As noted earlier, American global hegemony entered a new peak phase after World War II once the European empires that had dominated much of the world for several centuries self-destructed in two world wars. This left the United States as the sole superpower and the only global hegemon. While the Soviet Union was treated by American elites as a new hegemonic evil power that justified U.S. expansion, the Soviet Union never, despite its vast nuclear arsenal, significantly eroded U.S. hegemony after the post–World War II collapse of European empires.

America's global hegemony, the underpinning of its evolving immoral morality, has gone through a series of modern phases. The rise of transnational corporations, which sealed America's control of half the world's Gross Domestic Product in the 1950s, deepened the economic roots of hegemony. These corporations aggressively pursued new global markets and profits, intensifying the state's commitment to hegemony. In the 1960s and '70s, though, the American defeat in Vietnam was a critical setback to the hegemonic agenda, not only weakening American power but also catalyzing a "Vietnam Syndrome" that created major new obstacles to sustaining it. America's moral stories evolved to manage the new antiwar sentiment among Americans themselves, as well as the growing discontent in the developing world to American power.

Beginning with President Ronald Reagan, the American empire "struck back," fueled by Reagan's militarism, the collapse of the Soviet Union and the end of the Cold War, and what was perceived as a successful war—Operation Desert Storm—in the Persian Gulf by President George H. W. Bush. The first Bush president was photographed at the conclusion of that war, jumping jubilantly and saying "we kicked the Vietnam Syndrome once and for all."[6] The events of September 11, 2001, would also help eliminate the remnants of antiwar sensibility in the population, but the catastrophe of the second Bush president's war in Iraq created a potential tipping point toward American hegemonic decline. The anxiety among American elites about American power, as well as the anxiety among the American people about their jobs, education, and health care, required the explosion of immoral morality seen under the second Bush administration to calm the waters by moralizing America's increasingly tenuous and violent hegemonic order.

While this book focuses on the moral stories, these twists and turns in American hegemony underlie everything we describe. American hegemony itself, and its roots in the corporate and political system, has been widely described already. Our focus in this book is to show how the hegemonic developments have given rise to continuously evolving moral stories and the storm of immoral morality that's corrupting our entire social order.

While America's hegemonic power has escalated globally to produce the new storm, it is not new and has always given rise to immoral morality. Historically, such morality underpins the worst forms of American power and order. Think of the slave South, one of the most moralistic American regimes. Southern moralists filled Southern churches and town halls with ringing affirmations of the goodness of slavery. One Southern author wrote: "Although they are inferior, we took them to our homes and taught them Christianity, and how it protects, supports, and civilizes him. By taking them away from the savages of Africa, giving them a religion, and providing them with benefits, they have more liberty than a free laborer of the North could experience. Our Negroes are not only better off as to physical comfort than free laborers, but their moral condition is better."[7] Southerners explicitly described slavery as moral education, and thus it was an unselfish service or obligation that slave owners owed their slaves: "Slavery Christianizes, protects, supports, and civilizes him; that it governs him far better than free laborers at the North are governed … Never before has the black race of Central Africa, from the dawn of history to the present day, attained a condition so civilized and so improved, not only physically, but morally and intellectually."[8]

Such Southern moralism helped keep the Southern white plantation owners in power and made it extremely difficult for Southerners to challenge slavery on principled grounds. It stripped Southern whites of the moral language for even imagining that the slave state's goodness and values were immoral. Since force and terror are insufficient and inefficient for sustaining most exploitative regimes, virtually all turn to this approach—which Orwell called "reality control," involving immoral moralism.

In the early 1920s, the Italian political theorist Antonio Gramsci spent years trying to understand how the dictator Benito Mussolini captured power and the public imagination. Gramsci concluded that the answer lay less in arms than in moral argument. In his years in Mussolini's prisons, Gramsci wrote his *Prison Notebooks* that spelled out how such "controlled insanity" was created. He called it a theory of "legitimation"—explaining how vesting tyrannical power with moral sanctity was central to rallying masses of people behind Mussolini, who, like Hitler—as we show in Part Two—was a charismatic hypermoralist.[9]

Most leaders of great empires—from the Egyptian pharaohs and Roman emperors, to Lenin, Stalin, and Mao Tse-tung—have been, like Hitler, notorious immoral moralists who knew how to bathe their conquests in moral or spiritual legitimations. Conquests that simply plundered without resort to moralistic ideals seldom lasted long, as in the case of Genghis Khan, who proclaimed unapologetically: "The greatest happiness is to vanquish enemies, to chase them before you, to rob them of their wealth, to see those dear to them bathed in tears, to clasp to your bosoms their wives and daughters."[10] Such open embrace of evil is rare and rarely works.

The United States today is not George Orwell's *1984*, nor is it a slave state or Mussolini's fascism or Hitler's Nazi regime. But hegemonic immoral morality does not appear only in the most dictatorial or totalitarian states. The British Empire, for example, created a spectrum of immoral morality in the eighteenth and nineteenth centuries, many elements of which have strongly influenced the United States. In Part One, we track the evidence indicating how powerfully the British hegemonic story shaped the U.S. approach. And we show that virtually all empires, both relatively benign and horrifyingly evil, have come up with their own paradigms of immoral morality, although America's version has its own particularly seductive features.

Because the values propagated by immoral moralists often have long-sacred legacies in the nation, they can strike a genuine deep chord in sectors of the population. Values thus gain wide acceptance and legitimacy not only because of the lies or the cleverness of the spin but also because they resonate to long-established national and religious moral codes that offer a sense of security and identity. Immoral morality is often used as propaganda, but its credibility arises not just from lies and spin, nor even the threat of force, but also from its resonance with the nation's moral heritage. For example, the long-standing conceits that America is a divinely inspired "shining city on the hill," with a Manifest Destiny to lead the world helps explain the current American resonance to ideas of American goodness and our moral obligation to "spread freedom" and "protect civilization."

The greater subtlety of immoral morality, its resonance with American traditions, and the greater freedom to challenge the state's version of it makes the American approach even more potent and dangerous. For one thing, if the immoral morality is sincere and resonates with many ordinary Americans, it becomes far more difficult to define or reveal as illegal or unethical. And since the elites who promote it are often true believers, the immoral morality cannot be dismissed simply as an outright fabrication of the work of "lying liars."

In states that brutally repress any free media, or in ones that crush and kill dissenters—including Fascist or Soviet-style Communist states—thought control becomes more evasive. It is easier to recognize that the official media and morality are propaganda and lies. But in a system that permits relative freedoms of expression and dissent, and tolerates some degree of open debate about even the most fundamental moral axioms, it can be easier to persuade the masses that the liberty and goodness proclaimed by the state may actually be real. The velvet glove is always preferable to the iron fist. In this sense, Orwell may have misunderstood that the requirements of the most powerful forms of immoral morality do not require the dictatorial extremes of Oceania. There are more Winston Smiths in America than in Orwell's Oceania, and many of them will never come to love Big Brother, as Winston did. But for the majority of Americans, the real freedom to question many of the moral assumptions and policies of the state make it harder to see or challenge the core of America's immoral morality.

A personal example illustrates the grip of hegemonic morality on American emotions—and makes clear it is no academic matter. On my (Derber's) campus, the administration invited Secretary of State Condoleezza Rice to receive an honorary degree. It was May 2006, and Iraq was exploding in suicide bombs, sectarian violence, and anti-American insurgency. I joined a group of faculty, led by the Jesuits on campus against the war, which protested Rice's selection. But when I appeared on the Fox television program *The O'Reilly Factor,* hosted by Bill O'Reilly, and gave a short and modest argument for why a Jesuit institution might oppose giving an honorary degree to a spokesperson for a war that's been rejected by the Pope, the Jesuit order, and many non-Catholic students and faculty committed to social justice, I got scores of hate-mail messages like this one: "Yes, we saw you on TV. How dare you insult our wonderful president and his marvelous secretary of state. Who do you imagine YOU are? Just a phony worthless moron ... and the sooner you are kicked out the better.... You are a disgrace to Christ and to the American people. —*A World War II Vet and Catholic Patriot par excellence.*" Another wrote: "I am ashamed that people such as yourself live in this great country, which gives you the freedom to speak without persecution. It's guys such as you who are misguided, ignorant, and lowly. If all professors at Boston College think like you, the school is a disaster. As a former marine and retired chemical engineer, if I were to cross your path, I would puke. You do not deserve to live in this country."

The rage, here, suggests the depth of moral sensibilities that were offended. Simply to question the legitimacy of the secretary of state's appearance was an offense against the nation. It hinted at a weakening of the moral glue that keeps an imperial nation together: the moral authority of our leaders, the goodness of the nation, and its foreign policy. On national television, I raised questions that were not acceptable, such as whether Rice was patriotic and whether the motivations of the United States in the region were good. My hate mail came from people brimming with the righteous rage of immoral morality who cursed me and vowed to silence me in the name of their deepest values.

Of course, not all Americans agreed; all empires have their heretics and all nations their dissenters. One Boston College alumna, a nun, Sister Megan Rice, with a master's degree in biology, tore up her diploma when she read that the university was awarding Secretary of State Rice an honorary degree. She wrote this:

I had had hopes that attitudes at BC had changed when I discovered large contingents of students attending the School of America Vigils these past few years since returning from Nigeria in 2003. It is sad to think that the present Administration at BC cannot learn from the insights and inspirations of its students and numerous faculty members who rightfully speak by their lives for justice and compassion and above all, peace, in our suffering world as did their leader and servant, Jesus of Nazareth, with a similar Empire in his day.[11]

The differences between Sister Megan Rice and the angry veterans who sent me postcards is one expression of the "morality wars." Sister Rice views the veterans and the Boston College administration as blinded by false patriotism and regards Condoleezza Rice, as I suggested on O'Reilly's show, as unpatriotic or even a war criminal. The administration and veterans look at the same person as an inspiring patriot. All feel strongly about our moral views.

In this book, we bear the burden of showing that we are not just expressing our own moral sentiments, but that we are engaged also in challenging our own values and the movements that carry them. We will argue that American hegemonic policy, carried out not just by Bush but also by both Republican and Democratic presidents throughout much of American history, is a very serious and enduring form of immoral morality. In showing that Democrats are complicit, we argue that hegemonic morality rages on all sides of the political spectrum.

While our biographies inevitably enter into our analysis, we offer, as noted earlier, a serious critique in this book of the Left as well as the Right. We have long been part of the Left and the cultural tradition associated with the "Borscht Belt," the secularized Jewish communities that made a tradition of being self-critical, epitomized by comedians such as Woody Allen. A generation ago, socialists and other Leftists would congregate and vacation in the Borscht Belt resorts of New York's beautiful Catskill Mountains. Through its influence on the media, Borscht Belt culture has diffused throughout much of America, breeding resentment on the Right, especially in the Bible Belt. The conflict between the Borscht Belt and the Bible Belt helps define what the morality wars are all about.

But while we strongly critique the Right and the Bible Belt as sources of immoral morality, we also critique the Left and the Borscht Belt as deeply scarred by their own moral traditions. Immoral morality has flourished on both the Right and the Left. We do not hold back in our indictments of such morality wherever it comes from, and we argue that for liberals and those of the Left, it is suicidal to deny the pathology because it contradicts the very premises of critical thought and justice on which the Left is based.

We have divided the book into three parts, each devoted to one of the three main American stories of immoral morality. In Part One, we look at the morals of empire. All through history, empires have survived through the seduction and charisma of their lofty principles. In this first part, we look in some detail at the immoral morality of the Roman and British empires, which created the beliefs and religious templates of immoral morality that now flourish in America. Using Rome and Britain, we show how powerfully empire morality has permeated American thinking, how far back it goes in American history, and how it functions today. Empire—or hegemony—is the political religion of America, with millions of Americans, including those who oppose the Iraq war and much of the Bush administration's foreign policies, being true believers. The core doctrine of this immoral morality is the goodness of America as a nation and its obligation to serve as the "leader of the free world." A newly fashioned and seductive version of this hegemonic morality is enshrined in the "war on terror," and we look at the reasons why so many Americans resonate to it.

In Part Two, we look at "born-again" nations, those based on stories that have two chapters: decay and rebirth. Born-again stories often coexist with empire but are a different discourse. One version lies at the heart of fascism and Nazism as ideological systems, and created its greatest historical tragedy in Hitler's Third Reich. In the United States, a very different version of born-again moralism has held great authority. It reflects the long history of the born-again story in American history, one that has led today not to fascism but to what some commentators call theo-corpocracy. It is embodied most deeply in the Republican Party and the Religious Right, and it is the political driver of the culture wars. While the Religious Right may be sincere in its moral beliefs, its political morality is saturated with the moral intolerance, absolutism, and other contradictions highlighted above. In the wake of 9/11, the born-again narrative combined with empire morality to create an American dogma and power-breeding resentment around the world.

In Part Three, we look at the politically correct (PC) epidemic on both Left and Right. PC is a nonpartisan strategy for wielding power in the name of moral purity. Historically, the Stalinist Left as well as the Fascist Right embodied real-world versions of a PC nightmare. Today, PC is helping create its own crisis of immoral morality in the United States. The American Right has dominated the culture wars by its attack on Left PC, a very real disorder that contradicts the core Left morality of free and critical thinking and has done harm to the larger society while proving to be nearly suicidal to the Left itself. But the Right has conveniently ignored its own PC, which is far more entrenched and has the official backing of the state. While Left PC—about politically correct speech and attitudes toward women, gays, and minorities—is in the news all the time, the Right PC about capitalism and America is relatively invisible, a testimonial to its status as "common sense" that no sane American would question. Bush Jr. resurrected the idea that war is peace—his way of moralizing the war on terrorism—and it is a form of Right PC in which millions of Americans have placed their faith.

The current realities are bad enough, and the moral storm is still gathering strength. New 9/11-style attacks could bring us to a nightmare worse than we want to imagine. Nonetheless, other historical conditions are leading in an opposite direction and offer grounds for hope. Ironically, such hopeful change lies in the rise of adversity, with the country facing the most serious economic crisis since the Great Depression. The Great Collapse helped elect President Barack Obama, who we show in Part Four could be driven by the economic crisis and his own morality toward a new U.S. global role. Looming planetary catastrophes involving nuclear proliferation and global warming could transform the consciousness of both Americans and everyone else on the earth. This is another form of perfect storm that would initially create alarm and despair, especially in America itself. But it could lead to one of those rare awakenings that might, in the end, change our course, plunging us into barbarism or helping us find a higher moral ground.

PART I

Empire and the Morality of Winning

1

How to Be Chosen

What the Roman and British Empires Taught America

What enterprise that an enlightened community may attempt is nobler and more profitable than the reclamation from barbarism of fertile regions and large populations? To give peace to warring tribes, to administer justice where all was violence, to strike the chains off the slave, to draw the richness from the soil, to plant the earliest seeds of commerce and learning, to increase in whole peoples their capacities for pleasure and diminish their chances for pain—what more beautiful ideal or more valuable reward can inspire human effort?

—*Winston Churchill*[1]

Orwell's land of Oceania was one of three world empires in *1984*. Big Brother ruled the empire through the Ministries of Truth and Love, which invested the empire with absolute Moral Truth. People supported the Empire of Oceania because they lacked the thought or language to question its moral purity. They believed fervently in Oceania's goodness.

Orwell was on to something profound about empires. Virtually all empires have conquered, ruled, and killed in the name of a higher moral creed, a classic immoral morality that justifies war in the name of peace, conquest in the name of self-defense, and occupation in the name of civilization or God. While empires differ in many specifics, all purport to bring sacred order and defend secular honor and civilization itself. Imperial leaders suggest that *empire is not just moral—it is a moral obligation*.

Empire morality—whether with ancient Rome, the British Empire, or today's American superpower—is seductive. Empire morality can express partial truths, and it can bring some of the benefits that it proclaims. But it beautifully exemplifies the defining attributes of immoral morality. It

dresses up self-interested behavior—notably seeking and wielding hegemonic or dominating power—as virtue. It is selective, holding up one set of
values for itself and one for other nations. It is hypocritical, using brutality
while preaching civic virtue, practicing coercion while preaching freedom,
and waging war in the name of peace or offense in the name of defense. It
is inconsistent, applying its moral codes when it chooses. Its lofty rhetoric
disguises and distracts from its ruthless behavior.

In this and the next chapter, we want to look more closely at the moral
stories told by empires, notably those of Rome, Britain, and the United
States. These stories are classic forms of hegemonic morality, and they
operate with remarkable force and consistency in each of these three cases.
There are many unique features of the United States as a hegemon, or
dominant power, since it is, after all, a democratic and noncolonial nation, and it instinctively denies its very existence as an empire. But like
Rome and Britain, American hegemony arose because of its capacity to
exercise coercive power, and because it offers a compelling moral story. It
is a story that originates with the birth of the nation, as a "city on the hill."
The moral claims are very high, involving the embodiment of God's will
and the spread of civilization's highest values. What is striking, despite
America's unique conception of itself, is how its own claims track that of
earlier empires. Despite the widespread questioning of the Vietnam and
Iraq wars, classical Roman and British imperial moral axioms have taken
root in America. Questioning of tactics and strategies of war—even the
question of whether a particular war is a mistake—is tolerated, as in earlier
empires. But the core beliefs of America's imperial story, largely derived
from Rome and Britain, are not open to question: its fundamental goodness as a nation, and the principled character of its global aspirations and
power. These beliefs are seared deeply into the American character.

Rome, Imperial Morality, and the Constantine Syndrome

Rome is the prototype of empires of Western civilization. The Romans
wrote the moral script used by many Western empires up to the present
U.S. version. Moral claims sustained Roman power. Today's images of
Rome come mostly from Hollywood. In the film *Gladiator*, Russell Crowe
plays the character Maximus, who is a former general turned slave. And he
confronts emperors and their families who are a bloody lot of killers, assas-
sins, and schemers. Maximus is the only moral man. The emperors do not

waste time with moral homilies, and live and die by the sword. The whole Roman chronicle collapses into something like the reality show *Survivor*, where the only morality is "each man for himself" and "kill or be killed."

Yet despite the undeniable brutality of empires and the decadence of many famous emperors, including Caligula, Nero, Domitian, and Caracalla, Rome survived as much by its moral claims as its swords. Some Roman chroniclers refer to "Rome under Better Emperors 96–180," a period from Trajan to Marcus Aurelius and Hadrian, who were moral philosophers as well as emperors.[2] And there were the great moral essayists of the Roman age, from Cicero to Plutarch to Epictetus, who developed philosophies of restraint, stoicism, love, and cooperation. But these are not the forms of Roman imperial morality to which we refer. Instead, we are thinking of principles claimed by Rome as inherent in the empire itself. Rome asserted that its empire embodied the highest civic values and that the gods themselves blessed the empire. Empire was a moral obligation even for Rome at its most brutal, and it offered Romans their own winning team.

The moral story of Rome falls into two chapters, each with a seminal code of immoral morality that would be absorbed by later Western empires. One is the script of the pagan Roman Empire, from Caesar to Constantine, a secular code associated with civic virtue and the spread of Western civilization. The second is the script of the Christian Roman Empire, the code we call the Constantine Syndrome, that would eventually meld with the Chivalric Code of the high Middle Ages and offer divine moral justifications for the crusades and later Western empires from Spain to the United States. Both of these codes contained and required a view of honorable defense, a third "security" or military code that ensured protection of the chosen through the strategy embraced by the most powerful militaries (and sports teams) even today: "the best defense is a good offense."

The Pagan Roman Empire

Imperial pagan Rome began with Julius and Augustus Caesar and ended when Constantine wedded the empire to Christianity in 311 AD. A perfect storm gave rise to the greatest empire of antiquity. In the first century AD, an expansive Roman economy and agriculture required more land, resources, and slaves. Economics and greed are always driving forces of empire, and Rome was no exception. A growing military establishment fed Rome's appetites and was empowered by the Roman high technologies of roads, waterways, and warfare. At the same time, the Roman aristocracy that had governed Republican Rome through the Senate and the Forum was fracturing. The new economic imperatives of growth, the collapse of the existing political order, and the military's new capabilities and ascendancy came together in a big bang to produce an empire, a solution to Rome's internal and external crises.

An empire is defined as an alpha-nation, realizing its power and acting on it for its own ends. But if raw power and greed create and define an empire, they do not thenselves ensure and sustain it. Only immoral morality can do that.

An empire's immoral morality typically comes from a founding myth that defines the birth and destiny of a chosen people. Rome's creation myth was a synthesis of Mars and Athena, the God of war and the Goddess of wisdom and civilization. This Roman mythical invention recurs for more than two thousand years, up to the neoconservatives and President George W. Bush, who offered a hawkish morality of Mars to bring the Athena of democracy and civilization to the Muslim world.

Mars is Rome's creator. Romulus and Remus, the two brothers who founded the city, were Mars's sons, abandoned by him, and then nursed by a she-wolf, a favored animal of Mars. The brothers were possessed of Mars's war powers, and their martial temperaments led to Romulus killing Remus, attracting outlaws and warriors to the new city, and taking the Sabine women for himself and his fellow warriors. There is no disguising the spirit and fury of war in the founding story of Rome.

But in Virgil's *Aeneid,* an ode to the rule of Augustus Caesar, who was considered the first great Roman emperor, power and warfare take on a profoundly moral character. Virgil writes: "(Augustus) shall be born, who shall limit his empire with the ocean, his glory with the stars.... Then wars shall cease and the rough ages soften. The dread steel-clenched gates of war shall be shut fast."[3]

In a few lines, Virgil turns Mars and his war powers into *the policeman of peace.* Virgil patriotically announces that only the martial power of Rome can guarantee the peace of the world. Thus emerges the Pax Romana, a moral peace born of war. In Orwell's *1984,* the reigning mantra is "War is Peace." Rome created the first great immoral morality based on this slogan. War is great—the foundation of morality—because it is the means of peace. It is only war that can end war, the immoral morality still guiding empire today.

Embedded in this story of Mars is the melding of self-defense with empire. Without the empire, Rome and the civilized world would be under constant threat from the barbarians and, after Constantine, the infidels. Security required taking out the barbarians on their own playing field, before they got to Rome. This ancient "security" code—defense requires offense—becomes an underpinning of empire from Augustus and Virgil to George W. Bush.

But if Mars is the martial god fathering Rome, his marriage with Athena, a symbol of Athens, was necessary to sustain Rome's moral authority. Athens was the crucible of Western civilization and Rome's imperial ancestor, as much emphasized by Virgil in the *Aeneid.* As Roman scholar Wilfred McClay writes, Virgil blended Rome's "homegrown story with the Greek import," embedding the Roman Empire in the golden aura of Greek civilization.[4]

Rome had to claim Athena, along with Mars, as critical to its own founding story. If father Mars created the founding moral story of "War is Peace," mother Athena showed that Roman peace (Athena was also a goddess of military victory as well as wisdom) would mean the rule of wise civic virtue and the triumph of civilization over barbarism. Ironically, the role of Athens in Rome's imperial morality shows that the origins of Western civilization melded the history of Republics and empire in the same revered philosophical soil of classical Greece.

Athens symbolized all things civilized, but Rome had to show that Athena now favored Rome, whose martial temperament could bring civilized values to all the world, proving that those not within the empire could not be fully civilized and would henceforth be known as "barbarians," a theme still evident with empires today. By enslaving the barbarians, Romans were bringing them the freedom of civilized life. A Roman slave was at last free of the moral shackles of barbarism, free as a slave to imbibe the great moral values of Roman civilization. Athens thus added to Rome's founding moral story the Orwellian twist that "slavery is freedom."

The pagan empire of Julius and Augustus Caesar drew its morality from the Roman Republic, which drew heavily on Greek gods and the Athenian ideals of civic virtue. Rome conceived itself as a "city on seven hills," favored by the gods after Athens to create a chosen people who would embody the highest values. The pagan Romans made their morals universal, part of natural law and the design of the gods, presenting them as *"universally valid, as if inscribed in the natural ways of the world."* As two Roman scholars write: "The Roman political imagination imbued the city of Rome with a special significance as a place possessing its own spiritual gravity.... This gave its institutions and governing practices an assurance of their ethical rightness and superiority over vanquished enemies."[5]

There are a few core elements here. One is that Romans are a chosen people, possessed of the universal values on which all of civilization should rest. The empire emerged as the Republic crumbled, creating social dislocation and a vacuum of identity and community. Julius and Augustus, even as they sealed the fate of the dying Republic, gave Romans a renewed sense of their "chosen-ness," one that renewed the sense of belonging and community around a new state order, a new "winning team."

This new winning team, as highlighted by Virgil in the *Aeneid*, drew on Rome's inheritance of the Greek civilized virtues, as embodied in the Senate, the Forum, and Rome's remarkable legal order. A key theme is that the spread of Roman power meant the spread of justice and civilization itself. The Roman Empire would bring civic virtue and the rule of just law to all nations, and bring freedom to all "barbarians" beyond the imperial frontiers, while also restoring to all Romans a sense of community and moral superiority.

While Rome claimed universal values, it also permitted an ancient multiculturalism. While the empire required deference to core Roman values and to the emperor himself, it permitted local cultures and conquered peoples to retain many of their customs. Its pantheon of gods contributed to a tolerance that would erode under the monotheistic religion of Christian Rome.

We can summarize the pagan Roman Code as follows:

1. Rome, the city of seven hills, is destined by fate, fortune, and the gods to rule the world.
2. Rome's values are universal and represent the highest form of civilization.
3. Rome's values and majesty, embodied in the emperor, have their roots in ancient Greece, and the Roman people embody the rule of law, nobility, courage, wisdom, personal virtue, compassion, prosperity, and peace.
4. Rome has a moral obligation to spread these civilized values to all peoples, including barbarians and heathens.
5. Rome's greatness is shown also in its architecture, athleticism, recreation, and technology, which it will share with all people.
6. People worthy and loyal to the emperor can obtain Roman citizenship, regardless of their nation of birth.
7. Rome will respect the cultures of conquered peoples. All people are free to worship their own gods, as long as they bow down to Caesar as well. Indeed, Rome will incorporate the gods of conquered peoples in its own pantheon.
8. In return for the benefits of empire, Roman citizens, slaves, and subjects owe the emperor loyalty, obedience, and service, whether to the military or to their local rulers or owners.
9. Pax Romana is the only and best way to govern the world peacefully and spread civilization to all.

10. Rome's legions will be prepared to crush all people who defy its authority or resist its gifts. Rome's legions will also keep barbarians from its gates.

The great Roman writers could wax lyrical about empire as a moral blessing to the conquered and a moral obligation of the conquerors. The great Roman poet Ovid wrote:

There will be others to beat the breathing bronze with greater skill and grace,

So others too will draw out living faces from the marble,

Argue legal cases better, better trace the motions of the sky,

And so pronounce the cycles of the stars.

For you, O Roman, it is due to rule the peoples of your Empire.

These are your arts: TO IMPOSE PEACE AND MORALITY (our emphasis)

To spare the subject and subdue the proud.[6]

Ovid emphasizes that the Roman Empire is, most of all, a project of "peace and morality." This is a stark reminder that an ancient pantheon of gods, poets, and philosophers immortalized the immoral morality of empire. Empire existed to "impose" universal values and civic virtues, a concept that resurfaced nearly word for word in the Bush administration's occupation of Iraq.

The Christian Roman Empire

The pagan Roman Empire declined over centuries from military overstretch, political corruption, class warfare, confiscatory taxation, and economic depletion. But by the third century AD, despite internal warfare among scheming generals and emperors, growing revolts from the provinces, and increasingly destructive attacks from the barbarians on the periphery, the Roman Empire survived for two more centuries, but only with the help of a revolutionary new system of imperial morality. This new moral code—the Constantine Syndrome—survived the collapse of Rome itself and became a new foundation for empire in the Western world.

The Constantine Syndrome began with the Emperor Constantine, who embraced Christianity in 313 AD in one of the most famous and influential conversions in history. Like other emperors of his era, Constantine was mired in constant battles that sapped the empire. During the Battle of the Milvian Bridge, Constantine saw a miraculous vision, which was recounted in the famous text of Eusebius, an esteemed bishop and church historian who became one of Constantine's closest spiritual advisors and most important chroniclers.

> He said that about noon, when the day was already beginning to decline, he saw with his own eyes the trophy of a cross of light in the heavens, above the sun, and bearing the inscription, CONQUER BY THIS. At this sight he himself was struck with amazement, and his whole army also, which followed him on this expedition, and witnessed the miracle.[7]

Note that the vision of a "cross of light" instructed Constantine to "Conquer by this." But this was not a sign from the Mars of pagan Rome but from Jesus of the Christians who the Romans had been persecuting for centuries. From that moment, the Roman Empire would never be the same. Constantine felt that the pagan gods had failed the empire, but Jesus had assured it victory. Constantine believed that the future of the empire now rested on its divine sanction and mission from the Christian God. He immediately ordered the end of the persecution of the Christians and began to make Christianity the favored religion of the empire, vesting Christian officials with official powers. Henceforth, the empire would be seen as the instrument of divine will and would act to fulfill the commands of God. The empire would serve God and ensure that God's will be done on earth. Likewise, the Church would sanctify the empire with the authority and blessings of God.

Constantine created a new Christian Roman legion. Eusebius describes the new Christian symbols, which would now identify and inspire Roman troops:

> A long spear, overlaid with gold, formed the figure of the cross by means of a transverse bar laid over it. On the top of the whole was fixed a wreath of gold and precious stones; and within this, the symbol of the Saviour's name.... The emperor constantly made use of this sign of salvation as a safeguard against every adverse and hostile power, and commanded that others similar to it should be carried at the head of all his armies.[8]

After Constantine's death, Emperor Theodosius made Christianity the official religion of the Roman Empire, but it was Constantine who is considered the bookend of an era begun by Augustus. Constantine melded pagan with Christian themes, and began shifting the overall moral justification of the empire from pagan myths and civic virtue toward the vision of the empire as the glorification of the Christian God and realization of His will. Historian Alistair Kee, who described Constantine's rule as "a fundamental turning point," observes that after Constantine's conversion, "the imperial ideology, with all its implications for the accumulation of wealth and the exercise of power over the weak, was given religious legitimation by the Church."[9]

While many have questioned the sincerity of Constantine's faith, there is wide consensus among historians that he transformed the relation between state and church in a way that would fundamentally change Western civilization. In a theme strongly emphasized first by Eusebius, Western empire would now be blessed and protected by the Christian God. The Constantine Code can be summarized as follows:

1. The Roman Empire is chosen by the Christian God, the one true God, to rule the world.
2. No god, other than the Christian God, is to be tolerated.
3. The Lord's grace is to be bestowed upon the world through the emperor and the Church.
4. There is a divinely ordained hierarchy, enshrined in state and church, to which all ordinary people must submit.
5. Although He may have preached peace in His lifetime, Jesus's truth is to be spread by any means necessary, including the sword.
6. Roman victories are the victories of Christ. Anyone opposing the empire is opposing God.
7. All Romans must show obedience and loyalty to the emperor to serve Christ and the Lord.
8. The morals of Rome are those of Jesus and all Romans must live according to these values.
9. Rome has a moral obligation to defend and spread its empire to serve God.
10. True Christians must spare the heathen's soul eternal torment, but this may require the enslavement, torture, or destruction of his mortal body.

The Constantine Syndrome offered a vision that far transcended the Roman Empire, both giving divine sanction to the empire as well as making Rome a mere instrument of a much larger divine plan. The Constantine Syndrome created tension between the seat of government (Rome) and the universal Church, and it set the Church up as a potential rival to the government for earthly power, which early Christians had largely renounced for the afterlife. The church blessed the state but also subordinated it to larger purposes and the following religious script:

For the people's own good, resistance must not be tolerated. Conquest, slavery, and torture may be necessary and justified to bring heathens to the path of truth.

In the name of defense against Satan's aim of attacking and controlling everyone on earth, the Constantine Syndrome moralized a spiritual and secular imperial offensive to protect believers and convert infidels everywhere. The best defense against Satan was the good offense of the Roman legions. The Christian script reinforced and spiritualized empire while also building the Church.

This new Christian moral story of empire could not save Rome, which was already in a state of irreversible decline, and in some ways contributed to its decline. But the Constantine Syndrome has enormous importance because it survived Rome's collapse and surfaced in the Middle Ages during the Crusades. It survived in the great European empires as a dominant moral narrative unifying imperial state and Church.

Pagan Rome had offered ordinary Romans a sense of community and moral superiority based on their unique state and chosen destiny to bring civilization and rule of law to the world. But the Constantine Syndrome, rising as the pagan state was collapsing, gave Romans and Christians an even more powerful moral totem: a sense of being chosen as a universal Church by God to spread His word. A winning team chosen by God was even more powerful and morally reassuring than one chosen because of its civilizational superiority.

Fifteen hundred years after Constantine, in 1804, Napoleon would invite the Pope to Paris, France, to participate in Napoleon's imperial coronation. He feared that his new French Empire would lack moral credibility without the papal blessing. Two hundred years later, President George W. Bush waged the war on terrorism and the war in Iraq in the spirit of the Constantine Syndrome, claiming it a divinely sanctioned war against new barbarians. This war would invoke the Roman "security" code of Mars: the best defense is a good offense. Bush's invocation of God and his claim to spread the ancient Western civic virtues of freedom and democracy show that both pagan and Constantine Rome wrote the moral script of empire today.

The British Empire and the White Man's Burden

The poet Rudyard Kipling was the most famous moralist of the British Empire. In 1899, Kipling penned one of the most influential morality tales of any empire, called "The White Man's Burden." Kipling wrote it as a plea to the Americans to "develop" the Philippines, which the United States had acquired during the Spanish-American war. The poem summarizes perfectly the creed of the British, who explicitly conceived empire as a moral obligation, specifically the obligation of the most developed and cultured nation to civilize primitive peoples. The first famous verse of Kipling's poem reads:

Take up the White Man's burden—
Send forth the best ye breed—
Go bind your sons to exile
To serve your captives' need;
To wait in heavy harness,
On fluttered folk and wild—
Your new-caught, sullen peoples,
Half-devil and half-child.[10]

This captures the concept of empire as moral service to inferior peoples who are still savages. It is reminiscent of the Roman view of its obligation to civilize heathens or barbarians but, unlike the Romans, connects the concept of barbarians to race. In the second verse, Kipling describes the white man's burden as "to seek another's profit," making explicit that empire is a moral sacrifice by the British to help others. Empire is the British gift to its conquered peoples; it's not a gift to the Brits themselves. The latter assertion is a clear sign of immoral morality since nearly all historians view British commercial interests as the driving interest of the empire.

Kipling's work is important because (1) it captures so precisely the moral story of the British Empire, and (2) in its racist, paternalistic, and morally self-congratulatory tone and deceptions, it makes transparent its character as immoral morality. Kipling makes clear the essence of the British moral story:

The British Empire Code
1. Britain is a chosen and superior nation.
2. Although symbolically a monarchy, Britain has created modern democracy, civil liberties, and the rule of law.
3. The British have a moral mission to spread these values and raise up the heathen everywhere. The burden of civilizing the world now falls on the Anglo-Saxon race.

4. Some people must be saved from their own barbarism, as in the case of "widow burning" in India, the historic practice of widows expected to immolate themselves after their husbands' death.
5. Other nations must be taught the proper use of nature and its resources, as in the case of native peoples in the Americas who did not own private property.
6. The British must intervene to prevent uncivilized peoples from fighting tribal wars, as in the case in much of Africa, and civil wars, as between India and Pakistan.
7. Without the British, other advanced people may take advantage of the weak; thus the British must protect uncivilized peoples, as in the case of Native Americans who were attacked or killed by whites who colonized America.
8. Under Anglo-Saxon leadership, all peoples can unite into a world brotherhood, a commonwealth of nations based on Britain's universal values.

In this story, the British must be vigilant to defend the empire against savages who do not recognize they must submit to the superior race for their own benefit. They also have a moral obligation to fight other whites who establish rival empires, try to undermine Britannia, possibly seize Britain's colonies, and abuse and exploit inferior peoples rather than enlighten and civilize them. Cecil Rhodes put this succinctly: "I contend that we are the finest race in the world and the more of the world we inhabit the better it is for the human race. Just fancy those parts that are at present inhabited by the most despicable of human beings; what an alteration there would be in them if they were brought under Anglo-Saxon influence.... Added to which the absorption of the greater portion of the world under our rule simply means the end of all wars."[11]

Despite all the greed and cruelty of the British Empire, it did, in fact, end slavery, spread commerce, and bring to the world many of its finest civic and cultural achievements. But the threads of credible moral claims, seamlessly combined with self-interested material and psychological benefits, are exactly what make immoral morality so seductive and dangerous. The British could really believe in Rhodes's claims and Kipling's appeals to their own highest moral sensibilities, which reinforced their own sense of chosen-ness. Not only were the British delivering certain genuine moral triumphs—such as their abolition of slavery—but it was simultaneously enriching British traders and industrialists, spurring a renaissance of British evangelicals, and giving all Britons a totemic identity as a chosen people and the world's most winning team since Rome. Rhodes proclaimed at the height of empire: "Remember that you are an Englishman, and have consequently won first prize in the lottery of life."[12] It is hard to resist such benefits, all wrapped in such inviting and lofty morality.

As Rome brought "peace," the British Empire brought the Pax Britannica. This had at least two components: the first that the world could not remain peaceful without a higher power, the empire itself, to enforce it. Without Britain, there would be only warring tribes in Africa or clashing ethnicities and religions in Asia. Second, Britain's own self-defense became equated with the defense of empire. Britain conquered and then redefined those who fought for their freedom as terrorists. Defending the boundaries of the empire in India and Africa became equivalent in public discourse to defending Britain itself. Empire extended the "British nation" to mean the British Empire, and thus fighting in any of the colonies became part of the honorable self-defense of the British people. Adding to the immoral morality of this equating of empire as self-defense was the racial connotation underlying it. Britain had a moral obligation to enforce such an expansive concept of self-defense because the Anglo-Saxon race was the chosen one. To default on its defense anywhere on the planet was to undermine the chosen race at home, violating its sacred mission to protect itself and the civilized world at large.

If we return to Kipling, the overt racism, arrogance, and paternalism show the immoral morality at work here. Many of the nations that Britain conquered or ruled—from India to many of its African colonies and, of course, America itself—were highly developed civilizations. It was immoral morality that gave Britain the moral hubris to proclaim its own civilizational superiority, to express moral concern over the alleged backwardness of others, and to assert it was morally obligated to subdue and remake them. In the name of morality, Britain was in all these respects acting immorally, even according to many of its own moral precepts—of acting lawfully, civilly, and peacefully—which it applied to others but not to itself.

Here, the central attributes of immoral morality—selectivity, hypocrisy, exceptionalism—stand out. Had Britain straightforwardly conquered in the name of glory or commercial interests, it would have been simply ignoble. But by ruling in the name of morality itself, it indulged in the more degrading practices of immoral morality, undermining the very cultures and economies that it proclaimed it would elevate, and violating its own morality in the name of its own moral superiority and goals. The British devastated much of India's textile industry, turning the Indian economy backward in the name of development. The British created a slavish dependency of Africa on Britain, in the name of liberating the continent from slavery. The British also attacked Asian and African natives who fought for independence as aggressors, claiming the honor code of self-defense to crush them and disguise the empire's own aggression. Finally, the British prevented America itself from exercising the democratic self-government that it had nourished as part of Britain's own proud Enlightenment tradition.

Some British imperialists were willing to acknowledge the economic interests and greed that drove the empire. Cecil Rhodes minced no words: "We must find new lands from which we can easily obtain raw materials and at the same time exploit the cheap slave labor that is available from the natives of the colonies. The colonies would also provide a dumping ground for the surplus goods produced in our factories."[13] But the British found themselves in the bind of all recent Western empires. They could not primarily justify their empire in terms of the real commercial interests driving it and the totemic glories that it provided their leaders and peoples. Because of Britain's own moral codes, the British had to offer a moral defense of empire, something other than purely self-interested argument. Yet, even if one acknowledges some of these moral aims, they could never be reconciled with the underlying realities of empire that required a never-ending perpetuation of control or the risk of collapse of the British economy and polity. Thus, a Western empire morally based on civilizational superiority and, increasingly, representative government becomes wedded to permanent violation of others' sovereignty, as Indian historian Pratap Mehta argues well: "The dependence of the imperial state on its subjects leads it to indefinite extensions of its temporary rule, and leads it to impose more and more implausible 'requirements' for self-rule upon them. Britain, for instance, justified its rule on the grounds that it brought civilization, progress, the rule of law, and modern institutions to the natives; at the same time, the continuance of empire was premised upon the thought that the natives were as yet incapable of civilization, progress, and modern institutions."[14]

As the British economy grew and the empire expanded across the world, British political and military leaders feared that the British masses might become disenchanted with the burdens of global rule. Empire was expensive in both money and human lives. There was a concern that British urban life was becoming too comfortable and sedentary, drawing young British men away from the discipline and rigors required of the British imperial navy and army. Robert Baden-Powell, a British career officer military leader during the Boer War of the late nineteenth century, fretted that young British men were becoming "soft" "because they have comfortable houses, and soft beds to sleep in. Their food is prepared for them, and when they want to know their way they just ask a policeman."[15] Baden-Powell feared that the next generation would be unable to sustain the moral fiber necessary to sustain the empire and would lack even the physical strength and knowledge to fight successfully on far-flung native battlefields. "The truth is," he wrote, "that men brought up in civilized country have no training whatever in looking out on the velt or the plains or in the backwoods. The consequence is that when they go into wild country they are for a long time perfectly helpless."[16]

To inspire the younger generation with the moral ideals and physical toughness required to sustain empire, Baden-Powell started the Boy Scouts. He laid out the new scouting movement's morals in this formal Boy Scout code:

1. A Scout's honor is to be trusted.
2. A Scout is loyal to the Queen, his country, his Scouters, his parents, his employers and to those under him.
3. A Scout's duty is to be useful and to help others.
4. A Scout is a friend to all, and a brother to every other Scout, no matter to what country, class, or creed the other may belong.
5. A Scout is courteous.
6. A Scout is a friend to animals.
7. A Scout obeys orders of his parents, Patrol Leader, or Scoutmaster without question.
8. A Scout smiles and whistles under all difficulties.
9. A Scout is thrifty.
10. A Scout is clean in thought, word, and deed.[17]

The code's aim was to imbue Boy Scouts with the morals of empire. Baden-Powell recognized that the spirit of empire had to be cultivated early in life in order to move young boys smoothly from the playing fields to the battlefields. Baden-Powell's Boy Scouts would be trained in the ideals of British honor, civility, responsibility, loyalty, and obedience that the empire required, especially among its soldiers.

To keep sustaining empire, the British had to dig for deeper moral justifications. The rise of revolts, of competing empires, and of more transparent moral contradictions around self-government led, early on, to new moral stories to accompany the white man's burden. Evangelical groups flocked to India and Africa in the nineteenth century, and they linked the Union Jack of Britain's flag to the cross. As in Rome, the "civilizing mission" became linked to God's will. David Livingstone, one of the greatest

British imperial missionaries, wrote from the heart of Africa: "I am doing something for God. I have preached the Gospel in many a spot where the name of Christ has never been heard."[18] Here, Livingstone was resurrecting Constantine's marriage of Empire and Christianity. Livingstone offered the Constantine Syndrome as a defense of British Empire everywhere; after an Indian mutiny, he wrote, "I consider we made a great mistake when we carried commerce into India, in being ashamed of our Christianity.... Those two pioneers of civilization—Christianity and commerce—should ever be inseparable."[19]

Such "mistakes" were rarely made in Africa, where, even before Livingstone, as early as 1824, ardent missionaries from the London Missionary Society saw empire as God's plan. For the missionaries, the "civilizing mission" was always integrally connected with Christianizing the African natives. Ferguson describes the prototypical missionary society aim in the Kuruman project in Southern Africa, which "looks like a smart little Scottish village in the heart of Africa, complete with thatched kirk, whitewashed cottages, and a red postbox. The essence of the Kuruman project was simple: in turning Africans into Christians, the mission was at the same time civilizing them, changing not just their faith but also their mode of dress, hygiene and housing."[20] *Missionary Magazine* reported "The people are now dressed in British manufactures and make a very respectable appearance in the house of God."[21]

This represented the melding of the morality of Augustus and Constantine, marrying the civilizational virtues of pagan Rome with the Constantine Syndrome. Thus we see the continuity of both the moral discourse and immoral morality of empire across two millennia. The United States would carry this ancient moral story—the classic form of immoral morality—into the twenty-first century.

2

America's Moral Big Stick

How Thomas Jefferson, Andrew Jackson, Teddy Roosevelt, Woodrow Wilson, Ronald Reagan, and George W. Bush Taught Us to Police the World

If we cannot muster the resolve to defeat this evil in Iraq, America will have lost its moral purpose in the world.[1]
—*George W. Bush, March 28, 2007*

Americans see themselves as a "shining city on the hill," a moral beacon for all humanity, but not an empire. The British, while recognizing their empire, shared some of this blindness. Salman Rushdie observed wryly, "the British don't know their own history because so much of it happened overseas."[2]

But Americans have been particularly reluctant to see themselves as an empire—a startling fact given that the United States is the most powerful nation in history. While showing classic signs of overstretch and imperial decline, the United States remains a military, economic, political, and cultural colossus astride the world. Its power makes Rome and Britain, at their height, look pitifully weak.

The reluctance to acknowledge empire is also surprising because U.S. expansion and intervention have been so continuous and violent throughout its history. True, much of American imperial force has been exercised through what Harvard political scientist Joseph Nye has called "soft power," including economic and diplomatic influence; and the United States has been anti-colonial in its strategic approach to world power.[3] Empires based on soft power that do not acquire formal or legal colonies are still empires. Political scientist Dimitri K. Simes agrees, observing that empires, which are defined by their transnational exercise of "great authority over large and varied territories"—an obvious trait of America—"rely on a broad range of tools and incentives to maintain this dominance: political persuasion, economic advantage, and cultural influence where possible coercion and force when necessary."[4]

But the American Empire has been based on hard as well as soft power: hard power so brutal, persistent, and expansive that the pervasive denial of empire remains puzzling. In a recent book, former *New York Times* journalist Stephen Kinzer details fifteen different regime changes forced by American intervention, often through the CIA, and involving overthrows of democratic governments replaced by U.S.-supported dictatorships, from Iran in 1953 to Guatemala in 1954, to Chile in 1973 to Iraq in 2003.[5] American scholars and pundits all across the political spectrum have chronicled the endless imperial U.S. interventions, regime changes, and wars. On the Left, these include great historians such as Charles Beard and William Appleman Williams, and contemporary analysts such as Noam Chomsky, Chalmers Johnson, and William Blum. In the center are historian Andrew Bacevich and Kinzer, and on the Right are Niall Ferguson, Pat Buchanan, and the neo-conservatives Max Boot and Robert Kagan. Their work leaves little room for doubt about America as an empire. Yet in a 2006 survey of students on my own (Derber's) campus, a plurality of students, and a vast majority of those identified as conservative, say they do not believe that America is an empire, which national polls also confirm.

American denial of empire is startling for yet another reason: it has been an empire with increasingly global aspirations since its founding. In 1783, George Washington characterized the colonies as "a rising empire," and nearly all the Founders saw America as destined to become one of the world's great empires.[6] After 9/11, American leaders and neo-conservative intellectuals defined America as a new kind of democratic empire called on by God and the world to defend civilization, spread freedom, and combat terrorist barbarism. Of course, this moral story was not new at all since it mirrored the immoral morality of both Rome and Britain and is part of the American moral fairy tale.

From the beginning, Americans saw themselves as a chosen people destined for greatness. They were also always intensely moralistic, their moralism and religiosity a defining trait of the Puritans who arrived on the Mayflower as well as the early slaveholders in Jamestown. Because of its radical individualism, the United States also had special needs for the glue that the identity of a winning team provides. America's triumphant morality made a group of enterprising immigrants without strong roots or safety nets more secure about themselves and their community. Moreover, the ruthlessness and acquisitiveness of American capitalism intensifies the need for an immoral morality that moralizes global greed and global power.

While George W. Bush is often seen as the creator of the American Empire, nothing could be further from the truth. American capitalism and the religious and moral ideology of the Founders created an empire project that has defined the nation since its beginning.

American history is actually the story of *five* American Empires, each reflecting the capitalist imperatives of the era, as well as a particular story of immoral morality.

First Empire:
The Fledgling Constitutional Empire, 1776–1828

In 1776, Americans began a revolution to free themselves from the British Empire and to recreate themselves as an independent and great power. Alexander Hamilton, a leading architect of the U.S. Constitution, argued the thirteen colonies should unite to create an empire: "one great American system, superior to the control of all trans-Atlantic force or influence, and able to dictate the terms of the connection between the old and new world."[7] As noted earlier, Hamilton's boss, George Washington, saw America as "a new empire rising." A South Carolina planter of the era, William Henry Drayton, foresaw "a new empire, stilled the United States of Americas, that bids fair, by the blessing of God, to be the most glorious of any upon Record."[8]

The Revolution led quickly to melding the colonies into a new, vast nation. In its first fifty years, the United States would expand southward and westward with stunning speed and violence. The milestones after 1776 included the following:

- In 1783, in the Treaty of Paris, Britain ceded its territory south of the Great Lakes and east of the Mississippi River to the Americans.
- In 1803, President Jefferson completed the Louisiana Purchase, the biggest expansion in the New Empire's history, adding 526 million acres that constitute 22 percent of the land territory of the modern United States, including not just present-day Louisiana, but also "parts or all of present-day Arkansas, Missouri, Iowa, Minnesota west of the Mississippi River, North Dakota, South Dakota, Wyoming, and Colorado east of the Rocky Mountains ..." and parts formerly of Canada.[9]

- In the War of 1812, the United States tried to take all of Canada from the British but failed.
- In 1821, Andrew Jackson conquered Florida since slaves were escaping there to gain Spanish protection.

By 1789, virtually all of America's Founding Fathers had weighed in to support a vision of empire. The Founders drew on America's creation myth of a "city on the hill," a Godly beacon of freedom to the world pronounced by John Winthrop as the Pilgrims' creed and repeated by Jonathan Edwards, who said that "God might in [America] begin a new world in a spiritual respect."[10] In 1778, George Washington issued a proclamation from Valley Forge that it has "pleased the Almighty Ruler of the universe to defend the cause of the United States...." Washington added in his inaugural address to Congress in 1789 that "every step" of the new nation "seems to have been distinguished by some token of providential agency." John Adams wrote that the colonial era was just "the opening of a grand scheme and design in Providence for the illumination of the ignorant, and the emancipation of the slavish part of mankind all of the earth."[11] America was mythically born, like Christian Rome and Livingstone's Britain, as an empire constituted by God to serve His will, an imperial America that Ronald Reagan and George W. Bush, among many other presidents, would repeatedly call "God-blessed."

But as suggested by Adams, in his reference to "the illumination of the ignorant, and the emancipation of the slavish part of mankind," this early Constantine vision of a Godly American Empire was tightly linked to an equally ancient secular immoral morality, expressed in the British Empire as the White Man's Burden and earlier in pagan Rome as the moral obligation to spread civilization to the barbarians. The American Founders created their own version of empire, stressing freedom and the Constitution. We shall call it the Constitutional Code, and it has prevailed to this day as a central creed of American imperial, immoral morality.

Today's Constitutional Code, as we will soon see, speaks of America's moral obligation to bring freedom and constitutional government to the Islamic nations, as well as the rest of the world. Its core message is:

1. Americans are a free people on a free land.
2. Americans inherited the rights of Englishmen and are destined to develop them further, including rights of religion, conscience, expression, and equal rights under the law.
3. The Constitution is sacred and may have been sanctioned by a higher power.

4. All Americans have the constitutional right to freely contract with others and to protect and accumulate property.
5. Freedom, including the right to property, requires a state to protect it. However, the state should intrude upon that freedom as little as possible.
6. Freedom requires prosperity. Resources must expand, and the state must be prepared to help citizens acquire, trade, and market their goods everywhere.
7. Americans must be prepared to help people everywhere who cannot develop freedom and prosperity on their own. The truly unfit and dangerous may have to be eliminated.
8. As a beacon for the rest of the world, America has a manifest destiny to extend from sea to sea and, in fact, beyond the oceans.

As will be shown soon, the Constitutional Code evolved through all five American Empires. The Founders, while sharing the assumption (indeed creating it) that America radiated universal values of freedom and constitutionalism, did not embrace the rights of all Americans, such as slaves or Native Americans. They also had a particular focus, arguing that American Empire was necessary not just to bring freedom to the world but also to preserve liberty in America itself. As early as 1751, Benjamin Franklin wrote that expansion for surplus land was crucial to creating prosperity and liberty, and to avoid domestic corruption.[12] James Madison, the author of the U.S. Constitution, vigorously espoused this argument. Inverting the French political thinker Montesquieu's notion that freedom was possible only in a small country, Madison argued precisely the opposite, as paraphrased by Williams, that "empire was essential for freedom."[13] In a letter to Thomas Jefferson, Madison wrote that a republic "must operate not within a small but an extensive sphere." An expansive and expanding state would acquire the new, surplus land and resources necessary for prosperity, cohesion, constitutional rights, and freedom: "Extend the sphere, and you take in a greater variety of parties and interests; you make it less probable that a majority of the whole will have a common motive to invade the rights of other citizens."[14]

Here, Madison is using a version of the Constitutional Code that justifies a strong and expanding state as necessary to preserve the universal moral values of liberty and rights enshrined in the Constitution. But Madison's critics in the 1780s and beyond saw the immoral morality built into Madison's reasoning. Fellow Virginian John Taylor wrote that Madison's argument was leading to an "iron government" of an imperial nature. "The executive power of the United States is infected," wrote Taylor, "with a degree of accumulation and permanence of power, sufficient to excite evil moral qualities."[15] Taylor especially feared the executive branch's license in war making, reminding his friends Madison and Jefferson that "War is the keenest carving knife for cutting up nations into delicious morsels for parties and their leaders."[16]

Taylor did not prevail, but his critique worried Jefferson, who had moral doubts about empire but overcame them. In arguing for the Louisiana Purchase, Jefferson wrote that the people of Louisiana "were as yet incapable of self-government as children."[17] And in 1809, Jefferson wrote that "no constitution was ever before as well calculated as ours for extensive empire and self-government."[18] Jefferson's startling idea that the Constitution's supreme moral virtue of self-government required and justified empire is the core of the immoral morality in the Founders' Constitutional Code.

The colonists and Founders assembled both Godly (Constantine) and secular (constitutional) high morality to justify an imperial project rooted in mundane commercial interests. Expansion westward and southward offered both Northern merchants and Southern planters endless horizons of wealth. To disguise acquisitiveness in the discourse of Christian mission and liberty was, itself, a classic sign of immoral morality. But the most serious form of immoral morality among the colonists and Founders, as in Rome and Britain, was superimposing these high moral arguments on the dirty business of conquering, removing, and killing large "savage" populations, which in America consisted of more than twelve million Native Americans as well as enslaving millions of Africans. Since the commercial interests driving empire ultimately required what can only be described as genocide and terrible crimes of slavery, it is impossible to deny the immoral morality with which the colonists and Founders, and the Constitution itself, will be forever tarred.

Both colonists and Founders coped in ways borrowed from the Romans and the British. The colonists and Founders were deeply steeped in Roman classical history and moral philosophy and were British subjects, using long-standing British moral sophistry and self-deception integral to immoral morality. One involved the lie that much of the land was empty. The dimensions of that lie continue to grow as historical research shows that the size of the Native American population and African slave community were far greater than scholars have traditionally known, while also showing that Native Americans and slaves were key, by virtue of their skills and labor, to building America itself.

Another approach involved simply denying the humanity of the Native Americans and slaves, treating them as agents of the Devil or as animals. European Christians had often seen darker peoples—including Muslims, Africans, Asians, and Indians—as primitives or Satanic, and the Devil was always portrayed as black. Killing or enslaving was morally construed as "a sign of the Grace of God."[19] Both religion and racism played a role in this form of "hard imperialism" that could take the religious form of destroying Satan or a crude secular Social Darwinism that justified genocide and slavery as a form of natural law and the triumph of the morally fittest.

Another approach was "soft imperialism," which did not deny the humanity of the Native Americans and Africans, "acknowledged their achievements," and "considered it possible and desirable to elevate the Noble Savage into at least partial civilization."[20] Soft imperialism, a classic immoral morality of both pagan and Constantine Rome, and at the heart of the White Man's Burden, moralized conquest as religious or civic salvation, a moral service to the conquered. America's "city on the hill" radiated soft imperialism, both of the religious and secular variety. Winthrop's Christian community would deny the legal claims of Native Americans to their land but would treat them as potential converts. The Founders' Constitutional Code would treat self-government as a potential ideal for the undeveloped savages and justified conquering them as exposing them to civilization's highest blessings.

Second American Empire: Manifest Destiny Continental Empire, 1828–1898

In the Second Empire, America expanded westward all the way to the Pacific Ocean, annexing a good chunk of Mexico in the south and west and uniting a vast continent under one government. All this was done to acquire land, spread American Gilded Age capitalism from coast to coast, and create a beachhead for economic expansion across the Pacific. But the expansion was dressed up in eloquent immoral morality, the famous creed called Manifest Destiny, drawing on the Chosen People motif of the Romans, the White Man's Burden code of the British, and America's own vision of spreading democracy and civilization.

Nobody symbolized the immoral morality of the Second Empire better than General Andrew Jackson, whose rise to the presidency in 1828 inaugurated the new era. In this swashbuckling fighter, we see all the imperial populism and brutalism of the age. Jackson promoted violent expansionism mainly to help the Southern plantation economy that was depleting its own land and needed more. Jackson inaugurated the pre-bellum phase of the Second Empire, which unsuccessfully sought to reconcile expansionist interests of Northern capitalism and the Slave South.

Jackson expelled Native Americans from all land east of the Mississippi, but he did not always bother to provide moral justification—a reminder that empire sometimes uses raw force without pretences. In 1833, Jackson told Congress without any high moral rhetoric that the Natives "must necessarily yield to the force of circumstances and ere long disappear." While Jackson was describing genocide, his lack of moral posturing was almost refreshing since there is nothing more morally odious than the use of high moral arguments to slaughter indigenous peoples.

Nonetheless, Jackson could not keep removing and killing without resorting to high principles and creating his own immoral morality. In annual addresses to Congress from 1829 to 1836, he used several different moral arguments that later became integral to Manifest Destiny. One was virtually a clone of the British White Man's Burden, with the Indian Removal Act of 1830 discussing how "removed Indians" would, under U.S. guidance, advance "from barbarism to the habits and enjoyments of civilized life." Jackson told Congress of his own desires to uplift the Indians: "Toward the aborigines of the country no one can indulge a more friendly feeling than myself, or would go further in attempting to reclaim them from their wandering habits and make them a happy, prosperous people."[21]

In another congressional address in 1831, Jackson proclaimed about Indian removal, "It is pleasing to reflect that results so beneficial, not only to the States immediately concerned, but to the harmony of the Union, will have been accomplished by measures equally advantageous to the Indians." Jackson then offers this classic version of immoral morality: "That those tribes can not exist surrounded by our settlements and in continual contact with our citizens is certain. They have neither the intelligence, the industry, the moral habits, nor the desire of improvement which are essential to any favorable change in their condition."[22] Jackson concludes that they must accept their removal and control by the "superior race," for it will teach them the virtues of a civilized nation.

Here, Jackson describes Indian removal and subordination as service by Americans to an inferior race. This is extermination framed as moral education and civilizational uplift. The racism echoes the British White Man's Burden, but the emphasis on the obligation to help barbarians become civilized goes back to Rome.

Jackson melded this civilizational theme with motifs of self-defense of America against Indian aggression. In 1832, after a particularly brutal assault that killed numerous Cherokees who resisted removal, Jackson told Congress this: "Severe as is the lesson to the Indians, it was rendered necessary by their unprovoked aggressions, and it is to be hoped that its impression will be permanent and salutary." Here, Jackson equates Indian resistance to extermination as aggression and the U.S. fight against such "aggression" as honorable self-defense. This was analogous to the nineteenth-century imperial British, who defined Africans resisting colonization as "terrorists." The British viewed their war against such terrorists as the protection of civilization itself and thus essential to the survival of morality.

Three years after Jackson completed his second term, and the Indians had largely been eliminated east of the Mississippi, John L. O'Sullivan would expand on the larger meaning of Jackson's accomplishments. A prominent diplomat, journalist, and editor, O'Sullivan coined the term Manifest Destiny to explain America's great moral mission as a new hemispheric empire. In 1839, in an essay called "The Great Nation of Futurity"—one of the classic American doctrines of immoral morality—O'Sullivan argued that the United States was unlike any past nation or empire. "On the contrary," O'Sullivan argued, "our national birth was the beginning of a new history, the formation and progress of an untried political system, which separates us from the past and connects us with the future only; and so far as regards the entire development of the natural rights of man, in moral, political, and national life, we may confidently assume that our country is destined to be the great nation of futurity."[23]

America, O'Sullivan said, is destined for something entirely new—and far more moral than any prior nations or empires. "We are entering on its untrodden space," wrote O'Sullivan, "with the truths of God in our minds, beneficent objects in our hearts, and with a clear conscience unsullied by the past." But while O'Sullivan emphasized American exceptionalism, he actually makes the case for a new American Empire that sounds much like earlier empires—and has the hint of Orwell: "The far-reaching, the boundless future will be the era of American greatness ... its floor will be a hemisphere, its roof the firmament of the star-studded heavens, and its congregation an Union of many Republics, comprising hundreds of happy millions ... who will, what can, set limits to our onward march? Providence is with us, and no earthly power can [stop us]."

America's Manifest Destiny is power over all the hemisphere of the Americas, and O'Sullivan suggested this is just the beginning of a providential guidance by America of all nations of the world. This vision of U.S. power makes both the Roman and British empires look small, but theorists of Manifest Destiny, such as Stephen Austin, who led U.S. colonists into Texas to take it from Mexico, sees this as a moral mission, a principled obligation, in almost exactly the same sense that the Romans and British did. "It is so destined," Austin proclaimed, because America's principle of "equality is perfect, is universal."[24] Here, in pronouncing the radical newness of America, Austin and other Manifest Destiny moralists return to the argument of pagan Rome: that its values are universal. They are, Austin wrote, "the self-evident dictates of morality." As in Rome, and as reinterpreted by Madison, Jefferson, and other Founders, this universality of America's moral vision of liberty and equality—as codified in the U.S. Constitution—gave it both the right and the "duty" to expand its influence around the world.

Manifest Destiny was a reformulation of the immoral morality of the Founders' Constitutional Code, justifying endless American expansion to spread freedom: "We must onward to the fulfillment of our mission [i.e., spreading across the Continent and to all nations] of ... the principle of our organization—freedom of conscience, freedom of person, freedom of trade and business pursuits, universality of freedom and equality. This is our high destiny, and in nature's eternal, inevitable decree of cause and effect we must accomplish it."[25]

This secular moral imperialism became a license for U.S. expansion in the Second American Empire, involving war against Mexico and persistent extermination of Native Americans after the Civil War. Stephen Austin argued that "Texas was a wilderness, the home of the uncivilized and wandering Comanche and other tribes of Indians," and he wrote that it was necessary "to restrain these savages and bring them to subjection." His great moral justification for taking Texas from Mexico by force was "that it was due to the great cause of liberty, to ourselves, to our posterity, and to the free blood which I am proud to say, fills our veins." Here, we see the immoral morality of *justifying a war to expand slavery in the name of liberty*. Austin explicitly links this to the civilizational and constitutional code of the Founders: "Our cause is just, and is the cause of light and liberty—the same holy cause for which our forefathers fought and bled to resist and proclaim war."[26]

Austin portrayed the Mexican war as deeply moral, not only to spread freedom but also to guarantee the security of the United States. In 1846, President James K. Polk, who led Americans in the Mexican war, proclaimed that U.S. security required annexing not just Texas but all of Mexico, leading much of the public and Congressman Abraham Lincoln to oppose Polk's war as "imperialist." But invoking the Monroe Doctrine and the right of self-defense, Polk rallied Congress to support the war. Polk raised "national security" to a high moral imperative, his main contribution to American history.

Manifest Destiny, the Second Empire's main moral story, also carried echoes of the Constantine Syndrome, with America's great power, like that of Rome, seen as ultimately sanctioned by God. In defining Manifest Destiny, O'Sullivan wrote: "All this will be our future history, to establish on earth the moral dignity and salvation of man—the immutable truth and beneficence of God. For this blessed mission to the nations of the world, which are shut out from the life-giving light of truth, has America been chosen."[27]

The language evokes the constitutional secular moral code of the Founders. But the Second Empire emphasized that America is carrying out God's will, with O'Sullivan saying, "America has been chosen" by God. In O'Sullivan's seminal essay on Manifest Destiny, he continues, "In its magnificent domain of space and time, the nation of many nations is destined to manifest to mankind the excellence of divine principles; to establish on earth the noblest temple ever dedicated to the worship of the Most High—the Sacred and the True."

It is thus not just the U.S. Constitution but God who has ordained American Empire. In the Second Empire, American elites discovered, like Constantine, that divine will is the most compelling argument for military intervention, something that remains central in American immoral morality all the way up to President George W. Bush.

Manifest Destiny opened up the entire U.S. continent as a wild frontier. As Americans in their covered wagons rode across that "virgin land" in the last phase of the Second Empire, a new Frontier Code emerged. It justified the final taking of the West and was a marriage of the Constitutional Code and Manifest Destiny:

1. People, especially men, prove their goodness through valor, courage, and hard work.
2. Good men are entitled to their property, the fruit of their labor, but must be prepared to defend it.
3. Good men protect their family while they should expect respect and obedience as patriarch and provider.
4. Good people should bond together to form a law-abiding prosperous community, obeying the community's rules and leaders or sheriffs.
5. There are outlaws and savages, including rebellious Native Americans, who do not accept the rules. They are apt to cheat, steal, and resort to violence.

6. Men of courage and honor must control the outlaws, using violence if necessary, and removing savages who prevent expansion of law and order across the frontier.
7. Good men have a manifest destiny to bring civilization to the wilderness, even though it has a rustic beauty, which should be preserved as much as possible.

The Frontier Code masculinized the imperial impulse and became the American blueprint for heroes from Buffalo Bill and Wyatt Earp to John Wayne and George W. Bush. The American cowboy was born as an imperial hero. Teddy Roosevelt imprinted his own stamp on it in the Third American Empire.

Third American Empire: Allied Global Empire, 1898–1945

In the Third Empire, the United States expanded its reign from the continent to the world. Manifest Destiny was globalized and American leaders described their new empire as the source of the first truly moral global order. The Third Empire's contribution to immoral morality was to build global American dominance in the name of a new world, free of the evils of colonialism and enshrining universal values of American democracy.

This vision cloaked the economic interests that drove the Third Empire in high moral principles—the classic mark of imperial immoral morality. By the end of the nineteenth century, when financial crises and class struggles were destabilizing and saturating the domestic market, U.S. agricultural and industrial firms were already investors in Latin America and were hungrily eyeing trade in the Pacific and in China, as well as expanding trade in traditional European markets. America's imperial drive was fueled by commercial greed and interest like that of the Europeans, even as it claimed a moral rather than self-aggrandizing end. But the United States was not yet ready to displace the British or other great European empires. Instead, it rhetorically challenged European colonialism in order to supplant European influence, while also allying temporarily with Europeans in imperial wars that could expand U.S. access to resources and "free trade." The "open door" policy announced by Secretary of State John Hay under President Teddy Roosevelt became the economic mantra for free trade and U.S. expansion, but the broader argument for the Third Empire remained fundamentally moral. Presidents Grover Cleveland and William McKinley attacked the morality of Spanish and European colonialism, inaugurating a new thread of "humanitarian" argument for expansion; Theodore Roosevelt defined the morality of U.S. war and global policing as "civilizing" and essential to world order and "national security"; and President Woodrow Wilson defined a new American global order that would replace European colonialism, spread democracy and liberty, and a century later would become the hallmark of the neoconservatives and of the immoral morality of George W. Bush.

The Spanish-American War of 1898 over Cuba and the Philippines marked the beginning of the Third Empire. By the 1890s, the United States had already invested deeply in Cuban sugar plantations as Cuba's relation with Spain—its colonial master—became increasingly conflictual. The Monroe Doctrine and Manifest Destiny had already made clear that the United States claimed a high moral imperative to prevent European colonialism from taking root anywhere in the Americas. The Third Empire began with an American assault on Spanish colonialism and on the backwardness, cruelty, and evilness of the Spanish control of Cuba, thus implicitly invoking a contrast between greedy European empires and democratic American globalism. American Empire would be the anti-Empire, a conceit central to American immoral morality.

In 1896, President Cleveland, moving toward a war footing with Spain, noted the U.S. economic interests, observing that "$30 million to $50 million of American capital are invested in plantations and in railroad, mining, and in other business enterprises on the island." But Cleveland quickly shifted the discourse from economics toward morality, saying, "The people of this country always feel for every struggle for better and freer government," and proclaimed that America would act out of "considerations of philanthropy and humanity in general."[28] Cleveland joined the growing chorus of newspapers and pundits calling for America to help "liberate" insurgent Cubans from a despotic Spanish rule. In 1898, joining the "yellow journalism" of William Randolph Hearst, who was selling newspapers by railing against the Spanish as brutal torturers and imperialists, the *New York Times* described the Spanish national character as blending "civilization and barbarism." The polarity between American goodness and European colonial evil was the new American gospel. So, too, was the identification of the American anti-empire as a new form of global humanitarianism.

In his first State of the Union Address, in 1897, President William McKinley announced his intention to intervene against the Spanish for it is America's "duty imposed by our obligation to ourselves, to civilization, and humanity to intervene with force." Here, McKinley aligned himself four-square with the "civilizing" ethos of Rome, Britain, and the American Founders, invoking the Constitutional Code by saying that the United

States seeks "to see the Cubans prosperous and contented, enjoying that measure of self-control which is the inalienable right of man." Beyond echoing the Founders, McKinley adds the humanitarian thread: "Intervention upon humanitarian grounds has not failed to receive my most anxious and earnest consideration"—a theme that would become part of the standard immoral morality of American imperial intervention from Woodrow Wilson to, most prominently, George W. Bush.

Along with the constitutional and humanitarian secular arguments, though, McKinley added two other classic themes of immoral morality. One was an echo of Constantine, with McKinley arguing that Spanish cruel rule over Cuba and the Philippines "called forth expressions of condemnation from the nations of Christiandom." God, McKinley was suggesting, would be on America's side in its war on barbaric Spain, and he recounted praying about what to do in the Philippines: "We could not leave them to themselves—they were unfit for self-government—and they would soon have anarchy and misrule over there worse than Spain's was; and . . . there was nothing left for us to do but to take them all, and to educate the Filipinos, and uplift and civilize and Christianize them, and by God's grace do the very best we could by them, as our fellow-men for whom Christ also died."[29]

Here, McKinley melded the secular theme of "uplift and civilize" and the sacred them of "by God's grace," the two classic themes of imperial immoral morality since Rome. But there was also a third increasingly central pillar: the morality of imperial self-defense, a concept that expanded to encompass moral protection of anyone within the empire or moral attacks against those resisting it. Like President Polk in the Mexican war, McKinley emphasized that U.S. national security was at stake, especially after the explosion that blew up the *USS Maine* in Cuban waters on January 15, 1898. McKinley argued that war against Spain was necessary "when the lives and liberty of our citizens are in constant danger"—the Third Empire's first effort to frame its expansionism as honorable self-defense against aggression. The famous war slogan "Remember the *Maine*" turned the Third Empire's early overseas adventure into (1) a moral evocation of the need to protect Americans and the honor of fallen U.S. sailors, thus strengthening the national security religion developed in the Second Empire; (2) the expansion of "self-defense" into a moral doctrine protecting the Cubans, expanding the Monroe Doctrine that had already seen defense of South America as part of America's moral duty; and (3) a new symbol of American civic goodness versus European colonial evil, with the *Maine* coming to represent, as Brad Bauer put it, "the vessel of the democratic ideals of the nation," essentially a re-evocation of the Constitutional Code of the Founders.[30]

Defeating Spain in 1898, and securing dominance over Cuba, the United States acquired Guam, Puerto Rico, and the Philippines, gaining such a visible and initially embarrassing global imperialist profile that Andrew Carnegie offered to buy the Philippines for $20 million and give it its freedom. Mark Twain, initially a fervent American nationalist, now railed against the flagrant "imperialism" of his beloved nation. But the Third Empire's expansionism was unstoppable, fueled by U.S. corporate needs for overseas markets and for uniting the population around a nationalist "winning team" identity as class conflicts intensified under the robber barons.

The two most important Third Empire leaders were Teddy Roosevelt and Woodrow Wilson, who layered new, seductive, progressive, and immoral morality on American Empire. Roosevelt was to the Third Empire what Andrew Jackson was to the Second, a self-proclaimed warrior who championed bold new American expansionism without initially seeming to dress it up in morality of any form. Roosevelt had graduated from college and gone immediately to the Badlands of South Dakota to ride horses and shoot guns. In 1898, when the Spanish-American War began, he immediately resigned his assistant secretary of the navy position to volunteer as a Rough Rider. Leading a regiment up a Cuban hill into battle, without waiting for the approval of his commander, Roosevelt became a new American hero after his swaggering, bravado performance in what he famously called this "splendid little war."

As early as 1895, Roosevelt had written that the "greatest boon" he could bring America was "an immediate war with Great Britain for the conquest of Canada"[31]—a line that seemed consistent with a man who later became famous for the line, "speak softly but carry a big stick." In writing about the Spanish-American War and the Rough Riders, Roosevelt acknowledged that "I had preached, with all the fervor and zeal I possessed, our duty to intervene in Cuba."[32] While this might just seem naked warmongering, his use of language signals Roosevelt's evolving recognition that war and imperialism required strong, moral argument. Note that he says "duty to intervene," *making clear that his enthusiasm for the war reflected a moral obligation rather than simple lust for battle.* Roosevelt was explicit that the "duty to intervene" arose from the moral necessity "to take this opportunity of driving the Spaniard from the Western World," which became known as the Roosevelt Corollary to the Monroe Doctrine. American intervention was a moral imperative, the only way to protect the Americas against the colonialism of the Europeans. Here, Roosevelt, like Cleveland and McKinley, made European Empire his enemy and American Empire a moral crusade against the evils of the Old World. Expansion as honorable protection and self-defense—of both U.S. citizens and the millions in other nations requiring American protection—became Roosevelt's theme song and his legacy to the empire.

In his corollary to the Monroe Doctrine, Roosevelt wrote that "chronic wrongdoing or an impotence which results in a general loosing of the ties of civilized society may ... in the Western Hemisphere—force the United States, however reluctantly ... to the exercise of an international police power."[33] As corporate leaders close to Roosevelt spoke forcefully of their need to capture markets both in Latin America and in Asia, specifically China, only seven hundred miles from the Philippines, Roosevelt extended his vision of moral sheriff from the Americas to the world as a whole. When the Spanish-American War started, he sent a telegram to Commodore Dewey to strike the Spanish fleet in the Philippines immediately. Historian William Appleman Williams concludes that "Roosevelt did not restrict that police power to Latin America, noting explicitly that America's efforts 'to secure the open door in China' were part of the same effort to protect and extend (in TR's own words) 'the interest of humanity at large.'"[34]

Here, Roosevelt uses not just the Monroe Doctrine but also the ancient immoral morality of Rome, proclaiming the universality of the moral values and interests that American expansion would protect. Roosevelt seemed so entranced with warfare as the highest form of civil and moral conduct that he whimsically, but approvingly, quoted one of his fellow Rough Riders who asked for a haircut before battle, saying, "Don't want to wear my hair long like a wild Indian when I'm in civilized warfare."[35]

But Roosevelt was uncertain that Americans would maintain the character to pursue "civilized warfare." In a 1907 speech to the Harvard Student Union, after Harvard President Charles William Eliot proposed abolishing football at the school, Roosevelt pronounced, "We can not afford to turn out college men who shrink from physical effort or a little physical pain." For the nation needed men with "the courage that will fight valiantly against the foes of the soul and the foes of the body."[36] His athletic references helped him create a new character code for the Third Empire, synthesizing Manifest Destiny and the Frontier Code, which we now call the New American Team Code:

1. The team/nation is sacred and is destined to prevail over its adversaries and protect deserving peoples.
2. The nation's goodness, both military and non-military, is sanctioned by higher powers and is proven through victory.

3. Personal morality and the team's honor are intertwined and all-important.
4. A few who are especially strong or valorous—the nation's leaders and military—have been chosen to represent and protect the group in a dangerous and threatening world.
5. People prove their goodness through valor, honor, courage, hard work, and dedication to the team.
6. Everyone must identify with the team and see it as their representative and symbol.
7. Being chosen for the team is a special honor. Honor is an ineffable quality, which must be defended at all times.
8. The entire community must support the team. Anyone who doesn't should be ostracized or perhaps punished more severely.
9. A victory for the team brings glory to the entire community/nation.
10. Do not question authority or think for yourself in ways that might endanger the unity of the team/nation.

This was Roosevelt's original contribution to moralizing the Third American Empire, helping bring the experience of every boy's playing field to the battlefields of American's new empire. American boys would play to win but in the service of the highest moral values. Roosevelt came to symbolize a vision of American global policing to end the evils of European colonialism. But like McKinley and Cleveland before him, Roosevelt failed to disclose honestly the urgency of the self-interested economic interests driving Third Empire expansion. In 1901, McKinley had admitted, but downplayed, the economic motives: "Incidental to our tenure in the Philippines is the commercial opportunity ... the legitimate means for the enlargement of American trade."[37] Roosevelt also acknowledged the role of trade, but in his emphasis on moral policeman he did not forthrightly state the intensity of the U.S. corporate interests involved. The corporations themselves were more forthright. U.S. Assistant Secretary of the Treasury Frank A. Vanderlip—later president of National City Bank—said in 1900 of the Philippines:

It is as a base for commercial operations that the islands seem to possess the greatest importance. They occupy a favored location not with reference to any part of any particular country of the Orient, but to all parts. Together with the islands of the Japanese Empire, since the acquirement of Formosa [Taiwan] by Japan, the Philippines are the pickets of the Pacific, standing guard at the entrance to trade with the millions of China, Korea,

French Indo-China, the Malay Peninsula and the Islands of Indonesia to the south.[38]

Chauncey Depew—a financier who worked for Cornelius Vanderbilt and became a corporate-friendly U.S. senator—was also more forthright, speaking at the Republican National Convention in 1904:

> The American people now produce $2 billion worth more than they can consume and we have met the emergency, and by the providence of God, by the statesmanship of William McKinley, and by the valor of Roosevelt and his associates, we have our market in Cuba ... in Puerto Rico, in Hawaii ... in the Philippines, and we stand in the presence of 800 million people, with the Pacific as an American lake, and the American artisans producing better and cheaper goods than any country in the world.... Let production go on ... let the factories do their best, let labor be employed at the highest wages, because the world is ours.[39]

Nonetheless, despite the undeniable role of Roosevelt in promoting U.S. global expansion through classic forms of American immoral morality, his contributions ultimately appear restrained relative to Woodrow Wilson. Roosevelt became more cautious in his imperialist view over time, actually being the only candidate in 1912 to argue for withdrawal from the Philippines. In contrast to the crusading Wilson, Roosevelt evolved toward "realism," committed to expanding America's sphere of influence through what he described as "step-by-step" pragmatism.

An ongoing current debate about Roosevelt's role does not really bring into question his role in facilitating America's global expansion nor his contribution to the moral discourse, but it does highlight the more important role played by Woodrow Wilson, particularly constructing the modern forms of immoral morality that underlie U.S. foreign policy. Journalist Fareed Zakaria has written, "Almost every American president in the past half century has been, at least rhetorically, a Wilsonian."[40] Wilson not only crystallized the moral story of the Third Empire but shaped the moralism guiding U.S. empire ever since.

On April 2, 1917, in his speech to Congress in which he declared war, Wilson proclaimed, "The world must be made safe for democracy." This became a Wilsonian trademark and came to define both Wilson and America as "idealist." Wilson enthusiastically embraced this label: "Sometimes people call me an idealist. Well, that is the way I know I am an American. America, my fellow citizens—I do not say it in disparagement of any other great people—America is the only idealistic nation in the world."[41]

While echoing traditional ideas of American exceptionalism—a nation unlike all others dedicated to moral ideals—Wilson is actually repeating, here, much of the rhetoric of the British and even the Romans, who also defined their power as an expression of exceptional idealism and universal moral values. What Wilson accomplished was to take these classic Roman and British themes, integrate them with those of the Founders and the Manifest Destiny creed, and create both a secular and sacred American immoral morality suited for the modern age.

Wilson accomplished this synthesis in his 1917 war declaration to Congress:

> It is a fearful thing to lead this great peaceful people into war, into the most terrible and disastrous of all wars, civilization itself seeming to be in the balance. But the right is more precious than peace, and we shall fight for the things which we have always carried nearest our hearts, for democracy, for the right of those who submit to authority to have a voice in their own governments, for the rights and liberties of small nations, for a universal dominion of right by such a concert of free peoples as shall bring peace and safety to all nations and make the world itself at last free.

In a senseless war of European colonial empires that were killing off their own citizens for greed and glory, Wilson framed the anti-colonial American argument for jumping into the war. While joining the Allies, Wilson was making an immoral moral argument for U.S. global power, as a nation playing by different rules than the Old Powers, one standing not for colonial greed or exploitation but "for the principles that gave her birth." Here, Wilson embraced the Constitutional Code of the Founders and made it an argument for twentieth-century American world dominion. America would fight this war—and remake the world—"for the things we have always carried nearest our hearts, for democracy," for the right of all peoples "to have a voice in their own governments," all to "make the world itself at last free."

This, again, is empire as anti-empire: remaking the world to ensure that all peoples enjoy the universal moral values of self-determination and rights codified in the U.S. Constitution. It is imperial power as moral service. This is classic immoral morality, cloaking self-interest in the rhetoric of moral sacrifice. The hypocrisy is on display in his own view of a genuine peace: "Only a peace between equals can last. Only a peace the very principle of which is equality and a common participation in a common benefit."[42] Yet, at the signing of the Treaty of Versailles after World War I, when Wilson helped other European leaders carve up the crumbling Ottoman Empire and redraw the map of the world, it was anything but a "peace between equals." This was a victory dictated, as always, by the victors, and not just over the Germans and Japanese. It was a cruel peace in which the lack of generosity helped lead to World War II. The signing of the treaty also created a fraternity of wealthy nations—especially between the British and French—who cooperated with America, as historian William Appleman Williams writes, "to control the poor in return for the rich [Europeans] accepting the American rules for the international marketplace."[43] The poor nations, of course, had no voice at all, betraying the immoral morality of Wilson's proclamations of a "peace between equals" and a commitment to "the rights and liberties of small nations."

While Wilson largely expressed himself in the secular immoral morality of the Constitutional Code, he also embraced the Constantine Syndrome: "There is a spirit that rules us.... I believe that men are emancipated in proportion as they lift themselves to the conception of providence and of divine destiny, and therefore I cannot be deprived of the hope that is in me—in the hope not only that concerns myself, but the confident hope that concerns the nation—that we are chosen and prominently chosen [our emphasis] to show the way to the nations of the world how they shall walk in the paths of liberty."[44]

Fourth American Empire: The Good Empire versus the Evil Empire, 1945–1991

In the Fourth Empire, America justified its rise to global superpower as the only alternative to what President Ronald Reagan dubbed the "Evil Empire." In the face of new Soviet evil, America redefined itself as the indispensable free and good society, which became the core moral premise of both the Fourth and current Fifth empires. The Fourth Empire's contribution to American immoral morality was to announce a new titanic moral struggle between good and evil, aligning America with an unquestioned cosmic goodness, while covertly cooperating with the Soviet enemy and using Soviet barbarism as moral cover for its own imperial expansion. The Fourth Empire updated the Roman tale of empire as the only moral defense against barbarism, all the while disguising America's own increasingly savage global power.

The two bookends of the Fourth Empire were presidents Harry Truman and Ronald Reagan. In 1947, soon after the end of World War II, Truman announced the Truman Doctrine, which assumed America's "goodness" (a matter discussed shortly) and clarifies the unsavory truth that Truman created *a morality of self-defense that instantly became a morality of global interventionism.* Truman called for intervention in Greece and Turkey since "the very existence of the Greek state is today threatened by the terrorist activities of several thousand armed men, led by Communists, who defy the government's authority."[45] In the name of fighting Communism (loosely defined as supporters of Marxism and the Soviet Union), Truman led an intervention that would install an American-friendly, quasi-fascist Greek regime—a paradigm for the immoral morality that emerged in the Cold War. In the speech outlining the Truman Doctrine, the president laid out the underlying morality of this new "security"-driven intervention: "We should not realize our objectives, however, unless we are willing to help free peoples to maintain their free institutions and their national integrity against aggressive movements that seek to impose upon them totalitarian regimes. This is no more than a frank recognition that totalitarian regimes imposed on free peoples, by direct or indirect aggression, undermine the foundations of international peace and hence the security of the United States."[46]

Of the reactionary Greek regime he was supporting, Truman would acknowledge only that "No government is perfect." Truman, like most of his Fourth Empire successors, would accept the dictatorial impulses of the leaders (in this case Greek generals) he was aiding in the name of the all-important containment of Communism. The immoral morality here is at least triple: (1) the United States expanded its power projection and its right to intervene anywhere in the name of honorable self-defense against global Communism, (2) it put in place an authoritarian military regime in the name of democracy, and (3) it extended the sphere of corporate-friendly puppet regimes in the name of self-determination. Fourth Empire U.S. interventions that followed were all built on the model of Truman's Greek intervention. Examples of such interventions consisted of the following: the 1953 CIA overthrow of the democratically elected President Mohammed Mossadegh in Iran, replacing him with the Shah; the CIA overthrow of the democratically elected President Jacobo Arbenz of Guatemala in 1954, replacing him with a series of brutal dictators; and the overthrow and killing of the democratically elected President Salvador Allende of Chile in 1973, installing the dictator Augusto Pinochet. But these interventions added a fourth dimension to the immoral morality, claiming that intervening was self-defense against Communism when none of the governments involved were Communist or Communist allies. Such successful deception ensured that the Fourth Empire could expand anywhere, in the name of security and self-defense, as part of a moral crusade against Communism.

In 1950, Truman signed NSC 68, a National Security Council document that solidified Truman's view of the Cold War as a moral emergency: "The issues that we face are momentous, involving the fulfillment or destruction not only of this Republic but of civilization itself." NSC 68 proclaimed that the aim of the Soviet Union was "the complete subversion or forcible destruction of the machinery of government and structure of society in the countries of the non-Soviet world and their replacement by an apparatus and structure subservient to and controlled from the Kremlin.... The assault on free institutions is world-wide now, and in the context of the present polarization of power a defeat of free institutions anywhere is a defeat everywhere."

The last phrase locks in Truman's imperial definition of global interventionism as honorable self-defense. The entire NSC document reinforces the Fourth Empire's moral obligation to police the world since "a defeat of free institutions anywhere is a defeat everywhere." This was precisely Truman's language in the Greek intervention, but NSC 68 heightens the moral stakes involved, conceiving the new world as a cosmic struggle between good and evil. America is the bastion of goodness because of its Constitution and the unquestioned commitment to freedom that America represents. America's purpose, made explicit by NSC 68, is

> to maintain the essential elements of individual freedom, as set forth in the Constitution and Bill of Rights; our determination to create conditions under which our free and democratic system can live and prosper; and our determination to fight if necessary to defend our way of life, for which as in the Declaration of Independence, "with a firm reliance on the protection of Divine Providence, we mutually pledge to each other our lives, our Fortunes, and our sacred Honor."

Here, NSC 68 returns to the Constitutional Code of the Founders as the basis for certitude about fundamental American goodness, while also adding an allusion to the Constantine Syndrome and America as God's chosen. Truman had also seen the American system as God-blessed, saying, "The basis for our Bill of Rights comes from the teachings we get from Exodus and St. Matthew, from Isaiah and St. Paul." In contrast, the Soviet Union is the polar antithesis, a demonic slave system at war with the American ideal of liberty: "Being a totalitarian dictatorship, the Kremlin's objectives in these policies is the total subjective submission of the peoples now under its control. The concentration camp is the prototype of the society which these policies are designed to achieve, a society in which the personality of the individual is so broken and perverted that he participates affirmatively in his own degradation."

NSC 68 set the stage for *Star Wars*, with the Soviet Union portrayed as the evil Darth Vader. American elites thoroughly digested and embraced this stark morality, but since NSC 68 was a policy document for experts, it took a popular president to bring this moral message to the public. That president was Ronald Reagan. In his famous March 8, 1983, "Evil Empire" speech, Reagan spoke of a father he had heard reacting to the fear of Soviet aggression: "Communism and our own way of life were very much on people's minds. And he was speaking to that subject. And suddenly I heard him saying, 'I love my little girls more than anything.' He went on: 'I would rather see my little girls die now, still believing in God, than have them grow up under Communism and one day die no longer believing in God.'"

Reagan added, "There were thousands of young people in that audience. They came to their feet with shouts of joy. They had instantly recognized the profound truth in what he had said, with regard to the physical and the soul and what was truly important." Reagan said this father of three girls had also recognized the most important truth of our day: that the Communists "are the focus of evil in the modern world."

Reagan then honed in on morality as the central issue in the world, with the Soviets repudiating "all morality that proceeds from supernatural ideas—that's their name for religion—ideas that are outside class struggle." Quoting the writer C. S. Lewis, Reagan said "the greatest evil" now is created by these Godless Communists, bureaucrats who operate "in clean, carpeted, warmed, and well-lighted offices, by quiet men with white collars and cut fingernails." Reagan then warned that the greatest danger is "to ignore the facts of history and the aggressive impulses of an evil empire, to ... remove yourself from the struggle between right and wrong and good and evil."

These were the Fourth Empire's most important words. You cannot remove yourself from the new all-consuming struggle between good and evil. Nor is there any questioning the Soviets' evil or the Americans' good because the president has already firmly rooted these moral certitudes in God. Reagan proclaimed that the basis of moral "ideals and principles is a commitment to freedom and personal liberty that, itself, is grounded in the much deeper realization that freedom prospers only where the blessings of God are avidly sought and humbly accepted." Reagan melded God, morality, and global American policing in a seamless concept of American goodness. American Empire became a Godly imperative to expand U.S. military power across the planet in the name of fighting evil. The emphasis on God as the foundation of morality itself and of American goodness, as well as of building American military dominance, is especially notable, particularly in Reagan's Evil Empire speech. "The great triumph of our Founding Fathers," said Reagan, was "voiced by William Penn when he said, 'If we will not be governed by God, we must be governed by tyrants.'"

And Reagan cites Alexis de Tocqueville's famous quote: "Not until I went into the churches of America and heard her pulpits aflame with righteousness did I understand the greatness and genius of America." De Tocqueville's conclusion: "America is good. And if America ever ceases to be good, America will cease to be great."

In this reference to de Tocqueville, Reagan makes America's moral goodness (in perfect contrast to Soviet evil) the center of U.S. foreign policy, roots morality in God, and connects America's morality with her Godliness. It is America's belief in God and God's belief in America that make her good. *America's moral obligation is to defend the world against the Evil Empire and to spread America's own divine and democratic Goodness.* Reagan has joined Madison and Constantine in his version of America's hegemonic immoral morality. This melding of God, freedom, and the American way in a global contest of good versus evil—requiring American boots on the ground all over the planet—would be taken up with urgent intensity by George W. Bush in the Fifth and current empire.

The Fifth Empire: World Hegemon: 1991–Present

In 2002, John Bolton, who became George W. Bush's ambassador to the United Nations, proclaimed, "We are an empire now, and when we act we create our own reality."[47] In 2004, George Bush himself said, "I trust God speaks through me."[48] These words announced the coming of age of the Fifth American Empire, the most powerful empire in history.

The Fifth Empire began with the collapse of the Soviet Union in 1991 and assumed its most militaristic and moralistic form under President George W. Bush from 2001 to 2008. Whether President Obama will preside over the end of the Fifth Empire is something we take up in the concluding chapter. Here, we cover the Fifth Empire from its inception through the Bush Jr. years. The novelty of the Fifth Empire's immoral morality was (1) a synthesis that managed to integrate virtually all the classic themes from Rome and Britain as well as those of the earlier four American empires, and (2) the intensity of contradiction between its lofty moralism and religiosity and its actual global conduct, which increasingly mirrored that of the terrorists it fought.[49]

When the Soviet Union collapsed in 1991, it ended not only the Soviet Empire but also the American Fourth Empire. The two had existed as spouses in a codependent marriage, fueling each other's survival and sense of moral purpose. While they hated each other, they couldn't live without each other. Soviet aggression—sometimes real, usually exaggerated, and sometimes fabricated by U.S. leaders—gave the American Fourth Empire its main moral justification for global expansion and intervention. Likewise, "Yankee imperialism" gave the Soviets their moral argument for holding on to Eastern Europe and keeping tight control over their own people.

But while the Fourth U.S. Empire was so morally tied to the Soviet Union that it could not survive without her, the death of the Soviet Union created a unique opportunity. For the first time, there was no nation that could check American power. All obstacles to America's Manifest Destiny seemed to have been overcome. American elites now set about the business of creating the fifth and possibly final American Empire, reaching its greatest power ever, yet possibly, ironically, beginning its inevitable decline. Just as many had viewed the 1898 Boer War as the beginning of the end of the British Empire, America's war with Iraq could possibly be the beginning of the end of its reign.

The immoral morality of the Fifth Empire rests on classic forms of American imperial dishonesty. The Fifth Empire was driven in large part by corporate aims to radically increase profits through globalization. With the collapse of any Soviet deterrent, corporate elites were eager to exploit cheap labor everywhere on the planet, using the threat of outsourcing to break down the costly high wages, job security, health care, and pension plans that American workers had built up since the New Deal was put in place by President Franklin Roosevelt. But Fifth Empire leaders defined America's new power as a high moral imperative—for spreading democracy and saving civilization itself—rather than a ticket to huge profits for global corporations. This was greed disguised as God's will and moral sacrifice.

The key to the Fifth Empire was the view, largely associated with neoconservatives, that America must become permanently and overwhelmingly militarily dominant. But the first leader of the Fifth Empire was no neoconservative but President Bill Clinton. Instead of creating a "peace dividend" after the Soviet fall, Clinton built the foundations of an even greater empire, arguing that economic and military aims had merged and that the new globalization could only succeed if America dealt decisively with new global security threats of drugs, international crime, rogue states, failed states, and terrorism. "The very openness of our borders and technology also makes us vulnerable in new ways," the president said.[50] Clinton's national security advisor, Samuel Berger, proclaimed that, after the Cold War, virtually everyone now "believes we need a strong military to protect our interests in a world of continuing if shifting dangers."[51] As military historian Andrew Bacevich wrote, Clinton combined this premise with two others to define his foreign policy: first, "that the United States must possess military capabilities enabling it to prevail over any conceivable combination of adversaries,"[52] and the United States must proactively change the world in America's interests, thereby transforming, in Bacevich's words, "the Department of Defense . . . into a Department of Power Projection."[53]

After the Soviet collapse, Clinton would keep one hundred thousand forces in both Europe and the Asian Pacific, as well as thousands more in the Persian Gulf. In 1999, he proudly proclaimed, "We have people on the sea, people in foreign countries, all over the world on every continent. We are everywhere."[54]

Clinton had the honesty to discuss the U.S. economic stakes involved, speaking frequently about globalization and the benefits for U.S. companies and economic growth. Nonetheless, since empires are ultimately about the power to control and kill, a higher level of morality is required to legitimize them. This explains the persistent immoral morality of the five American empires, all fueled by a capitalist economic system whose greed and profits cannot be honestly acknowledged as the basis of U.S. foreign policy. A president cannot say, "We are killing for Exxon and to lower the price of oil." He must find a moral ideal lofty enough to justify war and sophisticated enough to compel belief.

Only after September 11, 2001, did the immoral morality of the Fifth Empire come into full view, preached to ordinary Americans by George W. Bush. Bush's moralizing of U.S. aims was not new, having its roots in the intensely idealistic and religious rhetoric of Ronald Reagan, Woodrow Wilson, and many other earlier presidents. But no other president has put immoral morality on such spectacular and stark display. Bush divided the world after 9/11 into heaven and hell. On the one side was an America that represented God and His fundamental Goodness, embodied in liberty and American democracy. On the other were terrorists, who embodied the evilness of Satan and who were out to destroy all civilized values. In the immoral morality of the Fifth Empire, one could challenge a particular war, but any challenge to America's basic goodness became religious heresy—an opposition to God and to His plan of liberty.

Bush's immoral morality was that of a crusade, a word he used in several of his speeches on Iraq and the War on Terrorism. "This is a new kind of—a new kind of evil. . . . And the American people are beginning to understand. This crusade, this war on terrorism is going to take a while."[55]

This new titanic struggle between good and evil of the Fifth Empire is familiar. Terrorists became the new Communists, and the relationship between Bush and Osama bin Laden was a codependent marriage much like that built by the Fourth Empire between American and Soviet leaders. Bush despised bin Laden but needed him as a symbol of evil to rally

Americans and to build support for U.S. intervention anywhere in the world. Bin Laden and al-Qaeda gave America a moral justification for any war that served U.S. economic or strategic interests, since U.S. leaders could always allege, as in Iraq, that their motives were to attack evil terrorists. Likewise, bin Laden had contempt for Bush but found him splendidly useful, a poster boy for jihad. American imperialism was the best possible recruitment tool for radical Islam, and Bush played the role perfectly.

To seek global dominance is immoral, but to do so in the name of fighting evil is worse—hypocrisy that is classic immoral morality. Bush repeatedly defined the War on Terrorism—his umbrella policy to expand U.S. global power—as a pure moral struggle to destroy evil and assure the triumph of goodness: "We're taking action against evil people.... Our war is a war against evil. This is clearly a case of good versus evil, and make no mistake about it—good will prevail."[56]

Bush repeatedly used the phrase "Axis of Evil," making clear that any future wars against Iraq, Iran, and North Korea would be part of his morally driven war on terrorism. And intervention, which expands the empire, is seen as the only moral way to protect the world against barbaric terrorists. In the process, Bush redefines global policing and expansion as honorable self-defense: "In a time of testing, we cannot find security by abandoning our commitments and retreating within our borders. If we were to leave these vicious attackers alone, they would not leave us alone. They would simply move the battlefield to our own shores. There is no peace in retreat. And there is no honor in retreat."[57]

If this imperial redefinition of honorable self-defense against global barbarism is Bush's first pillar of immoral moralism, the second was his focus on spreading freedom and liberty, the heart of America's moral goodness. As Bush was reducing freedom at home and working with murderous dictatorships abroad like in Saudi Arabia, Pakistan, and Egypt, his rhetoric on freedom itself intensified. He proclaimed, "I believe that freedom is the deepest need of every human soul." When weapons of mass destruction were not found in Iraq, he ratcheted up further his focus on liberty, saying that the war was driven by his "moral clarity" to bring freedom to Iraq and the whole Middle East. And this, he repeatedly said, stemmed from the historic truth that freedom was the moral value uniting all Americans: "America has never been united by blood or birth or soil. We are bound by ideals that move us beyond our backgrounds, lift us above our interests, and teach us what it means to be citizens."[58]

Here, Bush is returning to the civilizational claims of Rome and Britain, and especially the Constitutional Code of the Founders, updating it for the Age of Terrorism. The terrorists, Bush said, hated America most because it was the world's "beacon" of Constitutional freedoms: "Americans are asking 'Why do they [terrorists] hate us?' They hate what they see right here in this chamber, a democratically elected government. Their leaders are self-appointed. They hate our freedoms, our freedom of religion, our freedom of speech, our freedom to vote and assemble and disagree with each other."[59]

Bush added sacredness to America's secular creed of liberty, putting a particular stress on freedom as being God-given. In his 2003 State of the Union Address, Bush preached that "God has planted in every human heart the desire to live in freedom." God is the third pillar of Bush's immoral morality, as no president has made more frequent reference to God nor to His embrace of the freedom that America embodies. While he was careful not to say publicly that God chose America, Bush said repeatedly that the liberty America practices is a gift from God and one that God intended for all peoples. He thus crafts his own version of the Constantine Code: "Americans are a free people, who know that freedom is the right of every person and the future of every nation. The liberty we prize is not America's gift to the world; it is God's gift to humanity."[60]

This is Bush's way of aligning America with God in the War on Terrorism and the new American world order. But what is distinctive about Bush is not his belief in God or his view that the United States embodies God's will, and thus has a moral obligation to spread U.S. values through wars and global dominance, the classic form of immoral morality expressed by many presidents. The unique element is the intensity of his view that God speaks through him personally, as highlighted by Republican presidential counselor and critic Bruce Bartlett: "I think a light has gone off for people who've spent time up close to Bush; that this instinct he's always talking about is this sort of weird messianic idea of what he thinks God has told him to do.... He truly believes he's on a mission from God."[61]

This personalization of the Constantine Syndrome makes it yet more dangerous. The Constantine Syndrome is one of the most ancient Roman pillars of immoral morality. If Bartlett is correct, Bush moved toward a view preceding Constantine, one more like the Egyptian pharaohs who saw themselves as the Sun God. Bush does not see himself as a God, but his belief in himself as God's vessel was the foundation for new extreme forms of immoral morality leading toward an Empire that would control the world in the name of God and liberty, while breeding frightening political and religious authoritarianism at home, in the name of securing freedom in America.

3

The Mass Psychology of Empire

Why Bostonians Believe in the Red Sox and Americans Believe in America

I (Derber) have often asked students in my classes what they think would happen if a president gave this speech:

My fellow Americans:

Today, I have decided to ask Congress to declare war on Iran. It is the second largest oil producer in the world. It is unfriendly to our oil companies, and it's pushing up our prices at the pump. We have the power to take their oil for ourselves and control the whole region in our own interests. America does what is in our vital self-interest, and that is why I am commanding the U.S. armed forces to commence a campaign for regime change in Iran. God bless you, God bless Exxon, and God bless America.

While there are always a few students who say they find the speech refreshingly honest, most are appalled. They believe that U.S. wars must be waged for noble purposes and U.S. military forces must have a moral objective. If a president were to declare war for pure greed or profit, they say, he would be impeached.

My students are correct. American leaders cannot claim to wage wars for greed or corporate profit. Leaders of America—and all past great powers—have had to describe wars as rooted both in vital national interests and in the highest moral values of the nation. For any global hegemon, this requires immoral morality, recasting global dominance as service. As shown in the previous two chapters, leaders of the Roman and British empires practiced this moral sophistry for centuries, and American leaders flood the world today with modern versions of these ancient immoral moralities.

The question then becomes whether and why ordinary citizens "resonate" to immoral morality. From 2006 to 2008, the growing public opposition to President George W. Bush and the Iraqi debacle shows that citizens of the empire certainly do not believe all of a president's moral claims about his wars. Popular resistance to war and empire has always existed in America, and it is becoming intense and widespread after what many call "the Vietnam in the desert"—the meltdown in Iraq and the growing chaos throughout the Persian Gulf and the world. But President Bush was not impeached, and he retained widespread public support for his war on terrorism. Bush's claim of an idealistic America genuinely seeking to defend the world against evil continues to resonate even among many Americans who despise him. Through most of their history, Americans have maintained faith in the goodness of their nation and the benevolent influence of America on the world, even as the nation was persistently involved in crimes—from killing Native Americans and enslaving Africans to overthrowing democratic governments—that have been part of the long process of building American global power. But despite the fiery outrage at Bush and the Iraq war, which is spilling over into President Obama's fudging of how long he will keep troops in Iraq, the majority of Americans still sustain that faith in U.S. benevolence. The question is why. We believe there are three core reasons.

Historical Roots

The resonance of empire and its morality tales have deep historical roots in America, even back to the Mayflower. Eminent historian William Appleman Williams, former president of the American Historical Association, titled his wonderfully illuminating book on this subject *Empire as a Way of Life*. Williams's empire began with the Pilgrims who saw themselves as God's chosen people and continued, as shown in his last chapter, with the Founders, for whom empire became "synonymous with the realization of their [founding] Dream." Williams observed that "later generations became steadily less candid about their imperial attitudes and practices," but the empire kept expanding and the morality of American power became part of the national psyche. While empire was increasingly denied, the idealism underlying expansion became a taken-for-granted reality among ordinary citizens, inflating our identity and sense of self-worth.

Few nations start as empires. Rome was a republic for centuries before its empire stage. Britain was a small island contained by other European powers long before it became its own empire. The fact that America grew up as an empire from its creation, that it never experienced a period of nationhood prior to a sense of imperial destiny, has deep implications for popular resonance. To be an American has always been to have a moral entitlement of great power just under the skin. There was no historical era in which Americans could build an identity that was divorced from great power.

Popular resonance is linked also to the nearly uninterrupted success of the empire project. Since its founding, America has suffered few reverses in its manifest destiny. Each stage of American history has meant more land, power, prosperity, influence, and respect. Success breeds success. By the mid-nineteenth century, even America's most distinguished literary figures were caught up in empire fever and expressed the popular mood. In 1850, Herman Melville wrote, "We Americans are the peculiar, chosen people—the Israel of our time."[1] In 1860, Walt Whitman wrote, "I chant the new empire."[2] Most empires have suffered deep reverses even as they ascended, thus bringing some doubt to the empirical agenda and some weakening of popular resonance. But until very recently, the remarkable successes of American imperial history have reinforced an optimism of spirit and will, an unspoken sense that great power is what makes America great and that America's righteousness rightly destines it for global power.

But empire, even when deep in the historical bloodstream, must be persistently reinforced with stories that explicitly confirm the morality of the agenda. In the last chapter, we showed that every president has repeated some version of the same morality tale, thus creating a deeply entrenched ideological receptivity. Every schoolchild has read and reread some version of these stories, now etched deeply in the national psyche. Resonance, though, always depends on how skillfully these morality tales continue to be presented by leaders, historians, and other guardians of the nation's cultural and spiritual traditions, and how well they continue to correlate with the values and psychology of ordinary Americans. Resonance rises or falls based on an intimate dance between elites and citizens; in the case of American Empire, this dance, while sometimes thrown off rhythm by passionate antiwar movements, has tended to go smoothly as elites have created compelling moral stories that resonate with the mass psychology of the populace.

The Complicity of the Elites

Resonance depends crucially on the role played by the nation's ideological elites, those responsible for shaping the vision and values of the nation. They populate the Ideological Apparatus, the political and cultural institutions with the responsibility to ensure that the nation's ideology matches the interests of ruling elites.[3] The Ideological Apparatus plays a key role in legitimating the authorities and shaping popular values; in dictatorships it is overtly a propaganda machine, the kind that George Orwell immortalized. In formally democratic societies such as the United States, the Ideological Apparatus operates more subtly, but when immoral morality is required, the apparatus must produce the moral myths and create resonance. The elites within the Ideological Apparatus include not only political leaders such as presidents, whose ideological performance we explored in the last chapter, but also other leading politicians and policy elites, church leaders, journalists in the mass media, moviemakers in Hollywood, and the intelligentsia.

The Ideological Apparatus speaks not just for itself but its empire sponsors. In America, this has always meant the corporate and financial elites with the self-enriching economic interests of enormous global profits and wealth that fuel the empire. In the last chapter, we showed that corporate interests have always been the driving engine of the American Empire, along with the strategic political and military interests of the state and political classes. The economic engine—and especially the corporate force—has been paramount in America more than in earlier empires, reflecting the enormous growth of global companies and their new hold on both major political parties. Empire has been the political agenda of the Right in earlier times; in America, the distinctive feature is the extent to which it has become the project of both conservatives and liberals.

This should not distract from the reality that the moralist strategy of empire is one historically of the Right. It binds all mainstream parties and classes into a Grand National project, seducing those who are ordinary working people from the other forms of solidarity that might achieve their real needs. In America, it is a project of both mainstream conservatives and liberals since both have been absorbed into the political embrace of the corporate order. But let us not forget that the moralist strategy of empire is driven by the wealthy elites who have always dominated the economy and fear most the resistance of their own economically and spiritually disenfranchised populations.

Ironically, the idea prevailing in America is that today's cultural elites are subverting American power and patriotism. A narrow but influential group of conservatives tars the cultural establishment with the "liberal" brand, accusing the intellectual class of undermining U.S. foreign policy and attacking the very goodness of America. Conservative journalist Ann Coulter writes that Jesus Himself calls us "to do battle" with the "liberal intellectuals" since they "hate America" and are "treasonous."[4] Another conservative, Bernard Goldberg, in his best-selling book on the cultural elites, *100 People Who Are Screwing Up America*, calls the members of the Ideological Apparatus "snobby elitists" who look down on ordinary Americans "because they bowl and eat at Red Lobster" and "because they go to church every week and take the Bible seriously ... and because they fly the American flag on the Fourth of July."[5] Author Tom Wolfe writes that the cultural elites "do not have a clue about the rest of the United States" and "are forever trying to force their twisted sense of morality onto us, which is a nonmorality."[6]

This makes for entertaining reading, but it is wildly misleading. While the liberal intellectual and political wing of the "cultural establishment" has fiercely challenged President Bush's foreign policy, especially in Iraq, it actually reinforces the underlying moral premises of American Empire. As we show in Part III, the obliteration of the Left in the United States after the 1960s eviscerated the national debate, as has the absorption of many Democratic Party elites, along with virtually all Republicans, into the corporate system. The most important aspect of the American Ideological Apparatus is actually the broad moral consensus that now unites nearly all elites. The key groups—all of which have come together around the basic morality stories discussed in the last two chapters—are the political leadership of both parties, the policy elites in both conservative and liberal think tanks, the leaders of the country's major religions, including the Jews, evangelicals, and many Catholic leaders, the mass media, and many of both the conservative and liberal intelligentsia. This complicity is not new, but it is an astonishing convergence of diverse elites, uniting preachers, politicians, and intellectuals in unexpected and not obvious ways, encompassing the entire sweep of the Ideological Apparatus; it plays a key role today in explaining popular resonance. As we show shortly, this new consensus is masked in the bitter partisan divides and culture wars, but its nontransparency only increases the power of the ideological message and its capacity to stoke popular resonance. The elites, whether liberal or conservative, are all global corporcrats today, who embrace America as a great and abiding democracy with a moral obligation to exercise global power and leadership. They all believe that the United States must retain the world's strongest military and be prepared to use it to protect freedom and markets. On this, there is little difference between Barack Obama and Hillary Clinton and John McCain, between the *New York Times* and Fox

News, or between the conservative American Enterprise Institute and the liberal Brookings Institute.

The complicity of American elites—and the moral resonance to empire they help foster—is powerful today, as just noted, because it is masked in the appearance of great moral opposition to the empire agenda. The deep and angry divisions around the Iraq War are the most important example. The opposition to the war has been real and serious, not only outraging millions of ordinary American citizens but also alienating much of the intelligentsia and cultural establishment. But the dissent within the Ideological Apparatus was profoundly self-limiting. It questioned a war but did not challenge—and often reinforced—the underlying moral premises and hypocrisy sustaining American global power and dedication to freedom.

One illustration was the tack taken by John Kerry when he ran for president in 2004. Kerry and other Democratic and Republican Party leaders are the political wing of the Ideological Apparatus whose ideas carry special weight in shaping resonance. Kerry's famous flip-flopping on Iraq illustrates the contradictions and limits of elite dissent that challenges the means of exercising U.S. global power but not its morality or ultimate goals.

The problem was far deeper than Kerry's much-ridiculed linguistic muddle: "I actually did vote for the $87 billion (a supplemental funding bill for the war) before I voted against it."[7] Kerry was serious about his opposition to Bush's unilateralism and about the failure to build a stronger international consensus for intervention. But Kerry did not challenge the underlying intent of the war and the larger moral objectives of American global power. He certainly did not challenge or even acknowledge American Empire, which would have immediately made him the target of the entire Ideological Apparatus.

Hillary Clinton has taken a similar approach, initially supporting the war but criticizing the administration for numerous "errors of judgment." In 2006, in a congressional panel on Iraq, Clinton, in her strongest critique of the war yet, lambasted Secretary of Defense Donald Rumsfeld, but it was all about strategic blunders and tactical mistakes: "You did not go into Iraq with enough troops to establish law and order. You disbanded the entire Iraqi Army. Now we're trying to recreate it. You did not do enough planning.... You underestimated the nature and strength of the insurgency, the sectarian violence and the spread of Iranian influence.... Because of the strategic blunders and, frankly, the record of incompetence, you are presiding over a failed policy."[8]

This much-quoted statement, followed by Clinton's call for Rumsfeld to resign, seemed a strong war critique, but it never challenged the war itself and actually reinforced the view of a just cause. Clinton and Kerry have both embraced the role of superficial dissenters *who could not lead the nation into deeper questioning about the underlying purposes of the war or America's role in the world.* Kerry and Clinton have been glued to matters of strategy and tactics while Bush wrapped himself in the larger morality of American global leadership that Kerry and Clinton would not dare question.

Most of the Democratic Party leadership, including President Obama, and a significant part of the broader Ideological Apparatus eventually argued that the Iraqi war was a "mistake." A mistake is different than an immoral or criminal act. The mistake meant that the war was lost because of the failure to get international support or because of "errors of judgment" in equipping the troops or conducting planning and intelligence. *But the idea of a mistake does not imply evil intent or a larger critique of the United States' aims in the world; indeed, it suggests good intentions gone awry by poor execution.*

This is the way that division and dissent within the American Ideological Apparatus actually reinforce resonance. It challenges competence but not the moral agenda. Hillary Clinton, while denouncing the Bush administration's "incompetence in executing" Iraq, explicitly offered her own agreement with Bush's commitment to fight "tyranny." President Obama has made similar comments since assuming the presidency. Any genuine opposition to the Iraqi war and American Empire would have to challenge assumptions of U.S. benevolent aims, not just incompetent means. Obama, Kerry, and Clinton have never argued that the Iraqi war was waged to sustain U.S. hegemony in a critical oil-rich region rather than to forge "democratic transformation." They have not made clear that the United States has always worked with dictators and persistently overthrown democratic leaders for tyrants when it was the only way to sustain U.S. power and interests. There were many critics in America and around the world making these arguments, but those doing so in the United States were viewed as antipatriotic radicals and were more likely to be ordinary citizens—bloggers or street protestors—than oppositional political leaders or other dissenters in the Ideological Apparatus.

Since the dissent of the elites was framed around the language of mistakes and incompetence, it diverted visceral public concern of Americans about the morality and aims of American global power to concerns about strategic and tactical flaws. It silenced emergent popular doubt about the assumptions of America's good intentions in the world. It created the impression of vibrant democratic debate when the elites of both parties and in the broader Ideological Apparatus were tacitly supporting assumptions about

America's idealistic and moral character. Americans could hear the debate about Iraq for years, feeling terrible about the disaster U.S. intervention created in Iraq, but never seriously questioning the nation's global idealism and moral sacrifice of the United States in the Iraq War itself. America may have made a mess out of Iraq, but the terms of the debate never suggested that this was an inevitable consequence of a nation addicted to its own power and using moral language to disguise the addiction.

Kerry could have run as a Peace Hero rather than a War Hero. He had been a leader of the veterans' antiwar movement in Vietnam as well as a decorated soldier. His decision to abandon the identity of Peace Hero for War Hero speaks volumes about the contaminated dissent of the Ideological Apparatus and liberal political elites. The very concept of a Peace Hero has no place in an empire, which runs on the high-octane moral language of strength and moral sacrifice in war. War is peace in the world of empire, and peace is the rhetoric of weakness, incompatible with the moral toughness required to combat evil. Kerry's decision to run as a War Hero reflected his internalization of Orwellian immoral morality; had he run as a Peace Hero he would have become, like Orwell's hero Winston Smith, a heretic who would be savaged by both his conservative and liberal fellow members of the Ideological Apparatus.

Social Insecurity and the Winning Team

Resonance arises partly from the sophistry of elites but also from the mass psychology of the population. Insecurity and fear are key elements of a popular mindset that resonates with presidents and their Great Power morality. When community becomes weak and jobs insecure, the soil for resonance becomes fertile, easily plowed by the moralists of empire. In a society as radically individualistic and fiercely capitalist as the United States, empire moralists operate in a wonderfully resonant environment, stoking personal insecurities to exploit the moral triumphs and solidarity of a national winning team. Of course, when the team stops winning, resonance can erode quickly and the moral legitimacy of the empire can unravel.

Empire is essentially a winning nation—or at least one committed to and promising eventual victory. And Americans keep believing in America and resonating with the morality of its power for many of the same reasons that people in our own city, Boston, keep believing in the Red Sox. The resonance with the Red Sox would be clear if you wore a Yankee jacket at

Boston's Fenway Park and kept cheering for Steinbrenner's gang; you would be lucky to get out of the stadium alive. The resonance with America by its own citizen-fans is equally visceral, a spiritual and moral identity with an exclusionary and violent edginess.

Two of the founders of sociology offer clues about resonance that create Red Sox fever, as well as American super patriotism. Emile Durkheim, the nineteenth-century French sociologist, spent his life thinking about how societies jell and why people put their moral faith in their own nations. Durkheim would have well understood my (Derber's) experience on a sultry summer day in a suburban Boston neighborhood where few people know their neighbors. On this hot day, the Sox were playing in a high-stakes series, and suddenly people all up and down the street were out on their porches with their television sets tuned to the game. Everybody was glued to the screen, cheering wildly together when a Sox hitter blasted a homer, and moaning and groaning in unison when a ball hit by the other team dribbled through the hands of a Sox infielder and allowed the enemy to score. Soon, people were yelling out jokes, curses, and prayers from one porch to another, and neighbors who had hardly ever spoken before were in synch with each other.

Durkheim would find it easy to explain why the Red Sox are a religion in Boston. The Sox take a group of people who are separated by lawns, fences, and busy work—and suddenly jell them in a common cause. Most Bostonians know little about their neighbors, may be upset with them for leaving out the garbage, or are simply indifferent, too occupied with their own careers or personal problems to get to know them. This turns a neighborhood into a suburban wasteland.

But on that afternoon of high-stakes Red Sox baseball, this deserted street became a real neighborhood. People on one porch were constantly calling over to their neighbors on other porches, offering them a beer, or uniting in a collective cheer or jeer. I had never seen the street buzzing like this, a collection of strangers suddenly bubbling over together like a family.

Durkheim had a word that helps explain what is going on: *totem.*[9] The totem is the moral symbol around which a tribe, neighborhood, or society unifies. In primitive tribes, it was a pole carved into the shape of an animal sacred to the tribe. In Boston, the totem is the Red Sox, with Fenway Park recently voted by residents as the most sacred spot in town.

The totem represents the core moral values of the community. Durkheim saw it as the community's religion. Since the totem symbolizes the community's sacred bonds linking its members, it can function only as long as the morality of the community is itself beyond question. If the Red Sox cheat or disgrace themselves, we Bostonians call them "bums" but still honor them, upholding Boston's dream of inevitable triumph. Likewise, if a whole society is imperialistic or militaristic, its national totem must also still be seen as moral and sacred, or it will lose its "jelling" power. Armies are often totemic for their societies, expressing values of honor and moral sacrifice even when they engage in unjustified killing or conquest; the military totem, and the community it affirms, can be expressions of immoral morality, as it typically is in an empire.

As the ties that bind people together loosen, Durkheim argued that the totem would become even more important. In Boston, as in most American cities, the social ties have weakened, as people come from scores of different countries and backgrounds, move frequently, have less leisure time, and feel vulnerable to more crime and immoral influences. We are desperate for something to come together around, and the Red Sox fill the bill. It is one of the few sources of togetherness in a city crammed with ambitious individuals pursuing their own dreams.

When entire nations deliriously root for their teams, as in the Olympics, it's similar to that Boston neighborhood. On a national scale, sports fever can be one of the most thrilling ways of building a sense of belonging and common nationhood. Anyone who doubts this should have been in Italy during the 2006 World Cup, when nearly every Italian restaurant put up a TV screen for their patrons who might forget to eat their pasta in the heat of the excitement. Italy became one large cheering squad for its team, for a moment obliterating the many crises and problems that have divided the nation. The team's victory brought the whole country together, giving all Italians a sense of unity and moral self-worth, of being winners.

In America, sports have long played a similar role, but the crises of community that Durkheim highlighted are far more intense here. America is bigger and more diverse than Italy—and far more individualistic. Compared to Europe and most other nations, Americans really do "bowl alone." Durkheim noted this was a very personal crisis, for in his most famous work, he showed that societies with weak communities have high suicide rates, and that the most disconnected people have the highest suicide rates.

In a word, Americans are vulnerable to the deepest of anxieties that their society might unglue. The loosening ties to family and work create frightening personal insecurity and isolation. Collectively, we retreat into private cocoons, whether gated communities or fenced, private homes. As the divorce rate rises and the number of never-married increase, more people live alone and have less connection to anyone. The number of single households has exploded, now accounting for 46 percent of all U.S. households. A 2006 study by Duke and Arizona sociologists reported that the average American now has only two other adults to confide in about personal problems, and one-fourth of Americans have nobody as a confidant, a serious decline in social connections.[10] If Durkheim were painting a color-coated danger code, America would be in the red zone.

This helps to explain the sports fever that I saw in that Boston neighborhood, but it also helps explain popular American resonance to American nationalism and Super Power. Fenway Park brings together disconnected Americans, who feel the thrill of community in the stadium that they don't feel elsewhere. But a nation of disconnected people needs a broader and deeper connection than to a local sports team, one that cements a particularly intense moral tie between the individual and his country. An empire requires a passionate sense of patriotism and national belonging, connections that are particularly seductive to a disconnected populace.

This starts with the soldiers themselves, often young men from poor and broken communities whose only prior community may have been the Crips, the Bloods, or some other gang. But the military is the highest commitment community in America, knitting many of the most disconnected Americans into fiercely bonded combat squads. We now know from their own words that soldiers fight most of all for their buddies. Durkheim would not be surprised; the resonance of the empire that its own soldiers feel arises out of the identification with a nation of great power and respect, and especially the community of blood brothers that the military offers a group of young people who have known little sense of family or belonging. The military—the central institution of empire—is a dream for the disconnected, a model of codes of moral honor and solidarity that is fading in the civilian world.

As for the civilians, their resonance is much like that of the fans of the teams. They are not bound into the tight family of the players or soldiers themselves—living in a world apart from the team or the military. But fans "support the team" and civilians "support the troops" as a religion. And this religion offers precisely what Durkheim argued: the power to bring disconnected people together in a sacred bond and calm the anxiety of a populace fearful of social and moral breakdown and personal isolation. The religion may involve immoral morality, but the fan or patriot remains a believer and resonates to the moral and emotional rewards of bonding.

The team demands far less of the fans than players but still offers the rewards. The fans' daily isolation or disconnection is, for a moment, forgotten, as the fans meld together to support the team. When the team wins, they become number one, winners themselves. The psychic impact is so great that the fans often seem to go wild in the pursuit of belonging and victory. They paint their faces, tear down the goal posts, and often riot, especially after winning. This may be a mob mentality, but for the fans it is deep psychic healing, creating an almost primal link with fellow fans and offering a magical sense of community and self-worth.

The empire, while asking much of the soldiers, demands far less from the civilians—since they are not asked to sacrifice their lives. But from a Durkheimian view, the empire's global great power still offers dramatic psychic returns for civilians—which makes them soft targets for the empire builders. The disconnected American is searching for the totem that brings him into intense community. If that community is in Fenway Park, it provides temporary excitement and togetherness. But if that totem is the world's most powerful nation—the global team in a struggle of cosmic proportions between good and evil—the psychological payoff is greater than what even the Red Sox can deliver. The empire provides red meat for disconnected citizens in the following ways: (1) a reassurance of the moral goodness of the nation and thus of its citizens, (2) the connection to millions of other citizens who have banded together in a deep and lasting moral contract, and (3) a sense of belonging to the winning team that is more powerful than any other on earth.

Military and national power seems remote from everyday life, but it is everywhere. If you drive on any street or highway in America, you will find decals plastered on cars—often several on one vehicle—proclaiming "Support Our Troops." Americans are in love with their cars, and anything they put on them is important to their personal identity. The omnipresent "Support Our Troops" decal is one way Americans broadcast their morality and affirm their commitment to the national community.

The connection to the empire starts early for most civilians. Kids say the Pledge of Allegiance in school, and a flag flies in the schoolyard. The symbols of empire are in the young students' faces every day, even as they read about its great history in their civics books. Few escape the sense of pride that comes from living in the world's most powerful and righteous nation.

The mass psychology of empire is fired up on the playing fields of America. Before every game, civilians salute the flag and sing the national anthem. Hands are on their hearts as the flag flaps in the wind. Here, the community of fandom is being melded with the greater community of nation and empire. Sports fever and patriotic sentiment are united in what may be the most potent dose of moral community in an otherwise atomized and morally decaying civilian life.

In new stages of empire, resonance kicks in at a higher-than-normal level. Think what happened right after 9/11. The entire country rallied around the president and around each other. Flags appeared on every car and front lawn. People watched the buildings collapse. They held each other, wept, and engaged in a solemn covenant of revenge and redemption. The empire was renewed and every citizen became, for a moment, a soldier for freedom and for America. Most Americans felt morally cleansed and renewed. And the feeling was addictive. Political leaders see a big, silver lining in the cloud of Islamic terror, and it enables them to unite the nation in the orchestrated "long war" that President Bush calls "moral clarity." Moral clarity and immoral morality mesh and fuel popular resonance with an imperial war on terror, much as Orwell would have predicted.

Karl Marx, as a nineteenth-century founder of sociology, would agree with much of Durkheim's interpretation of the Red Sox and the empire. But Marx would offer some new insights, including the idea that these modern totems are "opiate" of the masses.[11] This veers closer to the idea of immoral morality: the American hunger for community, solidarity, and values is being manipulated in the name of morality itself. Resonance for the American winning team, whether at Fenway Park or after 9/11, is a hat trick that turns the fans into ultimate losers, who embrace their losses as moral uplifting sacrifice.

If Marx had been in that Boston neighborhood during the big Sox game, he would have observed that many of the working- and middle-class fans on their porches were not feeling all that secure. Many were facing downsizing or outsourcing. Some were students or young graduates having trouble finding any jobs. This was the famous "anxious class" and many had double trouble: not only insecure jobs but unstable personal or family situations.

Those in the anxious class worried about being a loser. As they chugged down their beer and got swept up in the game, they began to feel relaxed and good, sliding happily into the bubble of sociability that was taking over the street. This was good, clean fun, but it was also escapism, the opiate that Marx mentions, not so different from the bullfights in the Roman Coliseum.

The game also turned an anxious class into potential winners. It looked that day like the Sox, famous for seizing defeat from the jaws of victory, might actually score a big win. Bostonians always dream that the Sox are eventually going to win it all, as they finally did in the 2005 World Series.

This has personal meaning for every Bostonian, a city famous for nourishing big professional and life dreams. As long as they believe in the Red Sox, the Boston fans, even those in the anxious class, can still believe that they can personally win in the big game of life.

Marx would likely have pointed out that what the Red Sox do for Bostonians is what empire can do on a grander scale for millions of Americans who are also part of the anxious class. During the height of the British Empire, Cecil Rhodes wrote that just to be British was "to win the lottery of life."[12] American great power can feel to the anxious class like winning the lottery in America. Just to know that you live in the world's most powerful country—and one that is defending the world against the evils of terrorism—can be morally uplifting. And if a perennially losing team like the Red Sox can keep the dream of victory alive, even an empire suffering reverses in Iraq or elsewhere may still sustain belief that the American team and its patriotic believers will themselves triumph in the end.

Marx would share Durkheim's view that both Red Sox and empire resonate powerfully as community totems in a capitalist society. Marx famously proclaimed that the capitalist market would eventually dissolve all relations between people into a jungle of ruthless competition, destroying love, sentiment, and anything but egoistic market calculation.[13] The citizens in this atomized nightmare might buy the individualistic American Dream, but would also yearn for human connection and moral solidarity, something like the Red Sox were offering on the street and that Bush claimed to offer after 9/11.

But Marx would describe these totems as contaminated and manipulated. As the elites pile the costs of globalization on the workers in the anxious class, their rational totem is the community of the anxious class itself, the community of workers and employees destined to be losers. They could truly be winners only by uniting together in a broad social movement to make change in the global capitalist rules. The Red Sox and the empire provide the illusion of winning but can't deliver the goods. Since the empire is costly in tax dollars, diverting resources from the jobs and social services that the anxious class needs, it undermines the anxious class whose support it seeks.

The empire totem is based on immoral morality of leaders who fear most the unification of its own anxious class against the empire regime. A unified anxious class is the real enemy of empire. They could organize unions, progressive parties, and community movements that create an alternative solidarity, one that might genuinely advance the moral interests of the people themselves. In the United States, where both Republican and

Democratic parties have been so closely aligned with the corporate order, this advancement of moral interests must come from outside the mainstream parties, from the grass-roots popular movement that arises from the disconnected and anxious themselves and seeks the moral agenda not of empire but of peace and social justice at home. One sees such populist movements today beginning to blossom on the Internet: think of the diffuse world of anti-imperial bloggers, to the antiwar MoveOn.org legendary Internet movement, to thousands of other grassroots or 'net-based campaigners against the Bush plutocracy. To cope with this threat to the empire, the Ideological Apparatus, with intense ideological and religious fervor under Bush and a more nuanced secular morality of self defense and humanitarian aims under President Obama, has collectively organized a moralist strategy based on the seductive inclusive values of empire. It offers itself as a cross-class community that provides the spiritual promise of combating global evil and defending universal values of freedom. It unites Americans of all classes and backgrounds into a single national community, an America based on God and moral values.

As in any moralist strategy, elites put forth empire as an alternative and superior community to one based on the anxious class itself, precisely because it is based on moral and spiritual rather than economic foundations. If the disconnected people of the anxious class rally together for economic interests, they may find a measure of community, but it is materialistic and exclusionary, catering necessarily to the self-interests of that class alone. In America, Democratic elites have been fatally conflicted, not only supporting the empire agenda but also wanting to win by appealing to the economic interests of their base. In contrast, the Republican moralists of empire, fearful of any economic- or class-based community among the masses, offer the nation as an alternative spiritual community transcending and uniting the interests of all classes. Its promises of spiritual and moral uplift are higher than those of economic advancement, the trump card of all moralist strategies. Should the anxious workers choose the narrower material path, they may win some wage increases but lose their soul. The success of this approach was spectacularly on display in red (Republican) states in the 2004 presidential election, as Tom Frank wrote in *What's the Matter with Kansas.*[14] Kansans—including many in the Kansas anxious class—voted Republican because they had been persuaded that voting their religious convictions on God, family, and country morally trumped their economic anxieties. President Obama's election suggests the possibility that the severity of the 2008 economic meltdown may have changed the equation, a matter we take up in the last two chapters. But we need to look more closely at why it succeeded so powerfully in the Bush years, and why it may be taking a new form in the Obama era.

The core of empire's immoral morality is revealed in Frank's argument about Kansas. The Empire's economic elite makes grand moral claims to undermine a genuine moral cause of the class it seeks to seduce and control. It defines the economic needs of the anxious class as materialistic and amoral when they are central to social justice. To avoid meeting these moral claims, and to prevent the formation of the movement that could topple their power, they redefine morality itself, excluding the base "material" concerns of the anxious class and claiming a more universal and higher set of spiritual and moral principles—of liberty, self-determination, and democracy—that the empire itself violates.

Since the empire undermines its own workers' economic interests, the anxious class will continue to decline. In the guise of economic and moral uplift, the empire is actually undermining the prospects of the anxious class. Its decline—now reflected in more than twenty-five years of stagnant wages and drastic cuts in social services—is frightening. You work harder, longer hours at more jobs, but your debt just increases, and good jobs seem harder to get or hang on to. You see friends, family, and yourself perched on a precipice, some falling fast and hard to the bottom, deep in debt with no way to bail themselves out. Fifteen percent of Americans, you learn, declare bankruptcy every year. Fifty percent of Americans worry about losing their jobs, and the majority of them do not have enough savings to pay their mortgage or put food on the table after a few months of unemployment.

This creates a mass psychology of fear, the most richly resonant soil for empire and its morality tales. The fear of the anxious class is not an illusion or neurosis. It is a clear reflection of the long-term structural condition that ordinary working Americans now face. Our corporations and leaders have led us into a socioeconomic order that locks in social insecurity and throws away the key. Nobody who's rational in the anxious class can be unafraid.

Fear is empire's dream. In Orwell's Oceania, the omnipresent telescreens projected scary images, and the loud bomb explosions of the enemy armies bang, thud, and booooom throughout Eurasia all day long. All empires feed on fear, most directly the fear of being attacked, a fear that an anxious class is more primed to embrace. Fear of attack requires, first, an enemy: a nation or group that will attack you. Without an enemy, the most popular rationale for empire, even for the anxious class, crumbles—a prospect that sent American leaders into a near panic after the collapse of the Soviet Union. A desperate effort to define new enemies ensued and the Ideological Apparatus produced a laundry list of possibilities: global drug dealers, rogue states, failed states, nonstates, terrorists. Before 9/11, terrorists didn't make the cut.

This makes clear that who the "enemy" is usually involves ambiguity and interpretation, with the designation of the official enemy typically constructed by the political leadership, the Pentagon, and the entire Ideological Apparatus. The first test of empire resonance is whether the public finds the official enemy to be credible. A simple gut test comes into play for the ordinary citizen: do you feel afraid?

Here is where the mass psychology of fear—as carried by the anxious class and more broadly by a disconnected population—connects with the requirements of empire. Fear is a diffuse and generalized emotion. It can float in the psyche and is fungible, attaching first to one threat and then moving on to another. If you are afraid of losing your job, you live in a chronic state of aroused anxiety. It becomes difficult to know why you are feeling afraid, and you are more likely to become afraid of almost anything.

For the empire, this lowers the threshold of popular resonance to the official enemy. Diffuse anxiety is far easier to deal with when it is attached to a specific threat. The anxious class is looking for anything concrete to explain and focus its generalized discomfort. When the political leadership serves up an enemy, a fearful populace is far more likely to grab the bait. After 9/11, Bush fished for the anxious class with a terrorist enemy he called more evil and dangerous than Hitler and Communism, and the anxious class, indeed most of the country, swallowed hook, line, and sinker.

Fear made the country not only receptive to the new official enemy but to the inflation of the threat, a strategy essential to American Empire. A fearful condition like this can escalate to panic quickly, something leaders exploit with images of nuclear terrorism and mushroom clouds over American cities. Such inflation of a real but low-probability threat, more credible to the anxious class, also made Americans resonate to a response of clobbering the enemy, a response not only disproportionate to the threat but increasing the threat itself. When I (Derber) was in the dental chair after 9/11, having my teeth cleaned, the hygienist said she supported the president. She was ready to go to war anywhere and take out al-Qaeda and other terrorists. When I pointed out the obvious fact that Bush's war in Iraq was the best recruitment device that Osama bin Laden ever had, turning even many of the most pro-American Iraqis into zealots ready to sign on to the anti-American jihad, she said she thought we should nuke the whole country or region, if that was what it took.

Fear increases the resonance of my dental hygienist and many others in the anxious class partly because fear is fungible in a second sense: it can escalate to other emotions including rage. I learned that my hygienist's husband had lost a close, personal friend when the World Trade Center fell, and this made her both afraid and extremely angry. When the fear of the anxious class is converted to or melded with anger, it produces a population supportive of a president who is ready for revenge. Kill or be killed becomes emotional common sense, even if it is totally irrational.

Intense fear also diminishes people's ability to cognitively reason, making the anxious class less able or disposed to process critically the lies being dished out by the administration, such as the idea that Saddam Hussein conspired with Osama bin Laden to bring down the Twin Towers. I mentioned this to my hygienist, but she brushed it aside as a detail that she did not believe. I repeated the many reliable sources on the lie, including the president's own recent admission that Hussein had not planned or helped create 9/11. This cut no ice with her. A fearful, angry, or vengeful population is reluctant to withdraw support from its strong leader who is promising to protect and avenge them.

The combustible, emotional mix of anger, fear, and revenge ratchets up resonance with a core moral tenet of empire: that honorable and effective self-defense requires a strong offense. In the last chapter, we showed how this argument goes back to President Polk in the 1840s war of conquest against Mexico. *It now is the maxim central to American global Empire: that the defense of freedom in the United States is inseparable from the defense of freedom everywhere. This means taking it to the enemy, in President Bush's oft-repeated phrase, "whereever he is." In Orwellian terms: OFFENSE IS HONORABLE DEFENSE.* If we don't take the enemy out in Iraq or Iran, we will end up fighting him in Chicago or Kansas City or San Diego.

A fearful or angry population will be more resonant to the idea that security requires aggressive expansion. The downsized worker—or one fearful that he might be downsized—is told he has to get more aggressive in order to keep his job, or find a new one. Your own survival depends on your willingness to fight and expand your playing field. Track down possible job leaders anywhere in the country; cold call often and anywhere. If personal security is so closely tied to aggressive initiative and expansion, then it makes emotional sense to the anxious class that national security might require the same thing. This is music to the empire, which now depends ultimately on the popular belief that the defense of America requires American boots on the ground from Japan to Iraq to Colombia.

The litany of reasons why millions of ordinary Americans resonate with America's imperial morality tales does not imply they are lost permanently to the empire. A totem of a winning team loses its magical power when the team begins to lose and keeps losing. The American Empire may be on the cusp of a great turn, which could transform the long national history of victory into a quagmire of defeat and decline. Imperial decline can increase resonance, but it is more likely to have the opposite effect, particularly if the fall is fast and the landing hard. Later, we shall look at the prospects of immoral morality and its resonance in a permanently losing team, finding reasons for hope not only in that pessimistic scenario but in more sunny ones as well.

PART II
Born-Again Nations

4

Hitler's Born-Again Story
Fascism as an Immoral Moral Awakening

It is a strange experience to read *Mein Kampf,* Hitler's philosophical autobiography.[1] On one hand, the book can be seen as the racist sewer talk of a madman. On the other hand, its calls for moral and spiritual renewal are so passionate that it is hard not to be mesmerized. While Hitler has rightly become the symbol of pure evil, and *Mein Kampf* has been called the "Satanic Bible," fascism connected with the German people's deepest personal hopes and moral ideals. It affirmed the German nation as the founder of human morality and the natural leader of the world. It took a people's despair and promised a way in which the entire German nation could be born again. *Mein Kampf* is essentially a treatise on how the Germans could be collectively—and magnificently—born again.

This "born again" moral narrative is a second critically important paradigm of immoral morality. Like empire, it is an ancient form of hegemonic moralism, and has often been used to justify empire itself. But the born-again story, while often co-existing with empire, needs to be understood as a distinct system. Part II thus departs from the focus on empire morality of Part I and turns to different varieties of the born-again narrative. In this chapter, we show that fascism was rooted in an especially toxic form of the born-again story. In the next two chapters, we show that two other versions of born-again immoral morality—different from Germany and from each other—have risen in the United States, one in the South after the Civil War and one in the Religious Right and the Republican Party today.

Toward the beginning of *Mein Kampf,* Hitler wrote of his own personal faith: "I am acting in accordance with the will of the Almighty Creator. . . . I am fighting for the work of the Lord."[2] Hitler also wrote that the Fascist movement was, in essence, spiritual: "The young [Fascist] movement, from the first day, espoused the standpoint that its idea must be put forward spiritually, but that the defense of this spiritual platform must if necessary be secured by strong-arm means ... for the attainment of its goal no sacrifice can be too great."[3]

Hitler expresses here the two intertwined elements of his Fascist philosophy. The first was spiritual transformation of an entire people, going far beyond mundane economics and politics. The second was to implement this great spiritual aim by gaining power with violence, a form of Fascist moral "sacrifice" in which the German nation itself would have to die and then be reborn.

Before discussing Hitler and Germany in depth, listen briefly to Benito Mussolini, who brought fascism to Italy almost a decade before Hitler took power in Germany. Mussolini used almost identical language to Hitler's in defining fascism as a spiritual vision: "Fascism is a religious belief in which man is seen in imminent relationship with a superior and objective will that transcends the particular individual and raises him to conscious membership in a spiritual society.[4]

Mussolini precedes Hitler in defining fascism in spiritual terms, a movement in which *each citizen must die and be reborn* in the "complete spiritual existence" that alone makes life meaningful. You can achieve this by joining the Fascist movement and sacrificing for the spiritual nation that only fascism can create.

Mussolini saw fascism as a movement "more concerned with moral regeneration than with the equitable distribution of economic goods."[5] Although he had been a socialist before the war, Mussolini felt the war had proved that ordinary people are moved not just by their economic interests, that is, their "class interests," but also "by psychological and moral considerations that transcend them."[6] Socialism had forgotten the importance of morality and spirituality, Mussolini argued, and mistakenly put its faith in economics and class solidarity. Classes, though, would never be the basis of community for workers. Instead, Mussolini said, the nation is always the spiritual bond of the people. "Class," he wrote, "is based on the community of interests but the nation is a history of sentiments of traditions, of language of culture or race."[7] Later, he wrote, "The fatherland is the hard and solid ground, the millenarian product of the race."[8]

Mussolini saw the nation as a "moral union of individuals," the foundation on which morality itself rested.[9] And the institution that must express and enforce that morality was the state, the highest form of community. The individual, who Mussolini also claimed to respect, could only find his moral identity in solidarity with a morally reborn state and nation. Mussolini argued that the state was "the community of blood," whose function was "to conduct the struggle against nature, misery, ignorance, impotence and slavery of every form in which men find themselves in the state of nature."[10]

Mussolini promised that fascism would use the state to combat the moral decay that contributed to Italian malaise after World War I. Shortly after his march on Rome in 1922, Mussolini declared his aim to capture state power for moral and spiritual ends, arguing that "The state is a moral idea which incarnates itself and expresses itself in a system of hierarchies.... I intend to re-establish with all the means at my disposal a single national discipline binding upon sect, faction, and party."[11] Mussolini promised a moral rebirth in which the individual, "through the sacrifice of his own private interests, through death itself, realizes that complete spiritual existence in which lies his values as a man."[12]

Decay and Rebirth: The Morality Tale of Fascism

Fascism was a moral movement with a very specific morality tale: *decay and rebirth*. It is one of the classic stories of immoral morality, and exhibits the most frightening elements of the genre: the claim to spiritually create anew a nation by a movement committed to violence and evil. The rebirth story surfaces in various forms, not just in classical fascism but in religious politics around the world, including not only Islamic religious fanatics in the Middle East but the Religious Right in America and its political sponsor, the Republican Party.

Fascism was founded on the idea that Italy and Germany had both long been spiritually rotting and decaying, which explained the crushing and humiliating defeat of Germany in World War I. The Fascist movement would explain the causes of the decay and eradicate it. It would then catalyze a rebirth of the nation, one that would realize its historic moral and spiritual ideals and rise to great power and glory in the world.

In 1991, the influential British historian, Roger Griffen, wrote a work explicitly defining fascism as a morality tale of rebirth. Griffen argues the "mythic core" of fascism is "a palingenetic form of populist ultra-nationalism." Griffen defines the "palingenetic myth" as "The myth of renewal, of rebirth. Etymologically the term *palingenesis,* deriving from *palin* (again, renew) and *genesis* (creation, birth) refers to the sense of a new start of regeneration after a phase of crisis or decline."[13]

Griffen observes that the main source of palingenetic myth "in the wider sense is religion. The resurrection of Jesus Christ places one such myth at the very center of a whole faith." Moreover, myths of decay and renewal,

Griffen points out, are "a central motif of religious, mythical, and magical thought encountered literally the world over."[14]

However, fascism expresses a more specific form of palingenetic myth, one that has secular as well as religious meaning, which is applied to politics and is focused on historical decay and a moment of revolutionary change. Griffen argues that at the heart of the myth is the belief that we are living in a "turning point in the historical process." The "perceived corruption" and "decadence of the present" are "interpreted as the sure sign that a new order is about to emerge."[15]

The "populist ultra-nationalist" form of the Fascist rebirth myth is focused on rebirth of the nation or a people or race:

> Associated with a concept of the nation as a "higher" racial, historical, spiritual, or organic reality that embraces the members of the ethical community who belong to it. Such a community is regarded by its protagonists as a natural order which can be contaminated by miscegenation and immigration, by the anarchic, unpatriotic mentality encouraged by liberal individualism, internationalist socialism, and by any number of "alien" forces allegedly unleashed by "modern" society, for example, the rise of the masses, the decline of moral values, the "leveling of society, cosmopolitanism, feminism, and consumerism."[16]

Griffen sums up the Fascist essence as a vision of "the national community rising phoenix-like after a period of encroaching decadence which all but destroyed it."[17] As for the power of this vision to create resonance with the masses, Griffen has little doubt. The story of the reborn nation, under the right economic and social conditions, has "the almost alchemical power to transmute black despair into manic optimism and thus enable a party which promotes this vision to win."[18]

The Fascist morality tale, that is, has the political mobilizing power to create mass resonance and help its proponents seize state power, the purpose of all systems of political immoral morality. The popular appeal is of a deep order that Griffen compares, psychologically, to the passion of "falling in love." Its magnetism undoubtedly fueled Hitler's rise to power. But because the Fascist myth does not spell out the nature of the born-again nation, and because it is based on manipulation, duplicity, and other aspects of immoral morality, it involves "the heady emotions of 'falling in love' without any temperamental capacity to imagine or endure a steady relationship, let alone a marriage, which might eventually grow out of the passion when it cools."[19]

Hitler's Born-Again Story

Hitler wrote *Mein Kampf* while he was in jail, in 1924, after a failed armed putsch. It became a best-seller second only to the Bible. In an introduction to an English translation, German scholar Konrad Heiden calls it "a program of blood and terror in a self-revelation of such overwhelming frankness that few among its readers had the courage to believe it."[20] Heiden says, correctly, it was "written in white hot anger," a book of racist hatred, all true, but words that mask the appeal of the book as a spiritual tract appealing to the highest moral values of the German people. *Mein Kampf* is perhaps the most important book of immoral morality ever written, offering an intense moral and spiritual message to mobilize the masses, seize state power, and hold it through extreme violence, including genocide.

Mein Kampf is a central document in the study of fascism, defining the classical Fascist worldview from its most important source. And while most analysts have seen the book as disordered rantings of a lunatic, it actually has a coherent argument when perceived as an effort to spell out German fascism's morality code:

1. The German nation and the Aryan race are a higher force in themselves and more than the sum of individual people.
2. They have a spiritual value that is more important than their economic or material interests.
3. The greatness of Germany is embodied in the führer. All must submit to his will.
4. The Aryan race has been endowed with the mission to create and preserve all that is pure, beautiful, and meaningful.
5. All other races must submit to the Aryan and serve it or be destroyed.
6. There are vermin among the midst of the Aryan nation who undermine its purpose.
7. These parasites have produced decadence in the form of urbanism, materialism, "free expression," pacifism, and a preference for intellectualism over spirituality.
8. This plague has undermined Germany's strength and caused her defeat in World War I.
9. War is a moral good in its own right. It brings unity and strength.
10. The most threatening of the parasites are the Jews. For them, there is no redemption. They must be destroyed.

11. Once the sources of decay are eliminated, the Aryan race, through Germany, can take over the world for the good of a higher humanity.
12. The Aryan race will have the living space it needs to thrive and all other races will serve it.
13. The Nazi victory will give birth to a harmonious world order—a perfect thousand-year reich.

Mein Kampf, which spells out this code, is really a book in two chapters, one focusing on German decay that led to its catastrophic defeat in World War I, and the other focusing on the rebirth of the nation that would propel Hitler to power and Germany toward a great empire. The chapters come together as the backbone of a moralist strategy for permanent Fascist power.

Decay

After World War I, Germans were obsessed with defeat. National catastrophes gripped the soul of a nation, creating both collective malaise and a passion for a grand new vision. Moralist political movements, especially on the Right, have traditionally spun a morality tale to speak to this malaise and capture power. Hitler and fascism offered one compelling Radical Right story, with obvious parallels to Far Right morality tales today. It was a moral narrative of German decay and rebirth that could lead Germans from defeat to World Power.

Hitler devotes much of *Mein Kampf* to explaining Germany's long decay prior to the war. "Decay," "degeneration," and "decadence" are among the book's most frequently used words. Hitler means many things, but at the heart of it is the decline of moral values and spiritual degeneration of the German people, who he defines as a race that is the greatest on earth because it is the ultimate founder of culture; it is "culture-creating."[21] Other peoples use or consume culture or are parasites, says Hitler, but only the Aryan people are endowed with the gift to create the culture and moral values that elevate the human spirit as intended by nature and God.

While consumed by the German defeat in World War I—which Hitler describes as ultimately caused by "an ethical and moral poisoning"[22]—he views the war as a gift for exposing the decay: "For the German people it must almost be considered a great good fortune that its period of creeping sickness was suddenly cut short by so terrible a catastrophe, for otherwise the nation would have gone to the dogs more slowly perhaps, but all the more certainly. The disease would have become chronic."[23]

The "creeping sickness" was the spiritual decay of the "culture-creating" people that the war laid bare. It was a gradual but wholesale weakening of the creative essence and moral fiber of the Germans, the abandonment of their God-given responsibility to create the values Heaven intended. Hitler views this decay in the historic German national character as a kind of spiritual tuberculosis, which had infected and sickened all phases of pre-war national life. It eroded all the traditional values of German "blood and soil," of a people famous for its moral simplicity and discipline, its vigor, creativity, and iron will. In full moralist dress, Hitler now spewed forth endless pages on decay and decadence in every phase of life: economy, sexuality, family, the arts, education, politics, and religion itself. All would prove central to Hitler's argument for Fascist power and his own rule.

Hitler described a "spiritual" crisis of family values, especially of the young, embedded in the "moral plague of big-city 'civilization.'" Much of it is sexual, with nudity, prostitution, and easy sex—the "stifling perfume of our modern eroticism":

> Our whole public life today is like a hothouse for sexual ideas and stimulations. Just look at the bill of fare served up in our movies, vaudeville, and theaters, and you will hardly be able to deny that this is not the right kind of food, particularly for the youth. In shop windows and billboards the vilest means are used to attract the attention of the crowd.... This sensual, sultry atmosphere leads to ideas and stimulations at a time when the boy should have no understanding of such things.[24]

After the war, the rise of feminist movements, gay movements, and experimental forms of theater and dance accelerated this "spiritual madness." During the Weimar Republic of the 1920s, women in Germany gained more rights than elsewhere in Europe, including the rights to vote and to be educated; before Hitler came to power, there were 111 women representatives in the Reichstag, the most of any nation in Europe. When he came into power, Hitler endorsed the Kaiser's old phrase of *Kinder, Kirche, Kuche* (children, church, kitchen), driving women back into the home and celebrating a renewed cult of female domesticity and childbearing (with four children seen as ideal). He said in a speech: "Woman's world is her husband, her family, her children, and her home. We do not find it right when she presses into the world of men."

Hitler called the breakdown of women's traditional place in the family as a key to moral decay. In his first radio address after seizing power, on February 1, 1933, Hitler vowed to defend the family, along with religion, as the national rock supporting morality: "The National Government will preserve and defend those basic principles on which our nation has been built up. It regards Christianity as the foundation of our national morality and the family as the basis of national life."[25]

Likewise, Hitler denounced homosexuality as a decadent perversion of sexuality and the family. Homosexuals became more visible and public during Weimar, with many gays joining Hitler's movement, including Ernst Roehm, the head of the the Sturmabteilung, or SA, as well as other top Nazis like Rudolf Hess. But Hitler became an increasingly vocal moralist against homosexuality. The law against homosexual conduct had existed in Germany for many years prior to the Nazi regime as Paragraph 175 of the Reich Criminal Code, to wit: "A male who indulges in criminally indecent activity with another male, or who allows himself to participate in such activity, will be punished with imprisonment."[26] When Hitler came to power, he used this law as a means of tracking down and punishing those homosexuals who, in the words of one victim, "had defended the Weimar Republic, and who had tried to forestall the Nazi threat."[27] Later, he expanded the law and used it as a convenient tool to detain other enemies of the regime.

After gaining power, Hitler's rhetoric and policy against gays became increasingly punitive, embedded in broad moral and spiritual language about moral decay and the defense of family and religion. In 1935, Hitler amended the pre-existing law against homosexuals to toughen it, and many homosexuals were eventually sent to the concentration camps. The attack on feminists and gays as agents of moral decay is, of course, familiar today. Weimar's moral progress—offering new rights and tolerance for groups long discriminated against—was portrayed by fascism as moral decay. Moreover, violence against these groups was conducted in the name of moral values and spiritual purification. This is a sure sign of immoral morality: carrying out evil in the name of God and moral values. The Fascists' immoral morality is also shown by the use of anti-gay moral rhetoric as a strategy not simply for demeaning particular groups but for attacking political enemies and attracting popular support. Even in the 1930s, there was no easier way to achieve popular resonance than to attack gays as a symbol of moral decay.

Historian Walter Laquer has shown that, along with feminist and homosexual social movements, modernist and expressionist artistic movements flourished in the 1920s Weimer Republic, especially in big cities like Berlin. As shown in the famous movie *Cabaret,* dancehalls featuring nudity, sex, and experimental art or theater became common throughout

German cities associated with a loosening of traditional sexual mores and a breakdown of traditional female modesty and domesticity. Josephine Baker, the famous erotic dancer, symbolized the new ethos. And then there were the world-famous literary cafés of Berlin where "a great many people were to be seen dressed as poets with strangely growing beards, crazy ties, and long manes."[28] These cafés, says Laquer, led the world in a new experimental counterculture, similar to the 1960s and 1970s American counterculture: "It was a literary caravanserai. . . . For what was discussed in the Berlin literary cafés in the evening was repeated two days later in New York, London, Paris, and even Rio de Janeiro. School reformers were sitting there next to all kinds of fanatics, revolutionaries next to pickpockets, people on drugs next to apostles of health-food and vegetarianism."[29]

All of this new cultural experimentation—in arts, dance, literature, and theater—was seen by much of the world as a sign of a great German cultural renaissance. Who could not admire a brilliant playwright such as Bertolt Brecht, a towering symbol of the new German culture? Or the artist George Grosz? Or the actress Marlene Dietrich? But the German Far Right, including the Fascists, saw the new artists as decadent, soiling the great traditions of German art and literature, and subverting the sturdy rural culture that had sustained the German *Volk*, or nation. Hitler, who writes reverently in *Mein Kampf* of traditional folkish culture, sees this decadent "spiritual madness" spreading like a cancer, and promises to "master this disease" by destroying it in the name of preserving culture and morality, again a defining sign of immoral morality.

Hitler explicitly condemns the new modernist culture as a key part of the moral "creeping sickness." "Theatre, art, literature, cinema, press, posters, and window displays" all are "manifestations of our rotting world."[30] Hitler lambastes futurist art as an example:

> A cultural collapse . . . began to manifest itself in futurist and cubist works since 1900. . . . Sixty years ago an exhibition of so-called Dadaistic "experiences" would have seemed simply impossible and its organizers would have ended up in the madhouse, while today they even preside over art associations. This plague could not appear at that time, because neither would public opinion have tolerated it nor the state calmly looked on. For it is the business of the state . . . to prevent a people from being driven into the arms of spiritual madness.[31]

Hitler writes about such cultural innovation that, "Everywhere we encounter seeds which represent the beginnings of parasitic growths which must sooner or later be the ruin of our culture.... Such diseases could be seen in Germany in nearly every field of art and culture."[32]

Hitler writes often also of the moral blight of the modern big cities, and often described them as "Jew cities" and "sin cities." Hitler sees the new German cities as creators of a "rootless" lifestyle, created by the Jews, grotesque deformations of traditional rural life, which was rooted in "blood and soil" and created real moral community: "In the nineteenth century our cities began more and more to lose the character of cultural sites and to descend to the level of mere human settlements.... This is partly connected with the frequent change of residence caused by social conditions ... [current big cities] cannot lay claim to the slightest real vales. Masses of apartments and tenements, and nothing more. How, in view of such emptiness, any special bond could be expected to arise with such a town must remain a mystery."[33]

The rise of what today are called "secular humanists" who have broken from religion is, Hitler argues, another cause of these problems, creating a "weak" or soft cultural relativism and "humanitarianism" instead of iron moral discipline and submission to God's will. Beyond the traditional loss of faith is the erosion, even among believers, of religious dogma. Submission to the absolute authority of scripture is vital to Hitler to combat moral weakness and relativism, both in church and state:

> Also noteworthy is the increasingly violent struggle against the dogmatic foundations of the various churches without which in this human world the practical existence of religious faith is not conceivable. The great masses of people do not consist of philosophers; precisely for the masses, faith is often the sole foundation of a moral attitude.... But if religious doctrine and faith are really to embrace the broad masses, the unconditional authority of the content of this faith is the foundation of all efficacy.... The attack against dogmas as such, therefore strongly resembles the struggle against the general legal foundations of a state and, as the latter would end in a total anarchy of the state, the former would end in a worthless religious nihilism.[34]

Here, Hitler makes explicit the "dogma" and authoritarianism that he argues is the bedrock of both church and state. Less fundamentalist forms of religion may make possible a more democratic, tolerant, and flexible spirituality. But as befits an immoral moralist, Hitler argues that attacks on fundamentalism in either church or state lead to "anarchy" and needed to be destroyed in the name of preserving spirituality itself. Because the masses lack any solid moral anchor, they must be guided by strong religious and political leaders who are prepared to exercise the absolute and fundamentalist doctrine on which the people's very survival depends. Fascism is unapologetic about its spiritual fundamentalism and its political authoritarianism, and Hitler defines them as the only viable "foundation of a moral attitude." Where even genocidal violence is required, it is the wrath of a righteous spiritual sword.[35] Here, immoral morality is outed, since blatant evil—the violent persecution of religious liberals and democratic opponents—is carried out in the name of moral values and spiritual rebirth.

Rebirth

Rebirth requires, first, destroying the agents of decay. Hitler's virulent anti-Semitism targeted the Jews as the cause of all decay. The Jew "has no culture-creating force of any sort"[36] and is thus always a cultural "parasite," who "takes over foreign culture, imitating or rather ruining it."[37] Hitler saw Jews as infecting modern Germany like a parasitic microbe, poisoning the great cultural traditions of the *Volk*. The Jewish bacteria is responsible for all the decadence of modernism: corrupt cities, financial capitalism, Marxism, social democracy, liberalism, democracy, secular humanism, and the breakdown of traditional family values and authority itself. To permanently stop moral and spiritual decay, one must exterminate the Jews.

We remember Hitler for this incredible racism and for the Holocaust, carried out in the name of removing the root cause of moral decay. But we forget, at our peril, that Hitler gained resonance because there was a story of exhilarating rebirth to follow. Once the Jews were eliminated, the Germans were promised that they could begin the process of revolutionary spiritual rebirth: reclaiming their creative essence as a people, their moral values, and their destiny to lead the world.

This revolution begins with Hitler's view of culture—and the special place of the German or Aryan race in the very existence of culture. A people or nation is defined by its culture, and the Aryan people have a special destiny in the creation of the world's culture: "If we were to divide mankind into three groups, the founders of culture, the bearers of culture, the destroyers of culture, only the Aryan could be considered as the representative of the first group. From him originate the foundations and walls of all human creation."[38]

Hitler adds that the German people "provide the mightiest building stones and plans for all human progress." To all other peoples, it falls "only the execution," that is, following through on the great moral and spiritual visions created by the German "culture-creators."

The heart of the German gift for culture and world leadership, Hitler argues, is not intellectual but moral and spiritual power. Since it is the world's only creator of culture, the German community has a special destiny to lead the world. Hitler links cultural creation and German rebirth to this moral capacity to transcend the ego and serve the community: "This state of mind, which subordinates the interests of the ego to the conservation of the community, is really the first premise for every truly human culture. From it alone can arise all the great works of mankind.... Our own German language possesses a word which magnificently designates this kind of activity: *Pflichterfullung* (fulfillment of duty); it means not to be self-sufficient but to serve the community."[39]

Hitler, the moralist, clearly articulates the widespread sense that culture and national rebirth require going beyond "egoism and selfishness." But the immoral morality of his concept of duty comes in the call for absolute submission and obedience of the masses. Hitler says moral rebirth "requires willingness on the part of the individual to sacrifice himself for the community."[40] He means more than renouncing egoism but totally subordinating the self to the authority of the moral national leaders, that is, moral authoritarianism: "It alone leads men to voluntary recognition of the privilege of force and strength, and thus makes them into a dust particle of that order which shapes and forms the whole universe."[41]

This is something different than humanistic community, since it treats the individual as a "dust particle" who means nothing in relation to the leader and larger community. This individual is born again when he sacrifices readily for the leader, whose heroic vision of national rebirth will require the ultimate sacrifice of wars and patriotic violence. "The same boy who feels like throwing up when he hears the tirades of a pacific 'idealist' is ready to give his young life for the ideal of his nationality."[42] A great people, Hitler argues, "obeys the deeper necessity of the preservation of the species, if necessary at the costs of the individual, and protests against the visions of the pacifist windbag who in reality is nothing but a cowardly, though camouflaged egoist."[43]

There is only one true symbol of the morally reborn community that Hitler envisages: the army. Before the war, the army was the only German bastion against decay:

> The army trained men for unconditional responsibility ... it trained men in personal courage in an age when cowardice threatened to become a raging disease.... The army trained men in resolution while elsewhere in life indecision and doubt were beginning to determine the actions of men ... it meant something to uphold the principle that some command is always

better than none.... The army trained men in idealism and devotion to the fatherland and its greatness.[44]

The born again German nation will turn every citizen into a soldier of the German army. He or she will serve the nation obediently and sacrifice for the larger mission of the German nation: to recover its place as the world's greatest nation, which alone has the spiritual and cultural creativity, as well as the will to sacrifice and power that must guide and control the modern world. Hitler says repeatedly that German rebirth will require harnessing the spiritual vision of the Aryan to an organization of disciplined violence, something that only the Fascists can deliver.

The born again nation is a product of Fascist violence fueled by a great spiritual vision or idea. But as a moralist, Hitler emphasizes the priority of the idea or moral philosophy. "The application of force alone, without the impetus of a basic spiritual idea as a starting point," says Hitler, is doomed.[45] Only in the steady and constant application of force lies the very first prerequisite for success. This persistence, however, can always and only arise from a definite spiritual conviction. Any violence that does not spring from a firm, spiritual basis will be wavering and uncertain.[46]

Hitler emphasizes that violence must be driven by a positive moral philosophy that renews the national spirit. The fight against decay requires an optimism of the spirit: "Any attempt to combat a philosophy with methods of violence will fail in the end, unless the fight takes the form of attack for a new spiritual attitude."[47]

What Hitler and fascism offered was this "new spiritual attitude," the rebirth of the "new German man." Hitler argued that "the reason for the failure of the struggle against Marxism," which symbolized the modernist, Jewish ethos and was rotting the German masses, was the failure to bring a truly uplifting spiritual alternative: Marxism offers only superficial economic rewards and a "leveling" of the masses.[48] It does nothing to transform spiritual life; in fact, it degrades the spirit with its materialistic focus on economic and democratic social rights.

But fascism, and the *Volkish* (or folkish) philosophy that it resurrects, sees the superficiality of this modernist economic and democratic focus. It rejects materialism and envisages a reborn religious nation: "The Government, being resolved to undertake the political and moral purification of our public life, is creating and securing the conditions necessary for a really profound revival of religious life.... The Government of the Reich regards Christianity as the unshakable foundation of the morals and moral code of the nation."[49]

But Hitler's rejection of the modernist and Left's materialism and democratic equalities goes beyond just embracing religion: it speaks to the concept of "personality," the inequalities and "aristocracies" of nature, and the creative spiritual forces of humanity, culture, nature, and God embedded in folkish philosophy. Fascism emphasizes belonging to and service to the community, and it also holds high the creative essence of each individual personality; much of *Mein Kampf* is Hitler's testimonial to the vitality of each German, whose personality is sacred and to which fascism pledges its ultimate commitment. Hitler is a mesmerizing cheerleader for the German soul and what we would today call "personal growth" and "spiritual awakening":

> The folkish philosophy . . . extracts the importance of the individual personality, and thus, in contrast to disorganizing Marxist, it has an organizing effect. It believes in the necessity of an idealization of humanity, in which alone it sees the premise for the existence of humanity. . . .
>
> And so the folkish philosophy of life corresponds to the inner-most will of Nature, since it restores that free play of forces which must lead to a continuous higher breeding, until at least the best of humanity, having achieved possession of this earth, will have a free path.[50]

Fascism ultimately speaks of hope and redemption. And Hitler is the great moralist, giving every German the promise of being reborn in the "aristocracy of nature" that God has ordained. Capitalists and Marxists may offer bread sustaining the body, but fascism offers the true freedom that comes from rebirth in God's eternal embrace. Other parties, mainly of the Left, speak to the belly. Fascism speaks to the soul.

Why Ordinary Folk Resonated to Fascism

In discussing popular resonance with Hitler and fascism, we need to make three cautionary points. First, before gaining power in 1933, Hitler never did win acceptance among more than about one-third of the populace, although after gaining power the majority of the public embraced him. Second, much of the support he did gain had to do with his restimulation of the economy through military spending and creating jobs for unemployed Germans, essentially ending the German depression. And, third, Hitler gained support partly because of the most sophisticated propaganda apparatus ever created, one that generated endless lies, controlled the entire Ideological Apparatus, and served ever since as a worldwide model for effective propaganda.

In the Introduction and Chapter 3, we discussed resonance as a concept for understanding what helps make propaganda or moral visions attractive to the people. Propaganda involving immoral morality becomes resonant when it meets two criteria: (1) it connects with longstanding national ideology or cultural values, and (2) it emerges under conditions of desperate economic or social insecurity that make ordinary people receptive to moral or spiritual appeals.

Regarding the first, Hitler's tale of decay and rebirth exquisitely resonated with the *Volk* ideology that had become a dominant national cultural myth in late nineteenth-century Germany. In one form or another, the majority of Germans had assimilated and embraced the *Volk* story. The great chronicler of *Volk* ideology is historian George L. Mosse, whose work is critically important for anyone trying to understand fascism, the radical Right, and immoral morality. Mosse observes that *Volk* was the central ideological concept in Germany since the late eighteenth century, developed by leading German intellectuals to capture the essence of a people's spiritual identity: "*Volk* signified the union of a group of people with a transcendental 'essence.'" This "essence" might be called "nature" or "cosmos" or "mythos," but in each instance it was fused to man's innermost nature and represented the source of his creativity, his depth of feeling, his individuality, and his unity with other members of the *Volk*.[51]

Mosse argues that nearly all *Volk* thinkers, including Hitler, invoked nature and a deep connection to the land as central to vitality, moral values, and spirituality. "The essential element is the linking of the human soul with its natural surroundings, with the 'essence' of nature."[52] *Volk*ish thinkers, Mosse argues, saw the traditional German's rootedness in the land and nature as the key to German morality and spirituality:

The term "rooted" was constantly invoked by Volkish thinkers—and with good reason. Such rootedness conveyed the sense of man's correspondence with the landscape through his soul and thus with the *Volk*, which embodied the life spirit of the cosmos ... rural rootedness served as a contrast to urban dislocation, or what was termed "uprootedness." ... The concept of rootedness provided a standard for measuring man's completeness and his inner worth. Accordingly, having no roots stigmatized a person as being deprived of the life force and thus lacking a properly functioning soul.[53]

The ideology of the *Volk* is essentially an appeal to traditional moral values and spirituality, idealized among the German peasantry. As Mosse sums it up:

It used and amplified romanticism to prove an alternative to modernity, to the developing industrial and urban civilization which seemed to rob man of his individual, creative self while cutting him loose from a social order that was seemingly exhausted and lacking vitality.... It simultaneously gave new life to the possibility of individual self-fulfillment by making it part of the creative process of a higher life force. As this force, which streamed from the cosmos, was transmitted through the *Volk,* it was imperative that the individual be a member of the *Volk* unit.... It also made belonging to something larger than oneself a positive virtue indispensable to personal salvation.[54]

Fascism's morality tale of decay and rebirth draws deeply from the well of *Volk*ish thinking, with Hitler repeatedly and explicitly describing his political aim to create a reborn *Volk*ish state and culture. Hitler's goal was to re-create the higher moral and spiritual vitality idealized for decades by *Volk* thinkers. The resonance of fascism was both its familiar story of decay and its splendidly uplifting message that the spiritual vitality of both the German individual and nation could be heroically reborn.

Hitler's focus on moral decay had long been a central preoccupation of the *Volk* tradition, which lamented the loss of the rooted life of the simple, Godly peasant. For both Hitler and many *Volk* theorists, this was caused by the rootlessness of the Jew, originally from Middle Eastern arid lands and now a restless urban and commercial people: "According to many *Volk*ish theorists, the nature of the soul of a *Volk* is determined by the native landscape. Thus the Jews, being desert people, are viewed as shallow, arid, 'dry' people, devoid of profundity and totally lacking in creativity. Because of the barren-ness of the desert landscape, the Jews are a spiritually barren people. They thus contrast markedly with the Germans, who, living in the dark, mist-shrouded forests, are deep, mysterious, profound."[55]

Hitler's attack on the Jews—and his argument that they were the germ behind urban decay, the impersonality of the workplace and community, the degeneration of the arts, the "leveling" of personality by the Social Democrats and Marxists—resonated profoundly with a century of *Volk*ish thinking. When Hitler attacked Berlin as Jewish and rootless; when he attacked the artists, feminists, and gays as decadent Jewish egoism; when he attacked the Left, trade unions, and Social Democrats as urban, materialist, Jewish, political deformations, he was echoing a whole century of *Volk*ish myths and prejudices widely believed by ordinary Germans, especially those from rural areas, the "red states" of the German nation.

Hitler's concept of rebirth was also intensely resonant with the dominant *Volk* myth. Many *Volk* thinkers were hyper-nationalists who believed that

Germany could regenerate itself—and the very philosophy of the *Volk* presumed a spiritual essence in the German *Volk* that could not be suppressed forever. Hitler spoke to this Volkish optimism that the German spiritual creative essence could not be denied. The "rootless" Jews were out of sync with nature, and fascism was simply God's instrument for restoring roots and the morality and spirituality they ensured. As Mosse observed, rootedness "was viewed as the regenerative natural state of man which transformed the individual into a creative being."[56] In other words, the *Volk* philosophy assumed regeneration as part of the natural order, predisposing Germans to see rebirth itself as something ordained by God and nature. Hitler's decay and rebirth story could not have fallen on more resonant soil.

The second "resonating factor" involves societal conditions that breed extreme social insecurity. The depression, as it exploded into massive unemployment from 1930 to 1933, was the trigger. Millions of Germans lost their jobs, and millions more lived on the precipice. Vast numbers of Germans became part of an anxious class, whose economic and social prospects were far more dire than those facing America's anxious class today.

In the last chapter, we saw how social insecurity breeds resonance with empire. For many of the same reasons, social insecurity fuels resonance to fascism and its morality tale of decay and rebirth. An anxious class is looking for someone to blame. Fascism offers a whole set of enemies, starting with liberal elites who have sold out the nation and are spawning moral decay. These elites, the Fascists argued, are the mainly Jewish leaders of the Social Democratic Party who signed the humiliating Treaty of Versailles and ran the decadent Weimar Republic. German rebirth could be achieved only by a revolution against the materialistic, "leveling" rot of Weimar and ushering in an iron-willed Fascist state committed to the spiritual and military rebirth of the nation.

The Fascists had an appealing and familiar argument. Germany had been sold down the river by liberal urban elites, who had little connection to the moral values of the German heartland. The Treaty of Versailles was a national humiliation, and the punitive economic terms imposed by the Allies did contribute to hyperinflation and eventually the catastrophic German depression of the early 1930s. Wounded pride and economic despair made many Germans eager to fix on the leaders who could be tagged with both surrendering to the nation's enemies and destroying the economy. The fact that the Social Democrats were also urban, liberal, and disproportionately Jewish also played into the Fascists' cultural argument: that these were enemies of the German *Volk* who betrayed the nation because they were not truly members of the *Volk* but an alien elite propagating the urban decadence and decay and destroying the heartland.

The anxious class created by the German depression was overcome by fear. As discussed in the last chapter, fear eats at away at self-respect, intensifies the need for belonging, and increases the attraction of an authoritarian leader. The Fascists stoked popular fear while simultaneously offering antidotes to soothe the pain. Hitler's view of the German nation as the master race—the only culturally creative people—gave every German a sense of self-worth. The hyper-nationalism of fascism—which united all Germans in the great spiritual crusade for rebirth of the nation—gave every German a new sense of roots and belonging. In addition, Hitler's charisma as an iron-willed national leader, committed to defeating all of Germany's internal and external enemies, reassured the most frightened German that fascism meant national security.

Re-arming Germany created millions of new jobs, and this was a key reason why German workers came to embrace Hitler after he became the führer. Propaganda and moral or spiritual messages were not the only reasons for his support. Among the urban industrial working class, other reasons prevailed: Hitler delivered the material goods that the Left could only preach about. But among peasants, villagers, the large rural population, and much of the small business sectors—the majority of the German populace—Hitler's moral rearmament of Germany played a larger role than jobs and remilitarization in seducing ordinary Germans. Getting the people to love the great leader, as Orwell showed, is achieved by sermons from the mount.

Fascism, Conservatism, and the Moralist Politics of the Far Right

In Chapter 1, we defined the political strategy of the immoral moralist as one that seeks power and carries out evil in the name of moral values or God. Fascism proves that we need to take immoral morality very seriously and be prepared to combat it with all our resources.

It is comforting to think of fascism as historically unique—and something that we need not worry about today, especially in Western democracies. But political scientists have concluded something rather different: that while classical fascism is not likely to resurface, it is one branch of conservative politics, and, more specifically, a branch of the Far Right that mainstream conservatives turn to under extreme conditions that threaten their own power. Hitler came to power through the choices of the traditional German conservative movements, the German military and the great German corporations.

Political historian John Weiss, in his very important book *The Fascist Tradition*, argues that fascism, while profoundly radical, "is a conservative social movement."[57] Weiss notes there is a tendency among both scholars and laymen to want to see fascism as a uniquely German pathology, something utterly original and separate from the mainstream European political traditions. Weiss argues that nothing could be more mistaken. History shows that fascism is a product of conservatism under desperate social circumstances, when the survival of conservatism itself is at stake. Weiss, Griffen, and other scholars recognize differences between traditional conservatism and fascism, but demonstrate that fascism is one part of the broad conservative spectrum, a view now accepted by most political scientists. Fascism, Weiss argues, both "plays on the fears and represents the hopes of traditional conservatives."[58] In Germany, Hitler came to power because mainstream conservatives decided that he was their best hope for maintaining their own power, preserving their own vision of the nation, and destroying the Left.

Hitler was appointed chancellor in 1933, in a deal brokered by the venerable conservative aristocrat German president, General Paul von Hindenburg, in concert with other leading German conservative political and military figures. Successive elections from 1930 to 1933 had created no viable German leader, as German politics became increasingly unstable. As in all Western countries, the depression created an enormous crisis for traditional conservatives in Germany, since they could offer no clear solution for the suffering masses. While the Left-learning Social Democrats who had governed Germany through much of the 1920s lacked the vision or political will to offer their own solutions, popular support for the Communists skyrocketed in the early 1930s, just before Hitler gained power. The prospect of a United Front between the Social Democrats and the Communists—or even of an outright Communist victory—kept German conservatives up at night. By 1930, as the depression set in, parliamentary democracy eroded and Hindenburg chose a series of conservatives to rule through emergency decree, but no stable coalition survived.

Enter Hitler. For a decade, Hitler had been at the margin of German politics. The Nazis were only the most fiery and violent of multiple Far Right ultra-nationalist fringe groups that grew up during the chaos of the postwar 1920s. But Hitler—while attracting increasing public attention through his charismatic oratory, his spiritual calls for a *Volk*ish German rebirth, and his brutal violence, was still only able to win 2.8 percent of the vote in 1928[59] and twelve parliamentary seats before the national elections in September 1930, when his party jumped spectacularly to 107 seats.[60] But the Left also gained strength as centrist parties declined, with 143 seats for the Social Democrats and 77 for the Communists. The nightmare of a Communist Germany haunted German conservatives more than ever.

The years between 1930 and 1933 are crucial for understanding the political secret of fascism. In a series of elections in 1932 and 1933, Hitler won mass electoral support, winning 43.9 percent in his best showing.[61] The population was polarizing between the Far Left and the Far Right. The Social Democrats were an exhausted center-Left party, which had run out of ideas. Traditional centrist and right-wing conservatives were, likewise, proving completely incapable of running the country. Hindenburg and other leading conservatives in the military and economy feared anarchy—or worse, a Communist takeover.

In 1933, Hindenburg began serious negotiations with Hitler about his appointment as chancellor, finally agreeing to turn power over to him. The military, big landowners, and big business—the heart of the German conservative establishment—signed off on this agreement. On the one hand, they felt they could ultimately control Hitler. On the other, they shared a desperate fear of the Left and regarded the Fascists as an attractive alternative to Bolshevism.

Hitler's moralism and his politics of the *Volk* had challenged financial capitalism, but the Fascists had been careful not to threaten private property or a productive capitalist order. Hitler knew he needed a dynamic industrial base to support re-militarization. Reluctant capitalists increasingly threw their support to Hitler, as did the military, which distrusted Hitler but recognized that he had imperial plans that would support both German industry and the military. Moreover, the old conservative establishment had never been comfortable with the democratic principles of Weimar, which they saw as a threat to the old conservative aristocracy of earlier centuries. They shared Hitler's view that the entire democratic experiment was a plot of other Western countries and of the German Left.

Hitler's moralism was also broadly consistent with the old conservative establishment that had ruled through traditional appeals to God, family, and country. The *Volk*ish ideology that Hitler espoused was part of a broader conservative ideology surfacing among conservatives as early as the eighteenth century. The conservative establishment saw Hitler as a hothead, but they recognized him as a fellow conservative nationalist. Hitler's attacks on the decadent German city resonated with the old landed conservative aristocracy who shared the *Volk*ish ideology of rural virtue. Hitler's broader moral and spiritual calls to rot out decay and midwife a reborn Germany were more radical but consistent with their own worldview.

Beyond support from the old conservative elites, Hitler's electoral support also came from the traditional German conservative base. These included rural and small-town Germans, farmers, shopkeepers, and low-ranking white-collar workers, veterans, and lower-middle-class Protestants from both rural and urban life. They strongly resonated with Hitler's *Volk*ish moralism and had always shared his antipathy toward the Left and the secular, cosmopolitan culture of Berlin and other "decadent cities." Hitler's popular base was remarkably similar to the "red state" base of the American Republican Party today, a matter we will look at more closely in the next two chapters.

Before 1933, the majority of Germans never supported Hitler; his support was restricted to the largely conservative base that had always supported the Right. This makes clear that Hitler's morality tale of decay and rebirth did not resonate with all Germans, with the urban industrial workers turning increasingly to the Left. Had the Communists been willing to create a united front with the Social Democrats, as occurred in France, they might have prevented Hitler's accession to power. But the Communists blindly followed Soviet instructions to refuse the united front, with the insane assumption that Hitler's accession would intensify the depression to the point that workers would rise up for a Communist revolution. The Social Democrats, an exhausted party lacking vision and will, contributed to the suicidal tendencies of the Left, whose electoral base was actually larger than that of the conservatives.

Hitler's immoral morality succeeded because German mainstream conservatives embraced it in a period of extreme socio-economic crisis when the Left was imploding, incapable of any coherent moral vision, and organizationally impotent. The popular resonance with Hitler's moral narrative grew after he gained power, reflecting both his complete seizure of the Ideological Apparatus and brutal violence against anyone opposing him. As conservative leaders, the military, and large corporations rallied to support Hitler—backed by an academic intelligentsia itself largely complicit in rallying the population behind Hitler—more and more of the population fell into line. Even urban workers increasingly supported Hitler, as remilitarization stimulated the economy and created jobs, and as oppositional unions were destroyed. But the reborn Germany that Hitler began to build was broadly a product of the conservative establishment and popular base that had put their hopes in his *Volk*ish German dream, a nightmarish ideology of immoral morality.

5

Moral Calamity in Dixie
Rebirth of a Southern Nation

In the last chapter, we saw that the decay/rebirth myth was central to fascism, something that sets off alarm bells. The relation between the right-wing rebirth tales in Germany and the United States is a story of considerable interest. In this and the next chapter, we look at how the U.S. Far Right has engaged an old immoral morality in a way that will continue to severely test the survival skills of Americans and American democracy. This is a story of the strange twists of conservatism in America, the historic role of the Democrats as initiators of the rebirth tale, and the unexpected rise of a new Republican Party that appropriated the rebirth tale to help Wall Street resonate with the Bible Belt. It is a story of a nationalist rebirth myth that overlaps closely with Christian and evangelical rebirth myths about being born again and the Second Coming of Christ. It is also a story of the dangers of the rebirth morality tale in an age of a new anxious class and of a governing conservative elite unable to placate it. When conservatives face collapse, history tells us they can resort to the most extreme immoral morality, as seen in Germany and now in two closely related American stories: one of the historic South that we tell in this chapter and one of the Republican Party today that is the subject of our next chapter.

Rebirth of a Nation: The Film, the Slave South, and Southern Morals

In 1915, filmmaker D. W. Griffith produced *Birth of a Nation*, a movie that many critics see as the best American film ever made. Famed photographer James Agee called it "the birth of an art.... He achieved what no other known man has achieved."[1] America's best-selling film for many years, it is a gripping silent movie whose message echoes loudly in today's political landscape. It is a film about American morality and God in its most immoral form: the Slave South. It also is about the Southern Nation's morality tale of rebirth, which is the foundation of today's Republican rebirth story for America. The rebirth myth of the twenty-first century Republican Party is a historical evolution of the Southern rebirth myth, with each gaining popular resonance from powerful myths in evangelical Christianity, and each also linked to a conservative political agenda. In this chapter, we focus on the Southern rebirth story as essential prelude to today's rebirth myth that survives because of its intense Southern resonance.

The film is a love story about the daughter of an abolitionist Northerner romantically drawn to a son of the Old South who founds the Ku Klux Klan. It shows riveting images of the beatific Slave South, the wicked Northern carpetbaggers who came to plunder the South after the Civil War, their black stooges rising to control white Southerners, and the Ku Klux Klan, presented as the heroes who fought for the rebirth of the sainted Southern Nation. The film was based on the play called *The Klansmen,* which was a testament to the South's brave struggle to renew America's most noble moral and spiritual tradition.

The Old South was, in fact, an entirely different social order than the North. It was a slave economy rather than a capitalist system. It was agrarian rather than urban or industrial. Most important for our purposes, it was based on a quasi-feudal moral code entirely different from the capitalist morality code:

1. Nature or God has imposed a natural hierarchy of races and sexes.
2. Everyone has an assigned place with corresponding duties. Order and harmony require that they accept it.
3. White men of high station have an ineffable quality—Honor—to preserve, protect, and defend.
4. Men of honor must take care of those beneath them, be they of lower class, inferior race, or weaker sex.
5. For their own good, people lower in the hierarchy must submit to the will of those above.
6. The ideal community is provided by slavery and can be sustained by slavery or something as close to it as possible.
7. Although most blacks appreciate the kind good intentions of their white guardians, any who forget their place must be reminded of it.

8. Men of honor must protect the virtue of white women. Men must maintain their authority within the family. Above all, they must be kept from the lust of savage, animal-like blacks.

The moral identity of the South differed from the North not just in its racial values but also in its deep traditionalism, emphasizing a natural and eternal order. Everyone had a fixed place where morality required that they carry out the obligation of that station all their life. The landed aristocracy embodied a spiritual culture of honor and had an obligation to protect those beneath them—including women and slaves—much as the feudal lords hundreds of years ago protected their serfs. The worldview is medieval rather than capitalist, viewing Northern ideas of progress and industrialism as spiritual decay. It is a classic system of immoral morality, where spiritual concepts of honor and protection cloak a system of evil.

The Old South was so overtly racist that it might seem strange to call it spiritual in any respect. But that is precisely how millions of white Southerners, including Griffith himself, saw it. When he was accused of being against blacks, Griffith responded: "To say that is like saying I am against children, as they were our children, whom we loved and cared for all our lives."[2]

This racist paternalism is classic immoral morality, and it is at the heart of the intensely moral discourse of the Slave South. Protection of the weak and inferior has long been the moral cloak for control. The Southerners took this moralistic paternalism to the limit, arguing that their own moral commitment to protecting slaves was far greater than the moral attitude of Northerners toward African Americans, leaving them to sicken and die without mercy when they couldn't work. The moral ethos of paternalism was based on the classic immoral morality that slaves, like children, were incapable of independence, and needed protection from themselves. It created a self-image of an idealistic society rejecting self-interest with a morality of lifelong care for the weak.

The Southern Nation's rebirth story after the Civil War defeat has parallels to the German rebirth story after World War I. The crushing of a people led to a sense of unspeakable destruction of its moral essence, requiring wholesale political and spiritual resurrection. The morality tale of rebirth of the Southern Nation began right after the Civil War. It started with the concept of the South as a "people," race, or nation—a *Volk* as in Germany—and evolved into the idea of the South as an independent nation blessed with its own unique morality and philosophy. On March 21, 1861, Alexander Hamilton Stephens, who was elected vice president of the Confederacy, pronounced a racialized concept of the new nation: "Our new Government is founded upon … the great truth that the negro is not equal to the white man; that slavery, subordination to the superior race, is his natural and moral condition. This, our new Government, is the first, in the history of world, based upon this great physical, philosophical, and moral truth."[3]

As the Civil War began, the South finally birthed itself as a separate nation, a natural outcome of secessionist theory for many decades. Its foundation is racial—a people who constitute a "superior race," in many ways analogous to the racialized *Volk* in Germany. The new Southern Nation, Stephens argues, is a "moral truth" sanctioned by nature and God.

Jefferson Davis, the president of the Confederacy, had already made this the unchallengeable Biblical principle underlying Southern nationhood. In an 1858 speech in Boston defending slavery and a "free" Southern Nation, Davis was explicit that God would bless its racial foundation:

> Why, then, in the absence of all control over the subject of African slavery, are you agitated in relation to it? With Pharisaical pretension it is sometimes said it is a moral obligation to agitate…. Who gave them a right to decide that it is a sin? … Not the Bible; that justifies it. Not the good of society; for if they go where it exists, they find that society recognizes it as good … servitude is the only agency through which Christianity has reached that degraded race, the only means by which they have been civilized and elevated.[4]

The Southern Nation was founded on God and His morality, which rooted the concept of the new nation in racial superiority of whites, which was an earlier version of the Fascist story of race and racial purity as the core of nationhood. Davis becomes the ultimate immoral moralist when he says that slavery is "the only agency through which Christianity reached that degraded race, the only means by which they have been civilized." This is immoral morality at its worst, reminiscent of Rome's notion of "civilizing barbarians" and the British "White Man's Burden."

When Abraham Lincoln and the Northern armies crushed the new nation of the South, they did not crush the idea of Southern nationhood. Instead, the terms of surrender and Northern "occupation," much like that of Versailles as perceived in Germany, created the Southern sense of humiliation and defeat that led to the Klan and a new movement for rebirth of the Southern Nation. That movement was not classical fascism but grew from a new "decay and rebirth" moral narrative that can be viewed as an evolutionary ideological branch off the same ancient trunk of immoral morality.

Decay

The Southern rebirth myth, like that in Germany, is a two-chapter story of national decay and rebirth. The Southern decay story stems from the Northern invasion and its destruction of the South. The destruction of the South was catastrophic, obliterating the very foundation of the Southern economy, its honor code, and its sacred way of life. As in Germany, the sense of humiliation was extreme, and in both cases the terms of victory imposed by the winners deeply exacerbated the sense of dishonor and rage. In Germany, the punitive terms imposed by the Allies—including demand for reparations—were impossible for Germany to meet, ensuring economic disaster. Likewise, the era of Reconstruction immediately following the Civil War sought to impose a "Northern" way of life that Southerners interpreted as brutally punitive and decadent, violating white Southerners' identity and moral pride.

The Reconstruction's excesses helped create and feed a charismatic Far Right story of betrayal and decay, exactly as it did in Germany. *Birth of a Nation* is a cinematic portrayal of this story, where ex-slaves, encouraged by evil Northern Yankees, set up a culture of terror and gross racial and sexual immorality: "Secret clubs were established with the intent of raising the ex-slaves into political power over the Southern whites. It soon became almost 'anything goes,' with the ex-slaves abusing and threatening whites at every turn.... The Union League, militia, and ex-slaves patrolled all the streets, harassing and threatening everyone, especially all the wives and daughters of the towns."[5]

The theme of dishonoring women and degrading white Southern women—whose virtue constituted the core of Southern morality—recurs frequently in the Southern decay narrative. The Klan repeatedly emphasized how the Northern invaders abused Southern women: "Many of these ruthless Yankees have raped and killed your wives, your daughters, and slaves."[6] *Birth of a Nation*, as a film, is organized around the violation of Southern womanhood by the invaders and their black stooges. In one of the film's climactic scenes, a freed black proposes marriage to a Southern white woman:

HE: "You see, I'm a Captain now—and I want to marry ..."

(black approaches white with proposal of marriage.)

"Wait, missie, I won't hurt yeh."

SHE: "Stay away or I'll jump!" (She commits suicide by jumping.)

NARRATOR: "For her who had learned the stern lesson of honor, we should not grieve that she found sweeter the opal gates of death."[7]

The virtue and purity of white Southern women was always the symbol of white moral superiority and Southern morality itself. *Yankee notions of racial equality—and sex between black men and white women—meant the worst form of moral and spiritual decay.* Without the virtue of Southern womanhood, the Southern moral world would die.

The Klan and other Southern nationalists saw a broader decay—emanating from the moral poison of Northern secularism and urbanism. They introduced core themes of decadence that echo many elements of the Fascist decay story. A major theme of Southern nationalists involved the decay of religion itself, an inevitable outcome of Northern urban industrialism: "Religion can hardly expect to flourish in an industrial society.... But nature industrialized, transformed into cities and artificial habitations, manufactured into commodities, is no longer nature.... We receive the illusion of having power over nature, and lose the sense of nature as something mysterious and contingent ... the religious experience is not there for us to have."[8]

This view from Southern nationalists in the 1930s strikingly echoes Hitler's writings about the decay of religion. It also evokes the love of nature among the German *Volk* and the extreme decadence arising from the devaluing of land in the shift to an urban society. The theme of "blood and land" was central to both the Southern and German *Volk*ish philosophy. Both emphasized the moral essence of the simple, agrarian life in which people lived in close relation to nature and to each other. The *Volk* in both cases were physically and spiritually rooted, in a fixed and eternal moral order.

In the immortal film *Gone with the Wind,* a loving ode to the Old South, land is the "only thing" that has lasting value, as Mr. O'Hara expresses to Scarlett: "Do you mean to tell me Katie Scarlett O'Hara that Tara, that land doesn't mean anything to you? Why, land is the only thing in the world worth working for. Worth fighting for. Worth dying for. Because it's the only thing that lasts."[9]

Since land was so sacred, Southern nationalists stressed the immorality of decadent liberal cities—a theme also much stressed by the German Fascists. Southerners argued that Northern industrialism brought all the sins of urban life that Hitler emphasized: rootlessness, sterile materialism, and challenges to the verities of God, family, and country. As seen by both Southern nationalists and the German Far Right, cities were crucibles of liberal decadence, and urban civilization was as degrading to the Southern *Volk* as it was to the German *Volk*. Southern nationalism, while tightly linked to the Democratic Party from 1865 to 1965, ironically created the moralistic attack on secular urban liberals that would become the basis of today's Republican political strategy to discredit Democrats and the Left.

The Southern nationalists' general view of a decadent Northern culture and artistic life artificially removed from nature and imposed on the South also mirrors the Fascist critique of modernist art. "Nor do the arts have a proper life under industrialism, with the general decay of sensibility which attends it. Art depends, in general, like religion, on a right attitude to nature; and in particular on a free and disinterested worship of nature."[10]

The Fascist and Southern decay stories are broad-sweep pictures of spiritual, racialized civilizations—creatively inspired by nature and God—crushed by moral pretenders. The introduction to *Gone with the Wind,* appearing before the title on the screen, sets forth the nostalgic and intensely moral view of the South that had been destroyed: "There was a land of Cavaliers and Cotton Fields called the Old South. Here in this pretty world, Gallantry took its last bow. Here was the last ever to be seen of Knights and their Ladies Fair, of Master and of Slave. Look for it only in books, for it is no more than a dream remembered, a Civilization gone with the wind."[11]

The Old South appears a last vestige of true morality and honor. The Northern conquest destroyed this "gallant" civilization with its icy wind of moral decay, similar to the one Hitler said had corrupted and blown away the true nation of the German *Volk*.

Rebirth

The rebirth morality tale of the Southern Nation seeks to return sovereignty to the Southern *Volk*, a conservative Godly people with its own unique history of honor and racial pride. It comes in three versions. The first, emerging from the Klan's fight against Northern Reconstruction, was to preserve as much as possible of the Old South's economy, culture, and way of life within the context of a federated United States. The second was to secede a second time and create a new and independent Southern Nation. The third very recent form was to mount a transformation in the United States that would remodel the entire nation on the Southern moral code.

The first was based on recognition that a second secession to create a new and independent Southern Nation, however desirable, was not possible after the Civil War. Northern military forces were stationed throughout the South and would crush any such movement. Southern nationalists, including the former Confederate leaders, the Klan, and the White Line—a militia of organized whites to defend Southerners against Northern abuse—turned to a rebirth vision of a "nation within a nation," with the South accepting union with the North but pushing out Northern soldiers and rebirthing as much of the Old South as possible.

The key to this rebirth was to restore the moral order based on the superiority of the white race. But since slavery could not be reintroduced, the South sought to create rebirth through the new system of legal segregation. Jim Crow laws would re-create the natural order of racial hierarchy establishing the superiority of whites and their privileged role in a racialized order. Segregation would ensure sexual and racial separation essential to the purity of the South and its moral fabric. In this, Southern rebirth paralleled precisely the German Far Right view of racial purity as central to morality and to the rebirth of the nation.

The establishment of the Jim Crow South—which lasted nearly a century—constituted a genuine rebirth. The Jim Crow system had expectations like these:

a. A black male could not offer his hand (to shake hands) with a white male because it implied being socially equal. Obviously, a black male could not offer his hand or any other part of his body to a white woman because he risked being accused of rape.
b. Blacks and whites were not supposed to eat together. If they did eat together, whites were to be served first, and some sort of partition was to be placed between them.
c. Under no circumstance was a black male to offer to light the cigarette of a white female—that gesture implied intimacy.
d. Blacks were not allowed to show public affection toward one another in public, especially kissing, because it offended whites.
e. Jim Crow etiquette prescribed that blacks were introduced to whites, never whites to blacks. For example: "Mr. Peters (the white person), this is Charlie (the black person), that I spoke to you about."
f. Whites did not use courtesy titles of respect when referring to blacks, for example, Mr., Mrs., Miss, Sir, or Ma'am. Instead, blacks were called by their first names. Blacks had to use courtesy titles when referring to whites and were not allowed to call them by their first names.
g. If a black person rode in a car driven by a white person, the black person sat in the back seat or in the back of a truck.
h. White motorists had the right-of-way at all intersections.[12]

Jim Crow was, in Dr. Martin Luther King, Jr.'s view, clearly a resurrection of Old South morality, ensuring that freed blacks continued to treat whites as a different spiritual order of human. Whites required honor and respect that was not due to blacks. Stetson Kennedy, the author of the *Jim Crow Guide,* offered these simple rules that blacks were supposed to observe in conversing with whites:

1. Never assert or even intimate that a white person is lying.
2. Never impute dishonorable intentions to a white person.
3. Never suggest that a white person is from an inferior class.
4. Never lay claim to, or overly demonstrate, superior knowledge or intelligence.
5. Never curse a white person.
6. Never laugh derisively at a white person.
7. Never comment upon the appearance of a white female.[13]

These are another sign of the moral character of Jim Crow, essentially a moral code of interpersonal behavior ensuring respect and slavish deference to whites. But beyond the interpersonal realm, Jim Crow was a rebirth of the racial hierarchy and power structure of the Old South, from barbershops to burial grounds to buses:

- Barbers. No colored barber shall serve as a barber (to) white girls or women (Georgia).
- Burial. The officer in charge shall not bury, or allow to be buried, any colored persons upon ground set apart or used for the burial of white persons (Georgia).
- Buses. All passenger stations in this state operated by any motor transportation company shall have separate waiting rooms or space and separate ticket windows for the white and colored races (Alabama).[14]

While slavery was not resurrected, the new legal system of segregation restored white power in all institutional spheres. Freed slaves were reduced to sharecroppers—literally in the economy and metaphorically in the entire society. Most blacks were disenfranchised by poll taxes and black rebels were lynched with impunity. In the concluding scene of *Birth of a Nation,* rows of hooded, armed Klansmen stand between blacks and the polling places, assuring that blacks could not use the vote to challenge white authority. *The idyllic moral nation is reborn.*

The Klan and other Southern nationalists, including the white citizen councils that became the twentieth-century champions of white superiority, *created Jim Crow barbershops, schools, and hospitals in the name of God and moral values.* Jim Crow eradicated Northern decay and rebirthed not only the racial hierarchy God prescribed but also the broader moral code of the Old South.

While the second rebirth myth—of seceding again and giving birth to a new and independent nation—is a marginal movement in the South today, it expresses the fundamental rebirth morality story begun after the Civil War and still has some attraction to millions of Southerners. Southern Nation author and activist R. Gordon Thornton lays out this version of the rebirth creed as of the year 2000:

1.   Southerners are a conquered people, oppressed politically, economically, socially, and morally.
2.   The South is by definition a nation of its own, with its own unique language, culture, history, philosophy, and icons.
3.   Southern nationhood is practical as well as possible. The South will be better off as a free and independent nation.
4.   As a nation, it is our duty and obligation to practice our God-given right of self-determination. Once Southerners determine to free themselves, no force on earth can stop them.[15]

Thornton points out that 20 percent of Southerners share this philosophy, telling pollsters that they "would be better off as a separate nation." Dr. Michael Hill, the League of the South's president, states the aim in the language of *Birth of a Nation,* proclaiming that "one day, our flags will be unfurled over a new nation of our own making."[16]

The endurance of this call for rebirth of a Southern Nation reflects the continuing view of a Southern *Volk*: "Southern nationalism is a drive to preserve the social, religious, political, and cultural traditions of the Southern people. True Southerners denounce the secular humanist tendencies that have guided the empire since Appomattox. These Northern intellectual fantasies value nature above man and man above God."[17]

The Southern *Volk* is essential to the survival of Western civilization itself: "*The South is the last bastion of western civilization. We are the holdouts of Anglo-Celtic and Christian culture.*" This echoes Hitler's view that only the Aryan *Volk* was "culture-creating," and it alone could ensure the survival of culture and spirituality. Southern nationalist politics has now tended to reject a racialized story, although there remain virulent fringe white supremacist groups, but it remains a call for the Southern *Volk* to find God and save moral values by joining the struggle for rebirth of the Southern Nation: "Open your mind. Open your heart to the familiar warmth of our Southern Nation. The fire is a dear close friend who longs to dwell again in his hereditary home. As a Southron [sic], you are incomplete without the fire within ... That is the way God intended a Southron to be. His gift of fire makes us Southern. It makes us men; it makes us whole ... It is our birthright, given by the hand of God."[18]

The Southern nationalist movement is, in its own conception—and correctly so—a branch of Southern conservatism, with ancient roots in conservative thought. Thornton writes that "Southern nationalists draw its existence and its strength from a Southern conservative tradition with roots extending all the way back to the plain of Runnymede." It is viewed as different than conservatism in the rest of America."[19]

But the Southern Nation movement now also sees that its form of conservatism is beginning to appeal to American conservatives in all parts of the country, who see it as the conservatism born in the American revolution and U.S. Constitution: "As despair seeps into the ranks of traditional American conservatives, many are breaking their former political ties. They search for an alternative. Many are finding their answer in Southern nationalism.... Again, they look to the Southern bedrock of the original constitutional American republic as the answer."[20]

This leads to the third Southern rebirth story, rebirthing not a separate Southern nation but all of America in the great moral spirit of the South. The influential modern politicians who first saw this possibility of rebirthing the whole nation based on Southern conservative values were George Wallace and Richard Nixon. In his inaugural address as Alabama governor in 1963, Wallace began to make new bridges between Southern nationalism and a reborn conservative America:

> Today I have stood, where once Jefferson Davis stood, and took an oath to my people. It is very appropriate then that from this Cradle of the Confederacy, this very Heart of the Great Anglo-Saxon Southland, that today we sound the drum for freedom as have our generations of forebears before us....
>
> Hear me Southerners! You sons and daughters who have moved north and west throughout this nation ... your heart has never left Dixieland ... you are Southerners, too, and brothers with us in our fight.[21]

Wallace then makes clear that the true national fight is against the liberal decay brought on by secularist Northern elites:

We [America] are become government-fearing people ... not God-fearing people.... In reality, government has become our God. It [America] is, therefore, a basically ungodly government and its appeal to the pseudo-intellectual and the politician is ... to play at being God ... without faith in God. It is a system that is the very opposite of Christ for it feeds and encourages everything degenerate and base in our people.... Its pseudo-liberal spokesmen and some Harvard advocates have never examined the logic of its substitution of what it calls "human rights" or individual rights ... including the theory that everyone has voting rights without the spiritual responsibility of preserving freedom.... It is degenerate and decadent.[22]

But right after this decay story of how the North has betrayed America's spiritual and moral fabric, Wallace exhorts all Americans to join with him in a fight to rebirth America based on the great spiritual values of the Old South:

We intend to take the offensive and carry our fight for freedom across the nation, wielding the balance of power we know we possess in the Southland ... that WE, not the insipid bloc of voters of some sections ... will determine in the next election who will sit in the White House.... We intend, quite simply, to practice the free heritage as bequeathed to us as sons of free fathers. We intend to revitalize ... a government first founded in this nation simply and purely on faith.[23]

Although much closer to the corporate conservative mainstream of his time, Richard Nixon tried to recruit support among people sympathetic to Wallace's world view. Nixon would pick up Wallace's call in his appeal to the "silent majority." In his acceptance speech at the Republican National Convention on August 8, 1968, Nixon said he would speak for "the voice of the great majority of Americans, the forgotten Americans, the non shouters, the nondemonstrators ... they provide most of the soldiers who die to keep it [America] free."

This "silent majority" of "forgotten Americans" are the honorable and patriotic Americans from the South and the Heartland, whose voices had been drowned out by the bicoastal liberal "shouters" and "demonstrators." Nixon used the language of the moral majority to help build a new Republican base in the South and West. He set forth a version of a Reborn America that resonated especially strongly with the honor code and patriotism of the South:

For five years hardly a day has gone by when we haven't read or heard a report of the American flag being spit on, and our embassy being stoned, a library being burned, or ambassador being insulted....

America is a great nation. It is time we started to act like a great nation.... I see a day when Americans are once again proud of their flag; when once again ... it is honored as the world's greatest symbol of liberty and justice.

The time has come for us to leave the valley of despair and climb the mountain so that we may see the glory of the dawn, a new day for America.[24]

Wallace and, in a more modest form, Nixon laid the ideological groundwork for Ronald Reagan and George W. Bush. Both Wallace and Nixon correctly saw that American conservatism and the Republican Party itself were in crisis and on the threshold of fundamental changes. Reagan and Bush would complete the Republican Party's appropriation of the rebirth morality tale of Southern nationalism, making a reformed version of it the governing mythology of the entire nation. This would marginalize Southern nationalism by turning large parts of it into the hegemonic moral discourse of the entire nation. This was a genuine American revolution, transforming ownership of the moral discourse of the South from the Democratic to the Republican Party and harnessing the power of the decay and rebirth story from the Slave South to global corporate America.

6

God Bless America

The Republican Party and American Theo-Corpocracy

> During the more than half century of my life, we have seen an unprecedented decay in our American culture, a decay that has eroded the foundations of our collective values and moral standards of conduct.... To fundamentally change our culture we need a spiritual renewal.
>
> —*George W. Bush*[1]

The theme of decay is the headline of the morality tale of the Republican Party since Ronald Reagan. It is part of a new story about rebirth that George W. Bush has helped make the master narrative not just of his own life but of his party and large sectors of America.

Today's Republican Party was born in the 1960s and came to power under President Reagan, reaching its full ascendancy under President Bush Jr. It is "born again" in several senses. It is a product of historic realignment, a new coalition of religious and corporate groups. It brings together traditionalist Southern conservatism and progress-oriented Northern conservatism into a new unstable conservative hybrid. *It creates a new born-again morality tale at the center of its vision.* And it represents a new effort by mainstream conservatives to keep power by turning to the Far Right and appealing to the spiritual hopes and fears of an anxious class at the brink of despair. All of this has made a transformed Republican Party the carrier of immoral morality marked by dangerous authoritarianism.

This chapter shows how the Republican Party gained power under Reagan and ruled from Reagan to Bush Jr. through the charisma of its unique brand of immoral morality. It did more damage to the nation and the world than any American regime since the Slave South, all carried out in the name of God and moral values. Since the election of President

Obama, the Republican Party has been in disarray but the the immoral morality imprinted in the party by Reagan and George W. Bush remains its core brand.

We show that Republican immoral morality is rooted in a modern American version of the decay-and-rebirth narrative. It has surprising echoes of the Far Right German and Southern born-again stories described in the last two chapters. It is more politically dangerous than any other modern American political movement, and its immoral morality tale is likely to have a sustained resonance with an American people frightened by prospects of terrorism, economic decline, and domestic and global class polarization and violence.

The Two Conservatisms: A Prelude

To understand the reborn Republican Party, you have to understand the historic shift in American conservatism itself. Since the Civil War, and until the 1960s, America had been a nation of two conservatisms, one in the South and the other in the North. They are so different that for much of American history—from 1864 to 1964—they could not coexist in the same party. Northern conservatism, the conservatism of capitalists, was the core of the Republican Party. Southern conservatism wedded itself politically to the Democrats and reflected the precapitalist values of the Old South. When the Republican Party finally became a marriage of these two conservatisms, it was a truly reborn party, in fact, a rebirth of the entire American political tradition rooted in a morality tale of global rebirth.

We have already discussed Southern conservatism, a conservatism based on the idea of *tradition*. The tradition derived from the racist quasi-feudal morality of the Slave South, in which everyone had an assigned place reflecting God's natural order. Change meant moral decay, and Godliness meant preserving the eternal moral truths of the Southern *Volk* and its rural way of life.

Northern conservatism, in contrast, was based on the idea of *progress*. Dating back to Alexander Hamilton and the early Whigs—the predecessors of the Republicans—Northern conservatives were the party of Northern industrial capitalism. When the Whigs collapsed, they renamed themselves Republicans. They were the party of cities, technology, and secular commerce, all viewed as sinful in the conservatism of the Southern Volk. Northern conservatives—originally led by John D. Rockefeller, J. P. Morgan, and Andrew Carnegie—rejected the idea of rural stability and championed urban capitalist change.

Northern and Southern conservatisms are a clash between worldviews, so profound that it might be called a *clash of civilizations.* After all, it led to the Civil War. Since the reborn Republican Party has now united these two conservatisms, we need to understand a bit more about Northern conservatism, the gospel of the robber barons and America's modern corporate capitalists. Carnegie's 1889 *Gospel of Wealth*—a seminal ideological document—makes clear how central the theme of progress is in Northern conservatism—and how utterly contradictory it is to the traditionalism of Southern conservatism. Carnegie acknowledges that capitalist progress brings a huge "contrast between the palace of the millionaire and the cottage of the laborer," but that such inequality "has come with civilization" and "is not to be deplored but welcomed as highly beneficial." It is well, nay, essential for the progress of the race. Much better this great irregularity [inequality] than universal squalor. Without wealth there can be no Mæcenas. The "good old times were not good old times."[2] Here, Carnegie explicitly rejects the essence of Southern conservatism: the "return to good old times." He acknowledges the costs of capitalist progress—its huge inequality—but sees it as reflecting the moral virtues of material progress and meritocracy.

Northern conservatism is conservative not in its championship of change and progress but in its embrace of capitalist morality as the only path:

> The Socialist or Anarchist who seeks to overturn present conditions is to be regarded as attacking the foundation upon which civilization itself rests, for civilization took its start from the day that the capable, industrious workman said to his incompetent and lazy fellow, "If thou dost net sow, thou shalt net reap," and thus ended primitive Communism by separating the drones from the bees. One who studies this subject will soon be brought face to face with the conclusion that upon the sacredness of property civilization itself depends—the right of the laborer to his hundred dollars in the savings bank, and equally the legal right of the millionaire to his millions.[3]

Here, Carnegie does espouse conservative values of property and hierarchy that converge with the values of the Southern Volk. They would become part of the new morality tale of today's born-again Republican Party.

Carnegie is the ultimate Northern conservative—conservative because he defended the morality of private property and capitalism above all else and equated liberty and the Constitution with the "free market." Carnegie's moral order is embodied in the capitalist code:

1. Human nature is inherently self-interested and rational.

2. If people are allowed to act on their own self-interests, they will make good decisions for themselves and the community, allowing for both individual and social progress.
3. Let people, rich or poor, compete as equals and form voluntary contracts with whatever resources they have.
4. The results of such competition are freedom, progress, and prosperity, the moral foundation of capitalism itself.
5. Capitalism makes freedom possible. The core of liberty is the right to acquire property.
6. The market is an objective judge of merit. There is no need to appeal to extensive regulations or subjective moral codes.
7. The state must be committed to protect private property and help the nation acquire more property in competition with other peoples.
8. Freedom requires prosperity. Markets must expand. The state must be prepared to open markets at home and aboard.

Northern conservatism, as embodied in this code, was wedded tightly to the Republican Party for a century, becoming the morality of Wall Street and eventually Wal-Mart. But it was, in the main, a world apart from, and often contradictory to the traditionalism of the Southern Volk.

The Born-Again GOP

The born-again Republican Party that first came to power under Ronald Reagan in 1980 was a marriage of two incompatible visions of conservatism. They never truly resolved the contradictions between progress and tradition, as expressed in the clashing capitalist and Old South codes, but they have ruled America in a hegemonic Republican coalition for the last generation. The Republican Party settled for an ideologically incoherent coalition that sought to balance the values of Wall Street and the Bible Belt under the rubric of a global rebirth story with grand economic and moral claims that cloak global policies of evil in the name of good.

The coalition has three central players:

1. Wall Street and the Corporate Elite
2. National Security Elites and the Pentagon
3. The Bible Belt and Evangelical Christians

All three of these players have embraced immoral morality in their own overlapping stories of a reborn America. The internal tensions, stemming from incompatible conservatisms and moral claims, are now weakening the party. But they are still a potent political coalition, whether in or out of power. They are the hegemonic moralists of America and will remain the most dangerous political carriers of America's most dangerous immoral morality for years to come.

The new melding of corporate and National Security Elites with Southern Evangelicals was fueled by the Republican corporate crisis that climaxed in the 1960s and the 1970s. The U.S. economy was faltering relative to Japan; popular support for capitalism among Northern workers had been eroded by falling wages and the crushing stagflation of the late 1970s; globalization was leading many American workers to see U.S. corporations as abandoning America itself, and an evolving Left-leaning political revolution challenging the war in Vietnam and championing new civil rights had exploded on the scene. All these factors forced defensive conservatives and corporations to look in new places to resurrect conservatism and the Republican Party, leading to the totally unexpected and new alliance with Southern Evangelicals. When the Democrats passed the Civil Rights Act in 1964 and Barry Goldwater launched a Republican campaign openly appealing to the traditionalism of the South, a watershed was passed. For a century, Southern conservatives had hated Lincoln's Republicans and remained loyal to the Democrats. But when President Lyndon Johnson aligned the Democratic Party with the civil rights movement and passed the Civil Rights Act of 1964, it was too much for good, moral Southerners to bear. In the 1964 presidential election, Republican candidate Barry Goldwater swept the South, a revolutionary realignment that was the tipping point leading to the Reborn Republican Party and the rise of the Global Rebirth morality tale.

The Republican Party began a systematic "Southern strategy." Its immoral morality was summarized in 1981 by the legendary Republican political operative, Lee Atwood, as follows: "You start out in 1954 by saying, 'Nigger, nigger, nigger!' By 1968 you can't say 'nigger'—that hurts you. So you say stuff like forced busing, state's rights, and all that stuff."[4]

Atwood was a key to Reagan's election in 1980, with Reagan opening his 1980 campaign in Philadelphia, Mississippi, where three civil rights workers had been slain. During that appearance, Reagan proclaimed to cheering white Southerners: "I believe in state's rights."[5] Reagan didn't openly discuss race, but he appealed to the Southern sense of morality and nationalism described in the last chapter. With Reagan's election, propelled by white Southerners' migration to the party and a sweep of the South and West, the GOP was born again.

Each of the three coalition players of this born-again party had their own contradictory worldviews and moral discourse, but to win power they had to unite around a common morality tale. The corporate and National Security Elites, the carriers of Northern conservatism, wanted to preserve the core values of capitalism in its dynamic globalization phase. The Evangelicals wanted to return to the religious and traditional moral values of the Southern Volk. Under Reagan, an uneasy balance was struck seeking to equate capitalist progress with God and traditional values. But since the mass base of the party was increasingly made up of Evangelicals and other Southerners, the rhetoric of Reagan and Republicans increasingly veered toward traditional values of Southern conservatism, even as the actual practice and policies of the party hewed far more to the progressive theme of capitalist Northern conservatism. Reaganism meant full-speed global corporate power and militarism spiced with Godly born-again rhetoric.

But as globalization created a larger and more frightened anxious class, Republican power was threatened, creating under George W. Bush the prospects of a loss of the Republican Party's governing majority. While 9/11 allowed the corporate and National Security Elites to prop up temporarily the global capitalist story of Northern conservatism, the underlying crisis of the anxious class forced the Republicans toward increased reliance on their mass Southern base and its religious and Far Right leaders. Survival of the Northern corporate conservative establishment required a huge risk: ceding increasing power to the Far Right and the traditional conservatism of the Southern Volk.

Republicans responded to the growing national crisis of conservatism—symbolized at this writing by Bush's precipitous fall in popularity—by intensifying the path taken since the party was born again under Reagan. This involved (1) touting patriotism and the intensely moralistic war on terrorism that could appeal to a frightened citizenry and (2) moving Right to mobilize a minority of fervently faithful followers, mainly in the South, who were "born again." This meant reorganizing the Republican Party—and especially its hegemonic "morality tale"—increasingly around the myth of a born-again nation, the discourse with the most powerful resonance to Southerners and magnetic attraction to a large number of other religious and nationalist Americans, especially Evangelicals. The GOP embraced much of the traditional Evangelical Code:

1. Ultimate truth was revealed to us by our Lord and Savior Jesus Christ two thousand years ago.

2. There is no need for ambiguity or doubt. We know right and wrong, truth and falsehood, through His word.
3. Those who have received His truth have the duty to spread the word to rest of the world.
4. Anyone who chooses to reject His word after having been told deserves whatever fate our Lord imposes upon him.
5. Remember Jesus commanded, "Be simple like a child." Live by faith.
6. Freedom is following the will of the Lord and accepting His truth.
7. Satan is a real force, controlling much of the material world. Good Christians must devote their life to combating his evil.
8. Reward is guaranteed for whomever follows our Lord, if not in this world, then in the next.
9. We can be assured of ultimate justice through the goodness of our Lord.

The GOP did not embrace every precept of this code but incorporated its spiritual message into its moral rebirth story. While the Republicans' new morality tale is an evolution of the traditional Southern story, it has changed in basic ways, including its substitution of religion for race and its globalization of the born-again story into a worldwide battle for moral and spiritual survival against dark terrorists. Nonetheless, it is still, as it was in 1920s and 1930s Germany, a story of dangerous immoral morality seeking to invest an authoritarian and militaristic conservatism with a monopoly of moral and spiritual power, while demonizing and politically discrediting liberalism and the Left as agents of terrorism and moral decay. It remains a story with two chapters: decay and rebirth.

Decay

The decay headline—moral values are being threatened and betrayed!—has captivated pundits and bloggers in recent elections. Under Bush Jr., decay moved front and center to the Republican message, orchestrated by "Bush's brain"—Karl Rove. Rove has been the most prominent recent advocate of Republican victory through mobilization of the evangelical base, which sees its religion and traditional morals under attack by secular liberal and Democratic elites. Rove's ultimate strategy was classic immoral moralism: create an intensely moralistic story of rebirth. It promoted authoritarian change and military rule in the name of protecting the nation and the world from decay. His approach is widely understood, but we show here how this immoral morality tracks backlash narratives used both by Far Right conservatives in Germany and by Southern nationalists after the Civil War. Put simply, it is a story of the Christian American Volk morally subverted by a secular, rootless, and self-styled urban cosmopolitan elite and their liberal followers in unions, schools, and progressive social movements, all in the context of a global terrorist threat to the very survival of the nation and civilization itself. Despite key differences, Germany is a frightening precedent and the South is the base of the reborn party itself.

All three groups in the new born-again Republican Party coalition have embraced the decay story, but it is the Evangelicals who brought it front and center. At this writing, the leading Evangelical preacher of decay is James Dobson, head of Focus on the Family until his resignation in 2009 and an ultra-conservative political activist with great influence in the Bush/ Rove GOP. During the 2004 presidential campaign, Dobson had weekly conversations with Karl Rove. Dobson writes about moral decay sweeping across the nation and flooding schools, media, and the courts:

> What I was saying was that this godless and immoral curriculum and influence in the public schools is gaining momentum across the nation in ways that were unheard of just one year ago.... It's as though the dam has now broken and activists representing various causes, including homosexuality, are rushing through the breach in ways that are shocking.... It is aimed at the very core of the Judeo-Christian system of values, the very core of scriptural values.... Your people are going out into that world and your children are interacting every day with those that want to teach them contradictory concepts ... particularly the notion that there is truth.[6]

This touches on nearly all the themes that animate the Republicans' decay narrative. It is the godless humanists and liberal schools that are destroying the morality of youth, with the moral corruption of youth as a central theme of Far Right decay stories since at least the morality tales of German fascism in the 1920s. Much of the problem is sexual and symbolized by the gay movement, again an early Fascist preoccupation, and it is the theme that seems to energize Dobson and other Religious Right leaders more than any other. But beyond the definition of homosexuality and so-called equal rights for gays as evil is the sense of a broader tipping point in moral decay, with all of Christian morality and culture targeted for extinction.

Secularist evil is subverting the very possibility of moral values and "the notion that there is truth." Francis Schaeffer, an influential Evangelical writer, describes Secular Humanism as "the greatest threat to Christianity the world has ever known."[7] Since the Religious Right sees God as the foundation of civilization and Christ as the only authoritative messenger of truth, secularists—and particularly the liberal and Leftist movements since the 1960s—have set us on a course of complete cultural collapse, the "end of Christian civilization."

It should be noted that versions of this Evangelical argument, while it may appear hyperbolic and extremist, has deep roots in Western conservative thinking. In 1920, Winston Churchill made the argument that the Western enlightenment could create a moral and religious catastrophe. Churchill warned that liberal groups of anticlerical enlightenment humanist thinkers—the very thinkers who brought us human rights—were producing a dangerous and dangerously secular morality "as malevolent as Christianity was benevolent, which, if not arrested would shatter irretrievably all that Christianity has made possible.... [This humanist worldview] has been the mainspring of every subversive movement during the 19th century. This worldwide conspiracy for the overthrow of civilization and the reconstitution of society on the basis of arrested development, of envious malevolence, and impossible equality has been steadily growing."[8]

Building on these revered conservative roots, the American Religious Right's story of immoral morality—calling evil the humanistic movements for civil rights—has emerged in recent decades as the central American text of decay. Reagan and Bush Republicans appropriated this story to solidify their Southern base and make the GOP a dominant party from Reagan to Bush. The Republican Party today, while weakened by recent electoral and military defeats, has now de-racialized and refined the decay story so that it resonates not just in the Bible Belt but also in rural and exurban areas throughout the country.

Other sectors of the Republican coalition have amended the Evangelical decay story so that it appeals to all three wings of the Republican Party. Security Elites and the Pentagon have *globalized* the story. While the Evangelical decay-and-rebirth story has always had global implications for salvation of the world as a whole, the Evangelican story had focused traditionally on America. Evangelicals and Security Elites—in a new coalition we might call the "Theo-Cons"—have made the story of relevance to the whole world with a melding of American hegemony and the Second Coming. The Corporate Elites offer their own globalization of the story and have collaborated with Evangelicals and Security Elites to create a rebirth myth that makes global capitalism part of the natural order, or God's own work, and American militarism—in Iraq and elsewhere—as the key to global moral and spiritual rebirth.

For the Security Elites and global corporations, the real concern is the world and protecting America's endangered hegemonic status. The Security Elites have embraced the Neoconservative's Code:

1. The United States is the bastion of freedom and democracy and the ultimate source of good for the rest of the world, responsible for containing evil (today, the evil of Islamic terror) and restoring moral order.
2. Not only is it the most moral nation on earth, it is also the most powerful.
3. Destroying evil requires the exercise of decisive force. Our enemies do not listen to reason.
4. For the sake of world peace and security, freedom and democracy, as well as its own economic, political, and military interests, the United States must never hesitate to act or police any region of the planet.
5. The United States must maintain such overwhelming military and economic power that nobody dares challenge it.
6. Ideally, the United States should act with the cooperation of the world community, but if that is not possible, it should be prepared and willing to act alone.
7. The United States must not be permitted to hesitate acting upon its responsibilities and interests.
8. Misguided liberals have encouraged self-doubt, producing disastrous results in Vietnam and Iraq. This must never be repeated.
9. No one living within America's borders, be they citizen or alien, can be allowed to interfere with the United States seeking security or pursuing its interests and moral mission. If that requires an abridgement of civil liberties, it is better to sacrifice some freedoms than lose all.

The decay story here reframes U.S. imperial and militaristic foreign policy as a defense of the entire planet against evil and global moral collapse, while discrediting U.S. secular humanists and antiwar liberals, or peaceniks, as morally weak or traitorous. This is classic immoral morality. The Neoconservatives—including Paul Wolfowitz, William Kristol, Charles Krauthammer, Donald Kagan, Elliot Abrams, Richard Perle, and many other Pentagon officials and defense-related intellectuals—are intensely moralistic in justifying the Iraq War and American global dominance. They offer President Bush intellectual cover for his view of the Iraqi invasion and broader American militarism as a spiritual war against "Islamo-Fascists," code for the purest form of evil. *The new narrative suggests that America and the world face planetary moral and spiritual decay from linked external and internal enemies of the* Volk. In 2006, then–Secretary of Defense Donald Rumsfeld, in a speech emphasizing the evil of Islamic terrorists, linked the problem with moral relativism on the home front: "And that is important in any long struggle or long war, where any kind of moral or intellectual confusion about who and what is right or wrong, can weaken the ability of free societies to persevere."[9] That is, the moral relativism preached by secular humanists confused Americans about the absolute moral clarity of the war on terrorism and the war in Iraq, making clear that liberals are undermining the patriotism on which the nation depends.

The idea of foreign enemies catalyzing American moral and spiritual decay has deep historical roots in the United States, starting with Southerners who saw the invading Northerners as morally corrupting "foreigners." Chip Berlet, an expert on right-wing movements, writes that by 1900 nativist right-wing movements linked domestic secular humanists to the international Communist threat: "The nativist right at the turn of the century first popularized the idea that there was a secular humanist conspiracy trying to steer the United States from a God-centered society to a socialist, atheistic society. The idea was linked from its beginnings to an extreme fear of communism, conceptualized as a 'red menace.'"[10]

Political analyst Frank Donner discusses the "folkish" aspect of this linking of foreign enemies with internal moral decay: "The root antisubversive impulse was fed by the [Communist] Menace. Its power strengthened with the passage of time, by the late twenties its influence had become more pervasive and folkish.... A slightly secularized version, widely shared in rural and small-town America, postulated a doomsday conflict between decent upright folk and radicalism—alien, satanic, immorality incarnate."[11]

Neoconservatives now are re-creating this globalized decay story, turning the war on terrorism into a "doomsday conflict between decent upright folk" in the American Heartland and a tacit alliance of Islamic terrorists and the American liberal/Left.[12] Hitler repeatedly described German surrender as a betrayal by German Jewish Social Democratic leaders collaborating with the American, British, and Russian Allies, who would together destroy the moral fabric of the German *Volk*. The Security Elites in the GOP now argue that the American *Volk* is similarly threatened by urban liberal elites and labor and peace movements that are appeasing America's enemies. Led by the Democratic Party itself, the equivalent of the German Social Democratic Party, the liberals and Left are collaborating, wittingly or unwittingly, with terrorists, to subvert the religious and traditional values of America's Heartland.

In this globalized decay story, betrayal is a central theme, precisely as it was in the German Fascist story of decay and in the Southern National-ists' decay story. It thus resonates with special power in the South. The lead singer of the Dixie Chicks, a top country music group, found this out when she criticized the Iraq War. DJs refused to play the Dixie Chicks' records. Concerts were cancelled. Former fans, especially in the South, sent death threats.

In the 2004 presidential election, John Kerry, the Democratic candi-date and a war hero who helped lead a veterans' peace group, became the victim of the betrayal narrative. The "Swift Boat" Republican operatives and conservative veterans concluded this:

> Senator John Kerry committed acts that made him a Traitor to America after Vietnam, and likely subject to Court Marshall,... the "Vietnam Veterans Against the War" were not Vietnam War Veterans at all, not even their founder, Alan Hubble, was. Instead, the group was actually young antiwar activists and Communist Party members, some members had very limited military backgrounds. They were, however, PRETENDING to be Viet-nam Vets Against the War trying to strengthen a cause that trod upon the reputations and sacrifices of the American Soldier with a vicious political agenda steeped in Democratic Party guilt for having started the war.[13]

The Swift Boat attacks on Kerry involved two classic conservative decay themes integral to immoral morality. One is that liberal elites who oppose American wars are traitors, the same argument Hitler made about the leaders of the German Social Democratic Party. Second, Kerry and his fellow traitors were "antiwar Activists and Communist Party Members," pretending to be veterans. Here the decay narrative melds the internal and external carriers of moral decay; Kerry and other urban liberal Democratic leaders who opposed American militarism in Vietnam were actually Com-munist fellow travelers who morally degraded the country in league with the Godless foreign enemy.

Leading conservative members of the Ideological Apparatus have been explicit about how secular liberal elites betray America, since their immoral "relativistic" culture undermines patriotism and morality itself. One key figure is Lynne Cheney, wife of Dick Cheney and former head of the National Endowment of the Humanities. She writes sarcastically: "As American students learn more about the faults of this country and about the virtues of other nations, they will be less and less likely to think this country deserves their special support. They will not respond to calls to use American force and thus we will be ... able to return to the golden days of the late 1960s and early 1970s, when no president was able to build support for Vietnam."[14]

She adds that multiculturalism—taught by liberal professors, emphasizing diversity and equality—is clearly a form of moral decay with global implications: "Multicultural education may well be incompatible with patriotism, if patriotism means belief in the nation's superiority over other nations.... The advantage to the nation of multicultural education thus may be increased reluctance to wage all-out wars."[15]

Internal moral decay, wrought by secular humanists, is perceived as dooming national security. The moral weakness of a generation schooled by liberal elites will bring down both the American *Volk* and the American Empire. While corporate leaders are less vocal, they have accepted this framing since it discredits liberals and Leftists who oppose corporate globalization and capitalism. As just noted, the corporations have also long denounced unions, socialists, and now antiglobalization activists as immoral because they obstruct the moral progress and freedom that capitalism brings home and to the rest of the world.

The decay theme thus unites all three sectors of the born-again GOP—and is most explicitly framed by leading evangelists Jerry Falwell and Pat Robertson, who directly blamed the 9/11 attacks on morally decadent and permissive humanists, liberals, feminists, and gays: "The ACLU's (American Civil Liberty Union) got to take a lot of blame for this [the 9/11 attacks]."[16] Falwell went on to blame abortionists, liberal judges, and all the anticapitalist radicals from the 1960s, adding, "I point the finger in their face and say, 'You helped this happen.'"[17] Pat Robertson responded, "Well, I totally concur."[18]

The Republican decay story is classic immoral morality of the Far Right, with striking parallels both to the German Fascist decay story of the 1920s and the Southern decay story after the Civil War. In all three cases, it is crucial to recognize that the decay argument is a backlash against periods of great moral progress, essentially reframing liberal moral and political revolutions for social justice as evil. This redefinition of good as evil—leading to right-wing backlash movements seeking to undo human rights in the name of traditional morals and God—is the hallmark of immoral morality.

In Germany, the liberal Weimar Republic of the 1920s—that bred hysterical rage in the young Hitler—inspired a challenge in German history to traditional, repressive German values, most of all a shift from authoritarianism to democracy. Hitler and other conservative leaders redefined liberal democracy as moral decay, an immoral "massification" or

Communist leveling, threatening to destroy the creative spirit of the German *Volk*. The Civil War brought the most important moral advance in American history—ending slavery—but Southern Nationalists described it as the killing of America's most spiritual social order: the Old South. Today's Republican decay story is a response to the rise of the social justice movements of the 1960s and 1970s, including the civil rights movement, the peace movement, and feminist, gay rights, environmentalist, and other progressive moral movements that helped eliminate discrimination and promote human rights and equality. But Republicans—defining themselves as the "moral majority"—reframed the new Left movements for justice and peace as decay, with the 1960s seen as a moral and spiritual catastrophe, much as the German Far Right saw the liberal 1920s as a German collapse into insane decadence.

In all three cases, the Right used immoral morality to try to turn back the moral clock. The effort was to restore an immoral order in the name of morality itself: traditional German autocracy in the name of the virtuous *Volk*, the old Slave South in the name of traditional values of racial and masculine honor, and the Republican corporate order of the 1950s in the name of patriotism, progress, and traditional values.

As we will see shortly, Jews play a special and unique role in all three decay stories. In the German story, the Nazis branded Jews as the ultimate cause of decay and evil. In the South, Jews were also seen as an alien, decadent force, representing corrupt Northern capitalism as well as the perverse religious people who killed Christ. In today's Republican story, Jews have a contradictory role. On the one hand, they are crucial to the Evangelical story of moral salvation, since Israel's conquest of the Holy Land is part of God's Will for redemption of the world and the Second Coming. On the other hand, the "Borscht Belt"—the name for parts of New York and other areas where Jews are densely populated—is seen as the seedbed of the 1960s and all things immoral, and it is the breeding ground for decadence. In all three stories, Jews must ultimately be eliminated or converted to spiritually regenerate the nations.

The agents of decay in all three stories are remarkably similar. They are urban secular people with liberal or Left leanings, higher than average education, and a cosmopolitan tolerance or moral freedom subversive of the traditional values of the nation. They are the natural enemy of the "decent, upright" *Volk* in all three nations, who embody the classic values of God, family, and country. All these stories thus have a right-wing populist character, contrasting the simple *Volk* with arrogant elites.

In all three stories, the agents of secular decay are liberal or Left. The moral simplicity and conservatism of the *Volk* are contrasted with the decadence of an urban liberalism or Left that is subverting the eternal moral order of God, family, and country. *The decay story transforms the political conflict between Right and Left into a spiritual conflict between virtue and decadence.* As classic immoral morality, it redefines the Left values of equality and peace as morally subversive. This political theme is so central that we will return to it at the end of the chapter as the story behind the story.

Rebirth

The decay story is uplifting because it ends with rebirth, a moral cleansing, and creation of a "Promised Land." Hitler promised a new, purified Aryan Empire. Southern Nationalists saw a new Biblical South cleansed of Northern corruption. And the Republican rebirth story sees a spiritually reinvigorated America with traditional Western and Christian moral values, transforming the entire planet.

Historian Roger Griffin points out that the rebirth tale can be "restorationist" or revolutionary, that is, backward looking or forward looking.[19] There is always an element of restoration since the decay story is about the Fall from a more moral or spiritual age, a golden past. But Griffin argues that fascism and other right-wing rebirth stories tend to be revolutionary, looking toward a future purer and spiritually higher than anything in the past. This may reflect the Christian religious dimension of rebirth stories in the West, which promise a Second Coming of eternal salvation, something never before achieved on earth.

Hitler envisaged a kind of Second Coming of the Aryan race, which would not be simply a restoration of the nineteenth-century German *Volk*. He promised a "new man" in a "new Germany," a higher German race—purged of Jews and other decadent liberals—rising to create a great new spiritual German Reich that would rule the world. Southern nationalism has a more restorationist feel since it emphasizes the return to the eternal values of the Old South. But it also imagines a new Southern Nation that would finally be free of corrupt Northern liberals to express pure Southern conservative values and religion. Today's Republican rebirth tale also has strong restorationist elements since it emphasizes "traditional moral values," a return to the pre-1960s world in which Americans knew the difference between right and wrong. But it is fundamentally a revolutionary vision, especially in its Evangelical version since it imagines a purer Christian Nation purged of disbelievers and a free globalized capitalism that would spread the highest Western and spiritual values while destroying terrorists and traitors on the Left. All three of these rebirth stories are *purification narratives*; while all are framed in the name of moral and spiritual revival, they all function politically to purge liberal and Leftist forces from the Reborn Nation and ensure an authoritarian conservative rule.

There are several versions of the current Republican rebirth story, the most radical and populist being the Evangelicals'. GOP leaders, especially Ronald Reagan and George W. Bush, signal to their Evangelical base that they will quietly work to midwife the new Christian Nation that Evangelicals seek. They use coded or more general rebirth language, such as Reagan's "morning in America"[20] famous phrase and Bush's talk of bringing "God's gift of freedom"[21] to transform both America and the world. Both Reagan and Bush have spoken more frequently than earlier presidents of their personal faith driving their politics, with Bush, as shown earlier, the most explicit president in history to tie his own personal rebirth to his belief that God has chosen him to rebirth America as a mighty nation of arms and faith to "transform" the world. But Reagan and Bush, despite their intensely moral and spiritual discourse, have let the Evangelicals take the lead in framing the Republican Party's rebirth narrative, while offering both privately and publicly the assurance to their Evangelical base that they will do all in their power to midwife the a reborn spiritual nation purged of liberal, decadent, and secular influences.

The infrastructure of the Republican Party, in the local and state party councils and caucuses, as well as state legislators and Republican Congressmen, are far more openly committed to the Evangelical rebirth story—and to actually carrying it out. Deep down in the grassroots ranks of the party, this passion reflects the personal and often extreme religious views of grass roots New Right political activists. Journalist Christopher Hedges notes "Christian fundamentalists now hold a majority of seats in 36 percent of all Republican Party state committees, or 18 of 50 states, along with large minorities in 81 percent of the rest of the states. Forty-five senators and 186 members of the House of Representatives earned between 80 to 100 percent approval ratings from the three most influential Christian Right groups."[22] As one moves higher in the national party, the commitment to the Religious Right and its rebirth story becomes more strategic, a powerful legitimating story to discredit liberalism and the Left and perpetuate conservative power in an age of conservative crisis.

The most politically important version of today's rebirth story grows out of the theocratic school known as Christian Reconstructionism or "dominionism." While the word reconstructionism seems to suggest a return to the past (what Griffin called "restorationist"), it actually points to revolutionary new politics in which America would be transformed into a new theocracy. Religious and political versions of the Reconstructionist story have been embraced and spread by many of the Evangelical leaders most closely connected to the Republican Party, including Pat Robertson, Tony Evans (the founder of the Promise Keepers and one of President Bush's spiritual mentors), and James Dobson, chair of Focus on the Family. Reconstructionists see the Bible as literal and believe that God intended that all social and political life be reconstructed according to strict Biblical law. As Reconstructionist theologian David Chilton succinctly describes their view: "The Christian goal for the world is the universal development of Biblical theocratic republics, in which every area of life is redeemed and placed under the Lordship of Jesus Christ and the rule of God's law."[23]

Religious scholar and journalist Frederick Clarkson, an influential analyst of the Reconstructionist movement, describes it with these aims:

> Generally, Reconstructionism seeks to replace democracy with a theocratic elite that would govern by imposing their interpretation of "Biblical Law." Reconstructionism would eliminate not only democracy but many of its manifestations, such as labor unions, civil rights laws, and public schools. Women would be generally relegated to hearth and home. Insufficiently Christian men would be denied citizenship, perhaps executed. So severe is this theocracy that it would extend capital punishment beyond such crimes as kidnapping, rape, and murder to include, among other things, blasphemy, heresy, adultery, and homosexuality.[24]

The Reconstructionist's reborn America—in its purest form—will be a land governed by the Bible and purged of "labor unions, civil rights laws, public schools" and "democracy" itself. The connection between spiritual purification and elimination of liberals is a political key to the whole rebirth story that we will clarify later. But we should note here the purification of political and religious heretics is intensely punitive, with executions for blasphemy, heresy, homosexuality, or atheism reminding us of the Fascists' extreme violence in the name of moral purification. Secular humanists and liberals would be killed in the pure Christian Reconstructionist vision of a reborn America, much as they were in Nazi Germany.

A popular textbook used in Christian schools explains the Biblical basis of the "dominion" that the Reconstructionists advocate. It stems from Genesis (1:26) where it is written that mankind should "have dominion over the fish of the sea, over the birds of the air, over the cattle and over all the earth and over every creeping thing that creeps on the earth."[25] The Christian textbook writes that "When God brings Noah through the flood to a new earth, He reestablished the Dominion Mandate but now delegates to man the responsibility for governing other men."[26] It goes on to argue that the United States is called by God to be "the first truly Christian nation" and "make disciples of all nations."[27]

Here, Evangelicals begin to refocus on *global rebirth*, a theme critical to the Pentagon and global companies. To "make disciples of all nations" suggests that *a reborn Christian America has a responsibility to transform the entire world,* precisely the foreign policy agenda central to mainstream Republican corporate and military elites. Since Evangelicals have always sought to evangelize the entire world, there is a natural affinity between their theology and the Republican dream of American hegemony, helping pave the way for the "Theo-Con" movement.

This affinity emerges most strongly in the post-9/11 world. Evangelicals such as Tim LeHaye, the author of the hugely popular series of *Left Behind* novels selling more than 60 million copies, preach that global rebirth will emerge through a series of epic transformations. In LeHaye's *Left Behind* version, a Rapture occurs, in which believers are transported to Heaven while Left Behinds are left to suffer a Tribulation ruled by the antichrist, a long Christian symbol of internal and external evil, inflicting horrific scourges, plagues, warfare, and other violence.[28] A small group of the faithful wages war against the antichrist. In traditional Evangelical thought, the Jews eventually regain control of the Holy Lands and are then converted to Christianity. This signals the beginning of the final return of Christ to earth, and the Second Coming, the ultimate global rebirth.

President Bush and his neoconservative advisors have implicitly connected this enormously popular global rebirth theology—a theology driven by the vengeful and violent God portrayed in the Gospel of John and the Book of Revelations—with a militaristic vision of global transformation and American hegemony. Bush's most explicit Rebirth speeches are global, focusing on the Middle East. In these excerpts from his talk to the nation on the fifth anniversary of 9/11, on September 11, 2006, he frames his wars in Iraq, Afghanistan, Lebanon, and the broader Middle East as aiming at a grand rebirth:

> At the start of this young century, America looks to the day when the people of the Middle East leave the desert of despotism for the fertile gardens of liberty and resume their rightful place in a world of peace and prosperity.
>
> We look to the day when the nations of that region recognize their greatest resource is not the oil in the ground, but the talent and creativity

of their people. We look to the day when moms and dads throughout the Middle East see a future of hope and opportunity for their children.

And when that good day comes, the clouds of war will part, the appeal of radicalism will decline, and we will leave our children with a better and safer world.[29]

While it is not couched in explicit theological terms, Bush's vision of transformation of the Middle East has a Biblical rhythm and meshes relatively smoothly with the violent Evangelical global rebirth story. Islamic radicals and terrorists symbolize the legions of the antichrist, the main obstacle to global rebirth in the heart of the Holy Lands, while support for Israel as an ally against the antichrist is critical to achieving the Biblical path to the Second Coming. Evangelical leaders have connected the dots for their followers, ensuring that the Evangelical base remains loyal to the Republican Party's wars in the Gulf and Middle East. One Detroit preacher says: "It didn't take 9/11 to show me there is a global battle going on for the souls of men. When Islam comes into a place, it is intent on taking over everything, not only government but the business, the neighborhoods, everything."[30]

The Evangelical Right has taken the view that there will be no national or global rebirth, no Rapture, until Israel, with American help, has taken total control of all the Holy Lands. Several influential "Christian Zionist" organizations, with close ties to the Republican Party, have formed to lobby Congress and the White House for unqualified U.S. support for Israeli control of all Palestinian lands. Created by leading U.S. evangelicals such as John Hagee, pastor of the mega-church in San Antonio, Texas, these groups explicitly see Israeli domination of its Arab enemies as the Biblical sign that the Second Coming is imminent. Hagee is one of several powerful Christian Zionist leaders who support U.S. nuclear strikes on Iran and oppose on Biblical grounds any return of Palestinian land for peace.[31] This all points to a remarkable synergy between the Republican vision of American-led global transformation and the rebirth story at the center of the Evangelical movement.

Capitalism Reborn in the Strange Marriage of Evangelicals and Corporations

Soussas John Rushdooney, the founder of Reconstructionism, was a disciple of Princeton theologian Cornelius Van Til, who influenced Rushdooney and his son-in-law Gary North, also a leading Reconstructionist writer.

Van Til's epistemology was stark, as described by North: "By what standards can man know anything truly? By the Bible and only by the Bible."[32] This absolutist standard of truth sets the foundation for a fundamentalist religion—and when harnessed to politics, leads to an antidemocratic authoritarianism. This is where mainstream corporate conservatism plays with fire that could end up destroying capitalism and many of the orthodox tenets of conservatism itself. It symbolizes the conflictual marriage between the Right and the Far Right that occurs often in the creation of political immoral morality. It played out disastrously in the relation between German corporate elites and Hitler's firebrand Fascists in Germany, and is playing out now in a different way in America.

Capitalism requires science, free inquiry, and materialism—all at odds with Evangelical absolutism. How then could the political party of American corporate capitalism ally itself with a force so ideologically threatening to capitalism itself? Biblical law is not capitalist law, nor does Jesus's love for the "least among us" seem compatible with a ruthless global corporate economy. How, then, could corporate Republican leaders propagate a rebirth story that appears more medieval than postindustrial?

One explanation is the economic and political leanings of the Religious Right leaders. Robertson, Falwell, Dobson, LeHaye, and others are in the Southern conservative tradition. Moreover, since the early 1970s, these Evangelical leaders, despite their theocratic dogma, have provided corporate Republicans with thousands of grass roots foot soldiers, those who would rebuild the GOP as the dominant party in the South and the Heartland. Since the 1990s, they had infiltrated the GOP so deeply at the local and state levels that the national party leadership had become accustomed to their presence and confident that their rebirth vision of a Christian Nation would not jeopardize corporate America.

Equally important, the early Evangelical leaders and their successors espoused a rebirth story about the economy itself that was quintessentially capitalist. It had a dogmatic flavor, but one that was essentially a religious version of capitalist fundamentalism. The reborn economy preached by the Evangelicals re-created the conservative "free market" creed as literal religious orthodoxy, an economic system explicitly blessed by God. It calls for a definitive end to socialism and the welfare state and a return to the fundamentals of "free markets," precisely the argument that mainstream Republican corporate elites has been advocating since FDR's New Deal.

The Reconstructionists have written extensively about "Biblical Economics," laying out in exacting detail the Christian rebirth economy. Gary North, Rushdooney's son-in-law, speaks plainly in summarizing his own thirty-year project that resulted in six books and a life ministry devoted to Christian economics:

> The Bible mandates free market capitalism. It is antisocialist. The proof is here in over 8,000 pages of exposition, verse by verse.... The next time you hear someone say that the Bible teaches anything but free market capitalism, ask him or her which Bible commentary demonstrates this. You will get a blank stare followed by a lot of verbal tap-dancing about "the ultimate ethic of the Bible" or "the upholding of the poor in the Bible."
>
> Fact: There has never been an expository Bible commentary that shows that the Bible teaches anything but capitalism.[33]

North is the Christian Right's most prolific economic writer, but his vision of Biblical economics as free-market capitalism is shared by nearly all Religious Right commentators on the subject. In a Christian economics book titled *Let There Be Markets*, Gordon Bigelow argues that the free market is "a perfectly designed instrument to reward good Christian behavior and to punish the unrepentant."[34] The trials of economic life—the sweat of hard labor, the fear of poverty, the self-denial involved in saving—were earthly tests of sinfulness and virtue. While Evangelicals believed salvation was ultimately possible only through conversion and faith, they saw the pain of earthly life as a means of atonement for original sin.

Moreover, they regarded poverty as part of a divine program. Evangelicals interpreted the mental anguish of poverty and debt, and the physical agony of hunger or cold, as natural spurs to prick the conscience of sinners. They believed that the suffering of the poor would provoke remorse, reflection, and ultimately the conversion that would change their fate. In other words, poor people were poor for a reason, and helping them out of poverty would endanger their mortal souls. It was the Evangelicals who began to see the business mogul as a heroic figure, his wealth a triumph of righteous will.

From such writings, it becomes clear why mainstream corporate Republicans threw in their lot with the Evangelicals. The theology makes capitalism Godly. The notion of capitalism as divine or absolute truth is a form of fundamentalist dogma that corporate elites can embrace.

But the alliance goes further, since the Christian rebirth story explicitly lays out a purified, reborn "free market" capitalism that aligns almost completely with the Republican mainstream's own economic vision. Biblical Economics calls for abolishing the New Deal on divine principle. In *America's Providential History*, the Christian authors argue that Social

Security is unbiblical, that the New Deal programs "such as Social Security and other welfare agencies set up the state as provider rather than God," and that private pensions should replace Social Security.[35] They also argue that most taxes are unbiblical, calling the income tax "idolatry," the property tax "theft," and inheritances taxes Biblically prohibited. Prominent Evangelicals such as Pat Robertson have argued that Medicare and Medicaid are also immoral and unbiblical, joining many of his colleagues in the immoral morality who define government aid to the poor or elderly as outright "theft."[36]

A Christian reborn economy will give birth to a purified capitalism:

> The answer lies in the nature of voluntary free-market exchange, which is the very bargaining process through which each individual seeks to maximize his or her own welfare. As long as civil government is restricted to its biblically mandated role of punishing wrongdoers, rather than transferring wealth from one set of pockets to another through "legalized theft," the system of voluntary free-market exchange will flourish to the benefit of all concerned. In summary, biblically based principles naturally produce true free-market economic exchange that benefits all who take part in the voluntary process.[37]

Yet, corporations depend so heavily on government subsidies that they do not actually want to see such a "purified" capitalism purged of big government. Corporate capitalists at the center of the Republican Party work hand in glove with the government to manage the global economy in their own interests. Might the Evangelical reborn economy, then, be actually too capitalist for the corporations? Corporate elites realize that they have much to gain from this Godly free market rhetoric and little to fear. Evangelicals do not typically challenge corporations because Evangelical churches are themselves increasingly corporatized. The leading Evangelical pastors are wealthy CEOs of huge multimillion-dollar corporate religious empires. Corporations also believe that they have enough power over the actual running of the economy that they need not worry about Evangelical free market rhetoric at odds with the actual managed system of corporate capitalism; this is a contradiction long existing between their own rhetoric and practice that has not undermined them. Of course, German corporations had the same views about their control over German Far Right activists and their ability to manage and contain the political rhetoric; they turned out to be catastrophically wrong, something that could conceivably happen again.

The Evangelical Economic Rebirth story has now been personalized, greatly decreasing any tension, and increasing the comfort level between corporations and Evangelicals. In late 2006, *Time* magazine ran a cover story called "Does God Want You to Be Rich?" The story covered the boom of a new wave of Pentecostal and broader Evangelical preaching, which has come to be known as "Name It and Claim It," "Health and Wealth," or "Prosperity Theology." "It allows," *Time* notes, that "Christians should keep one eye on heaven. But the new good news is that God doesn't want us to wait."[38] Prosperity Theology draws from the Gospel of John 10:10: "I have come that they may have life and that they may have it more abundantly."[39]

Prosperity theologians interpret this as God's approving the American Dream and the race to get rich. Three of the four pastors of the four largest mega-churches in America have embraced Prosperity Theology, including Joel Osteen, T. D. Jakes, and Creflo Dollars, all in the South. But the message has percolated well beyond the South. Osteen's book *Your Best Life Now* has sold 4 million copies and is read in congregations all over America.[40] Prosperity Theology and capitalist ideology are melded here into a single rebirth story that resonates with millions of Americans and creates a functional marriage in the GOP for both corporations and Evangelicals.

Why Americans Resonate: The Bible Belt and the Borscht Belt

Over the last generation, the decay-and-rebirth story helped turn the GOP into the governing American party. As the historic ticket to political power of the Far Right, including Fascists all over Europe in the 1930s, this is deeply disturbing. It raises the question of why Americans are attracted to what we have described as a classic and dangerous narrative of immoral morality—and what might lead them to reject it.

The majority of Americans are far more progressive than the Republicans on virtually all issues, from economics to morality, and the rebirth myth has limited resonance with most of them. But the strategy of the GOP—and other conservative parties that face crisis—has been to excite, enrage, and mobilize its base. It can win in America without majority support in the entire population by turning out a highly enthusiastic and intensely politicized minority. As discussed in the next section, Republicans found a way to gain power by advancing a nonmajoritarian story that resonates charismatically to what might be called the "Immoral Minority," a strategy similar to that used by the German Fascists who never received more than 44 percent of electoral support before Hitler took power.[41]

Despite the progressive views of the American majority, the Republican base in the South and the Heartland—a huge if minority sector of the population—has proved in recent decades to be deeply resonant with the decay-and-rebirth story. Recent Pew public opinion polls on U.S. attitudes on politics and religion help to document the fertile soil. Approximately two-thirds of the American population agree that the "United States is a Christian nation." Moreover, 78 percent of all Americans say the "Bible is the word of God," although only 35 percent say it's not only "the word of God" but "is to be taken literally."[42] This points to the broad religiosity in the American population that makes it quite different from Europe and other advanced nations, but it is just the beginning of the story.

Within the religious community, there is a smaller but critically important group that is the real target for Republican resonance. This group shows up in the polls in response to vitally provocative questions: "What should be the more important Influence on U.S. Laws? The Bible or the People's Will?" Thirty-two percent of all Americans answer the Bible, while 63 percent say the People.[43] This might appear to be comforting to liberals or secularists, but it shows that there are millions in America who admit to be openly theocratic and reject the constitutional premise that the popular will should be sovereign.

The demographic group with the highest percent choosing the Bible over the People is white Evangelicals, among whom 60 percent choose the Bible. Among all Protestants, 44 percent do so, a still very significant minority. Education is inversely related to preference for the Bible, with 46 percent of those not completing high school choosing the Bible, compared with 20 percent of college graduates.[44] Interestingly, it is those who identify as conservative who are most likely to agree, whether they are Republican or Democratic, with moderate Republicans (a dwindling group) and liberal Democrats most likely to disagree.

These data show (1) that religion has become an intensely significant force in American politics and (2) that millions of conservatives have now embraced theocratic and antidemocratic principles that were less defining of conservatism in earlier eras. They also show the large minority of Americans who are potentially resonant to the Far Right decay-and-rebirth story and its authoritarian dangers.

Several factors explain why so many millions of Americans are resonant to the rebirth story. The first is that the rebirth story was part of the creation myth of America. The Puritans who originally landed at Plymouth Rock and settled the nation saw themselves as creating a new Christian nation, purged of the corruption and decay of old Europe. America would be the city on the hill, a reborn spiritual community guiding the entire planet. Their decay-and-rebirth narrative grew out of their own theology, as they had inherited the Calvinist, reformed Presbyterian, and other Protestant traditions from Europe that were closely tied to evangelism and the born-again experience. America, in short, was based on a rebirth story from the very beginning, and successive waves of Evangelical Awakenings kept the rebirth spirit alive throughout American history.

The Puritans had a secular as well as religious foundation for their rebirth story. They were immigrants and carried in their own personal bi-ography the drama of remaking their lives. Their own experience presaged the making of America as a nation of immigrants, all living out a form of secular rebirth in moving from the Old World to the New. This legacy of an immigrant nation is a second factor, a secular, moral force—since immigration is often experienced as a courageous and morally inspired sacrifice for one's children—that has heightened America's resonance to the rebirth narrative.

Moving toward the modern era, several transformations have created precisely the toxic mix that has given rise to Far Right power and immoral morality in the past. Ironically, these involve a combination of economic decline, military humiliation, and liberal moral progress. These circum-stances led to Far Right rebirth narratives in Germany and the American South, and they are now creating resonance to similar dangerous stories in America, although the Economic Collapse of 2008 shows that economic decline can also create progressive turns, giving rise to the election of President Obama.

Economic decline may be the most important precipitating factor, giving rise to the anxious class that can shift either toward the Right or the Left. For all the reasons discussed earlier, most notably the end of the American domination of the world economy of the 1950s and continuing weaken-ing of economic hegemony relative to Asia and Europe, and most recently the 2008 econoimc meltdown, a vast sector of the American working and middle classes are struggling to find good jobs and keep them. The spread of outsourcing and downsizing, and the adverse impact of globalization and new technology on millions of American workers are tied to a broader experience of personal uncertainty and disorder in American families, neighborhoods, and the world. Republican policies that systematically cut middle class protections and lower class safety nets have increased the fear of the anxious class and hiked the resonance to the rebirth story that the Republicans themselves are promoting—at least until the 2008 meltdown.

When economic decline—and the inevitable disordering of personal and family life that it brings—becomes acute, it can become a basis for a shift to the Left, as with Obama's election in 2008. But it can also become a third and intensely powerful resonating factor for the Far Right's rebirth story. This was most apparent in Germany in the 1930s, when a catastrophic depression was clearly the precipitating factor propelling Hitler to power. Severe economic crises create a powerful need for order and certainty, as well as both anger at the old order and passion for national rebirth. While economic decline in the United States is far less severe than it was in Germany, it has created chronic uncertainty among the anxious class, a search for blame, and a new quest for moral clarity and political and spiritual transformation. The Republican rebirth narrative offers someone to blame, a new authoritarian doctrine of truth and government, and a broader sense of moral and spiritual renewal that can restore the eternal reassuring verities of God, family, and country. Should Obama's economic policies fail, there is a serious danger of a Far Right resurrection.

National defeat and humiliation, particularly when it accompanies economic decline, is another historic source of resonance to the Far Right rebirth stories. The Slave South's crushing defeat in the Civil War and the German defeat and humiliation after World War I both gave rise to intense yearnings for a revolutionary national spiritual rebirth. This is what the Klan and Hitler offered their respective nations, hungry for respect and victory.

Today, Americans have suffered three critical military defeats and humiliations: Vietnam, 9/11, and Iraq. Taken together, they represent the first time in history that the United States has suffered cumulative military defeats both at home and abroad. While the Republicans have been hurt badly by the Iraqi catastrophe, the Republican decay story offers both internal and external enemies to explain America's recent military defeats, while its rebirth tale offers the psychological balm for the wounds they have inflicted. A nation suffering repeated defeats is angry and searching for pride. The GOP decay story offers a target for anger: the barbaric terrorist enemy and the liberal, "morally relativist" elites at home who are "appeasing" them, a word increasingly used by both George W. Bush and Dick Cheney as the situation in Iraq deteriorated. Victory for America—both in Iraq and the war on terrorism—is a critical element in the Republican rebirth story of a new moral clarity that can restore American pride.

The "appeasers" are a key to the story and its emotional resonance with the Republican base. The Republican story essentially creates two Americas: the Bible Belt and the Borscht Belt. Geographically, the Bible

Belt is centered in the South and the larger prairie Heartland but includes rural, exurban, and other religiously oriented areas around the nation. The "Borscht Belt" is traditionally the lovely New York mountainous area where liberal Jews took vacations and now more broadly refers to the secular, liberal East and West Coasts. In the GOP story, the Bible Belt is the home of the traditional good and simple American *Volk* (with demographics and lifestyle remarkably similar to the rural, religious, and patriotic German *Volk* idealized in the German Far Right rebirth story). In the GOP story, the Borscht Belt is the home of the appeasers and the decadent multiculturists and relativists remarkably similar to the urban liberal or Leftist regions that the German Far Right story targeted as the source of national decay.

As noted above, decay and rebirth stories arise from a combination of economic decline, national defeat, and liberal moral advance. The Borscht Belt plays a key role in the American story of moral advance. Far Right narratives of decay and rebirth virtually always follow a period of dramatic moral progress. In America, this moral revolution took place in the 1960s and 1970s, with the Borscht Belt the main source of the young activists who aligned with the civil rights movement and created the Vietnam antiwar movement, the women's movement, the gay movement, the environmental movement, and other radical forces for change. The Borscht Belt movements of that period created one of the most rapid changes in morals and human rights that America ever saw, a transformative egalitarian and progressive moment that challenged almost all traditional morality associated with sexuality, patriotism, capitalism, religion, and truth itself. It swept away sex, race, and class discrimination that had existed since the founding of the country, and proposed new ideals of equality, peace, and human rights. It proposed a new "way of knowing" that substituted critical thinking and free thought for dogma and infallible authority.

Polls show that the majority of Americans have come to embrace ideas of racial and sexual nondiscrimination and favor greater equality of wealth and power, as well as a less militarized role for the United States in the world.[45] In other words, the majority of Americans, however they might see the 1960s or the Borscht Belt activists, have embraced much of the new egalitarian ethos and human rights morality as genuine progress. But the Borscht Belt—and its moral revolution—nonetheless deeply unsettled vast numbers of Americans, especially in the South and West who felt their way of life was being attacked and undermined. These were the "moral majority" that Nixon first identified and became the resonant base for the immoral morality of the Republican Party.

As noted earlier, Far Right decay and rebirth stories virtually always are backlashes against accelerated moral transformations of the kind ushered in by the 1960s. The Republicans had to face the reality that this moral progress was not likely to be easily reversed in the end among the majority. Nonetheless, the Republicans—in the era between Reagan and George W. Bush—were able to exploit the Bible Belt/Borscht Belt divide to their own advantage. First, because the moral revolution had been so fast and dramatic, even many in the North were threatened and willing to initially accept the Republican's story that the Borscht Belt's "moral progress" actually represented decadence and decay. The acceptance of equal rights for women, gays, and other causes of the 1960s and 1970s was slow and is still a work in progress.

Republicans also successfully seized on charged identity issues separating people in the Bible and Borscht belts. The Borscht Belters are more secular, urban, and cosmopolitan than Bible Belters, and they tend to be more educated and have higher incomes. The Borscht Belters are disproportionately represented in the universities, the liberal wing of the national media, Hollywood, the courts, and other elite institutions that Evangelicals had come to identify with decay.

These differences played into a right-wing populist tradition long powerful in the South and the West. The Borscht Belters could be easily labeled in the Republican story as "elites" because they are, in fact, powerful in certain sectors of American society, primarily in the value-generating Ideological Apparatus. And many act like it, looking at those with lower education in a patronizing or disrespectful way, particularly if they are from the South or from the "fly over" states between the coasts. Respect plays a key role in politics, particularly in a society where the anxious classes are losing their security and status and are looking for a new source of self-worth.

The Republican decay story kindles the resentment of the Bible Belters and resonates to the historic conservative populism tradition that has long tried to turn the economic or status anxieties of Bible Belters into anger at liberal cultural elites. The Republican story begun by Goldwater and Nixon, and consummated by Reagan and George W. Bush, targeted these largely Northern elites as responsible for the broad decay of the nation, a theme resonating with Southern nationalism as well as the conservative populist tradition in both the South and the West. Second, by offering a rebirth story that would remove these elites—who tend to occupy the Democratic Party—from power, they tell a story of moral purification and renewal that will restore the *Volk* to their rightful position of respect and power.

As Thomas Frank has shown in *What's the Matter with Kansas*, this strategy shifts the anger of the anxious class from conservative corporate elites to liberal cultural elites through the Reagan and Bush Jr. years.[46] It allowed a Republican Party promoting narrow corporate interests to gain the allegiance of the anxious class, whose well-being they are jeopardizing. More broadly, it allowed the Republicans to use their decay and rebirth story to shift political attention from class divisions to the cultural divide between the Bible Belt and the Borscht Belt.

While there is much truth to this argument, it overlooks several important issues that we examine shortly. One is that the moral revolution of the 1960s and 1970s did carry real seeds of moral ambiguity, if not decay. Liberals and the Left have sought to portray some issues, such as abortion, which are morally complex, as black and white. This is part of a broader crisis of "political correctness" on the Left that plays into the Republican decay story. Moreover, the genuine cultural elite standing of Borscht Belters is a highly emotional basis of stratification in American society that Borscht Belters have been reluctant to address. Frank and others have also sometimes pounced too heavily on a "false consciousness" theory of the Heartland of the Bible Belt that erroneously ascribes a choice by conservatives to prioritize cultural over economic issues as sheer stupidity. This has also played into the Southern sense of being "dissed" and into the conservative populism that Republicans have exploited so effectively with their base.

An anxious class, in a period of national decline, is ripe for the conservative decay-and-rebirth story. In the Bible Belt, conditions for resonance with the GOP story, particularly among white workers, business leaders, and Evangelicals, have been overwhelmingly powerful. The Evangelical base, aligned with the corporate elites, will remain a passionately conservative and well-funded force in America for years to come. But the debacle in Iraq—and President Obama's stunning victory in 2008, along with an expanding Democratic majority in both houses of Congress—suggests that while their rebirth story will remain a powerful Republican tool for many years, it faces major challenges. As discussed further in Part Four, the majority of the country rejects the born-again moral discourse, sees through its immoral morality and has embraced new moral visions that can potentially move America in a more peaceful and democratic direction.

PART III

Political Correctness as an American Tragedy

7

The Invisible Political Correctness
The Right Is Your Big Brother

We have never escaped one or another form of political correctness (PC) since the Puritans. But after the 1960s and 1970s, interest in PC soared and became one of the hottest potatoes in the culture wars. Thousands of books and articles have been written since 1980 about PC as a plague ruining politics and everyday life in America. We argue in Part III that PC is a third form of immoral morality, found abundantly on all sides of the political spectrum. Since it is an effort to silence—and sometimes kill—others in the name of truth or values, it is yet another form of evil done in the name of good.

PC is rampant in empires and among the Born Again. They depend on PC for their very survival. But PC also exists in other political and social contexts, being rampant on the very Left that fights against Empire and the Born Again. It is thus a distinct system of immoral morality that deserves treatment on its own terms.

PC has emerged today mainly as a devastating critique by the Right of the American Left. A veritable army of conservative pundits makes a career attacking the Leftist effort to impose its own views about affirmative action, sexism, and homosexuality on the U.S. public. But if the Right has been effective because it has seized on something real about the Left, a matter that we discuss in the next chapter, then it has ignored something equally important about itself. PC is as much a phenomenon of the Right as it is of the Left. In fact, the very success of the Right attack on Left PC reflects the extent to which Right PC now pervades the entire culture and is the primary system of thought control in the United States. While Left PC is water-cooler conversation everywhere, Right PC is invisible to most people. That, in itself, is a sign of just how powerful Right PC is.

The most effective PC is always invisible. It is so deeply ingrained in people's minds that they can't see it. Right PC, which defines how Americans ultimately think about patriotism and capitalism, among other matters, is the most powerful PC in the land. It has become so widely accepted that ordinary Americans take it for granted, most liberals also accept it, and even some sectors of the Left buy into it. Right PC is the hegemonic system of thought control in America. It is used to justify America's most immoral foreign policy and economic practices in the name of morality itself.

PC as Immoral Morality

There is a "Politically Correct" dictionary from which we learn the following PC linguistic etiquette:

Bald: follicularly challenged
Criticism: unjust self-esteem reducer
Failure: nontraditional success
Ignorant: factually unencumbered
Mugging: unforeseen funding of underclass
Short: altitudinally disadvantaged; vertically challenged
White: melanin-impoverished[1]

The PC dictionary is marketed as the way to keep yourself out of trouble. It's funny enough to make the whole thing seem trivial. The linguist Charles Osgood cracks that being "politically correct means always having to say you're sorry."[2]

But the famous novelist Robert Louis Stevenson once said: "To know what you prefer, instead of humbly saying Amen to what the world tells you what you ought to prefer, is to have kept your soul alive."[3] This gets closer to the deadly serious nature of PC. When we lose our desire or ability to think differently than the prevailing wisdom or ruling authority, we have lost our humanity.

PC is more than just politically fashionable language or routine conformity to the norms of society. It is a strategy used by ruling elites and other influential groups to keep others in line. It seeks power by controlling thought and morality, and it does so typically in the name of lofty values or God. George Orwell takes Stevenson's point and puts it in political perspective. In Orwell's book *1984*, Big Brother refashioned the language of Newspeak to make it impossible to think thoughts contrary to the moral code of the regime. To think contrary to Big Brother was successfully defined as the most immoral act possible, and surveillance and censorship were defined as the highest morality. Oceania was the ultimate politically correct society.

This helps clarify why PC is immoral morality. PC places limits on the range of acceptable thought and morals, seeking to outlaw or marginalize ways of thinking that might challenge the powers that be. The limits that are imposed are almost always established by the Ideological Apparatus in the name of protecting basic moral values and the survival of the moral order of society itself. But since PC is a power tool using morality to keep others powerless, its use of values and beliefs is immoral. And since silencing dissenters or imposing broad-based censorship is itself immoral, and since the official morality being protected is often evil, as in the case of the Slave South, PC is immoral morality in many senses.

The Slave South was the quintessential PC society. No respectable Southerner could criticize slavery as evil or view it as anything but a sacred trust. Anyone, including slaves themselves, who saw slavery as immoral were viewed as sinning against God and betraying the South's core moral values. For this reason, there was no public debate about slavery in the South. All white Southerners took slavery as a moral good for granted. There was no need for censorship since whites lacked a moral discourse for seeing slavery as anything but a part of God's Plan for the superior race protecting an inferior race who needed their care.

But PC is immoral morality even if used in the service of a moral order that is not evil, as will be seen in the discussion of Left PC, which is often devoted to defending moral values of equality or social justice. The validity of the moral code being defended does not make the exercise of PC any less immoral. Any effort to silence debate about values in the name of morality is immoral.

The immoral morality of PC is pernicious because it is a common way in which political values are brought into everyday life, alienating and dehumanizing its victims and helping to explain why so many Americans hate politics. If a student doesn't feel free to speak her own views in a professor's classroom, whether the professor is Right or Left, this is PC—and it is a serious form of immoral morality. If children in a family feel unsafe expressing political or moral views contrary to that of their parents, this, too, is PC, whether the parents are liberal or conservative. Typically, parents enforce such prohibitions in the name of protecting their children's values, a paternalistic and very important form of immoral morality. Many professors and teachers, as well as journalists and political leaders, carry out the same form of paternalistic PC.

Many of the most disturbing forms of PC lack the drama of George Orwell and the transparency of the immoral morality of the Slave South. But they are no less serious, and the immoral morality involved is no less dangerous. In the United States today, relative freedom of thought and expression may seem to reduce PC, of either Right or Left, to a modest and often humorous annoyance. But it serves the same aim of silencing dissent as in Orwell's *1984*, and, in the end, it is intolerably dehumanizing.

PC and the Ideological Apparatus

Creating political correctness is one way of describing the aims of the Ideological Apparatus in most societies. The Ideological Apparatus, as described in earlier chapters, is the set of institutions—government information offices, mass media, churches, schools, and universities—that shape a nation's culture and values. Ruling elites set up the Ideological Apparatus to produce ideas and morals that sustain their power and increase the commitment of ordinary people to the larger society they rule.

In dictatorships and theocracies, the Ideological Apparatus typically functions as a pure propaganda system. The intellectuals, journalists, priests, and other culture-shapers will simply transmit the ideas and morals dictated from the top. In these societies, as Orwell suggested, thought control will be extreme. There will be only one "party line" and everyone will subscribe to the official PC or be eliminated.

In more democratic societies, including the United States, the Ideological Apparatus functions with relative autonomy. This means that there is relative freedom of thought and moral belief. In liberal Western democracies, there is considerable diversity of ideologies and substantial freedom of speech, giving the impression that PC is a haphazard or unofficial problem. It does not appear to be tightly orchestrated and controlled through ruling elites.

But in Western democratic, capitalist societies, especially the United States, the Ideological Apparatus still creates a PC that operates as a nuanced form of thought control and immoral morality. It is a set of fundamental ideas and values that legitimates the ruling elites and the existing social order. As we show shortly, this is Right PC, and it operates with great power on the most important beliefs and morals shaping the nation. While it permits diverse views and a carefully crafted range of respectable opinion, it creates a form of party line that has great power precisely because it operates with less formal coercion and thought control than in dictatorships.

In Western democracies, PC remains a systemic phenomenon essential to the legitimacy of the power elites. The party line it creates is more elastic and invisible than in dictatorships, with a broader spectrum of views on which differences are accepted. Nonetheless, on the most basic ideological beliefs and moral principles, an official PC is created and enforced. It constitutes the limited but crucial set of views that Noam Chomsky has called "necessary illusions," the set of values and beliefs that cannot be abandoned without leading to the crumbling of the regime.[4]

As shown in the next section, these necessary illusions, which sustain the power of the ruling elites and the perpetuation of the existing capitalist order, are Right PC. They are produced by a particular sector of the Ideological Apparatus and are largely invisible. They are not treated as PC in most of the American discussion about PC, but their very invisibility makes them particularly powerful and effective. Since Left PC is challenged and debated, it is always in jeopardy. Since Right PC is invisible and rarely debated, it is uniquely powerful.

In dictatorships, the Ideological Apparatus creates a single ideological vision and moral discourse. But in Western democracies, such as the United States, the Ideological Apparatus is more diverse. There are sectors that promote right-wing ideology and Right PC, and also sectors that are Left leaning and produce Left PC. The very diversity of the Ideological Apparatus appears to undermine its standing as a coercive organ of the state and a creator of PC. But this, again, is misleading. The divisions within the Ideological Apparatus do not weaken the power of the various PC systems propagated by different sectors. They create the impression of clashing ideologies and of free thought. But the outcome is actually more complex, leading to extreme thought control on matters of key importance to state and power elites, as well as disconcerting forms of thought control among key groups challenging them.

Right PC 1: Love It or Leave It

The two most important areas of Right PC involve patriotism and capitalism. These have become forms of invisible theology in America, and they are the core of Right PC. Faith in America and capitalism are so taken for granted that the thought control behind the faith gets no attention. That, in itself, makes it urgent to raise Right PC as a crucial form of immoral morality. We have already discussed many examples of Right PC in the empire section of this book, specifically, ideas about the goodness of American global power and of America itself that cannot be questioned by "respectable" people. Here, we look at the ways in which these views function as the Right's form of PC.

The power of Right PC, especially about patriotism, is reflected in how strongly even the Left now feels required to prove that they love America.

Of course, many Leftists do love America and it is not just Right PC that might lead them to want to demonstrate their patriotism and redefine it in new terms. But for many liberals and others further on the Left, there seems almost a sense of terror, as if they have to live up to the Right's PC idea of patriotism—or be completely disgraced. Antiwar activists put decals on their cars saying they support the troops, something that almost nobody on the Left or Right argues against. After 9/11, prominent Leftists began to fly the flag on their house or car, with progressive intellectuals such as Todd Gitlin, a former 1960s New Left leader, writing a whole book on why he put a flag up after the 9/11 attacks, and why the whole Left should start displaying this form of patriotism.[5] It has become unacceptable for any group in society, including those deeply opposed to U.S. wars, not to make displays showing one's patriotism. In the 1960s, the antiwar Left did not make these displays and were met with a clear message: "love it or leave it."

But this only scratches the surface of Right PC on patriotism, which like all PC is an effort to silence dissent or close off debate in the name of higher values. President Bush's mantra "you're either with us or against us" is stark Right PC. You have only two choices: support America and its wars or else you're on the side of barbaric terrorists. Bush claimed often that he doesn't question the patriotism of dissenters to the Iraqi war, but his slogans give the lie to this. There is no middle ground; one must take America's side or be America's enemy. The patriot in Right PC supports America "right or wrong," but America is always on the right side.

Right PC limits critical debates about what patriotism is, whether it is always a good thing, and ultimately what America itself is all about. The Republicans' trump card since the war on communism has been to paint Democrats and the Left as weak and anti-American. Principled opposition to war, in a nation not controlled by a Right PC, would itself be viewed as a high value requiring no defense; it signifies the courage to assert oppositional values and hold one's nation to global moral standards. But in America, Democrats and the Left find themselves constantly on the defensive against the charge of betrayal of their nation, finding it difficult to prove their patriotism as defined by Right PC and unable to question the very concept or morality of patriotism itself.

I (Derber) experienced this Right PC myself in my television conversation with Bill O'Reilly about Boston College's award to Condoleezza Rice, as already discussed in the introduction. His first question to me was, "Do you think Rice is a patriot?" If I said she was a patriot, I would have no standing to oppose her honorary degree. If I said she was not a patriot, I would be seen as ridiculous, since how could a Secretary of State's patriotism be reasonably questioned. Either way, the Right PC regime that

O'Reilly exploits shamelessly would mark me as a person who has no clue about what it means to love one's country. Had I offered another answer, that she was patriotic, and this is what is wrong with her since patriotism in an imperial nation is immoral, this would have completely eroded any "respectable" standing in the conversation.

Right-wing pundits such as O'Reilly, Sean Hannity, and Ann Coulter have made careers of equating the Left with anti-American and dissent as unpatriotic and thus immoral. Anybody who says U.S. wars are unprincipled and unjust—not just a "mistake"—is an America-hater. In Right PC, there can be no debate about whether patriotism itself is moral, a very serious issue discussed below. Moreover, Right PC has succeeded in narrowing the debate about U.S. foreign policy to questions of strategies and tactics, with questions about the underlying goodness of U.S. power and of the United States itself taken off the table. More broadly, it is part of a remarkably successful campaign to discredit liberalism and the Left as hating everything America stands for. One of the greatest triumphs of Right PC has been to (1) force liberals and the Left to kow-tow to ideas about patriotism that they don't believe and (2) to undermine the very existence of a "respectable" Left in America, making the Left synonymous with anti-Americanism.

We ultimately know PC by which questions are off the table, defined as "out of the mainstream," and thus discrediting those who raise them. To understand Right PC on patriotism, consider a few "unrespectable" questions that the Right PC regime successfully defines as immoral even to ask:

1. *Is patriotism always good?* This seems a foolish question because of the power of Right PC, which unequivocally equates patriotism with morality. It takes for granted that one should fly the flag at football games or in classrooms. It never questions singing the National Anthem or saying the Pledge of Allegiance at school assemblies. There is no debate in America about the morality of such patriotic displays or of American patriotism itself. Among the Right, even raising this question would be deemed outrageous.

But at least two questions need to be raised that Right PC has silenced. One is whether it is moral to be patriotic in a country carrying out an immoral domestic or foreign policy. At the extreme, one might ask whether patriotism would be moral in Nazi Germany or Stalinist Russia. But even in less extreme cases, there are reasons to question the automatic assumption that patriotism is moral. One is that many countries, particularly hegemons like the United States, are engaged over long historical periods in global expansion and control that are morally problematic. Patriotism in such countries is not obviously a moral virtue. Is it obvious that Romans during the Roman Empire owed Rome patriotism? Or that Spaniards owed Spain patriotism when the Spanish Empire was committing genocide against the natives of the New World? At minimum, it deserves serious debate in any hegemon, a debate that Right PC makes impossible in America.

Second, in a globalizing world, the question of how much loyalty one owes one nation, relative to loyalty to either smaller or larger communities, is becoming increasingly important. Global U.S. companies are increasingly uncoupled with America and legally act with no particularly loyalty to the United States. Is this immoral behavior? Is it moral? This generates some discussion about whether transnational firms are—or should be—patriotic. But it does not open up space for a discussion about whether individual citizens should be patriotic. Right PC ensures that anyone raising this question is deemed a heretic. We are not suggesting that patriotism is immoral in America. Rather, we are arguing that the question deserves discussion and Right PC rules such discussion out.

2. Is America a Good Nation? This is the most fundamental question ruled out of bounds by Right PC. In the United States, it is acceptable to challenge nearly any specific domestic policy on war, and one can question whether a particular administration is basically good or bad. But it is not acceptable to question whether the United States is a fundamentally good nation. It is simply assumed to be so, and anyone questioning this is seen as immoral and antipatriotic. As noted earlier, the view that liberals and the Left see America as a bad country, hate it, and therefore are immoral has become a drumbeat of the Right. Ironically, virtually no liberals and few members of the Left even raise the question of whether America is a basically good country, even if they are highly critical of a large spectrum of U.S. policies. Liberals and Democrats are terrified that they will be accused of not being patriots, leading to a timid and hugely constrained public debate.

Right PC is so powerful that the question whether America is good seems almost nonsensical. Because it is never raised, most Americans would be baffled by why anybody would even think to ask it. But this is a sure sign of PC, which is designed to make certain questions seem nonsensical or immoral.

Many Americans learn to think of particular nations—such as North Korea or Iran—as "bad" regimes or countries. President Bush explicitly labeled North Korea and Iran as part of the "Axis of Evil."[6] Right PC in America strongly promotes the idea that some nations are good and some not. But it does not accept the morality or patriotism of anyone who even raises the question of whether the United States is a good nation.

This affects debate about serious matters in dangerous ways. Since the United States is assumed to be good, Right PC discredits anyone who might ask why the United States should be allowed to have nuclear weapons while threatening other nations, such as North Korea and Iran, who might want them. Right PC makes the American arsenal of nuclear weapons morally unproblematic because American goodness assures that these ultimate weapons will not be used for evil. Since Right PC defines North Korea and Iran as evil, the opposite assumption is made. This makes it impossible to have an honest and globally credible argument about the subject of nuclear threats and arsenals, since nobody on the American side of the debate will be able to say what many other nations believe: that the United States is not fundamentally a good nation and does not have a better government than other countries that have or aspire to build weapons of mass destruction.

I (Derber) have sometimes asked my students whether the United States is good—and students tell me they have never had a teacher bring it up before. Even progressive students view their nation as basically good, with current policies such as the Iraq War seen as deviations from the fundamentally idealistic values of the Founders and the Constitution. When I remind them of the genocide of the Native Americans and the enslavement of millions of Africans on which the country was built, they begin to see the possible legitimacy of the question—and it often has a deeply distressing and eye-opening impact.

Polls around the world, though, suggest that people outside the United States are increasingly asking exactly this question: Is America good? This is creating a very large gap between how Americans and the rest of the world learn to talk and think about America itself. In other nations, people inevitably question hegemons that historically have always defined themselves as not only good but "chosen." To silence debate about the fundamental moral nature of a hegemonic nation is clear immoral morality. Historically, hegemons silence such debate as a form of Right PC, since to question the goodness of a hegemonic nation is to question the legitimacy of its global power.

The absence of conversation about whether the United States is a good nation makes impossible a set of systemic critiques that might change the fundamental values or direction of the nation—and challenge its legitimacy to be "leader of the free world." It profoundly reduces the scope of democratic debate inside the nation, taking off the table such issues as whether the United States should be a hegemon and whether it promotes freedom and democracy. It creates debate about public policies that always start with assumptions that are morally questionable and flawed. A war gone wrong is reduced to errors in judgment rather than a predictable result of systemic flaws or evils. Thus the debate about Iraq is about whether the United States made "mistakes" in execution or whether the administration lied. But it's not about whether the United States had fundamentally immoral or evil intentions in Iraq and the region, something that no Democrat has openly suggested. Any respectable discussion of the United States as a hegemon is about the exceptionalism of the country, which allows it to be described as hegemonic without the moral tarnish associated with imperial powers.

American exceptionalism is a critical feature of Right PC. If the United States is openly described as an empire, it is a "Democratic Empire," the Right PC language exonerating the country of guilt by association with its most relevant historical counterparts. The United States might, indeed, be a freer and better hegemon than its predecessors, but it also might be the same or worse; this is an important conversation that should be widely aired but does not take place in Congress or in the mass media, churches, or schools. Right PC curtails the debate about values and American morality in a drastic way, since one cannot question the underlying motives or benevolence of the nation. Only the Left hints at this question and by doing so it immediately discredits the Left under Right PC rules. This has turned the Democrats into a party so fearful, cautious, and self-censoring that it cannot play the role of an honest oppositional party, let alone a forceful critic of the U.S. hegemonic system.

The question of whether a nation is good or bad should be accepted as legitimate in any nation, and especially a hegemon. It is a foundational question in any ethical discussion, whether about a person, a community, or a nation. In powerful countries that never accept the legitimacy of the question, such as Germany between the wars, it took a complete catastrophe and destruction of the country to make the question legitimate. One does not want to wait for such a catastrophe to make it possible to ask this question in America.

3. *Is the United States a terrorist state?* The U.S. war on terrorism has credibility only if the United States is assumed to not be a terrorist state. Indeed, all official U.S. foreign policy is based on this unchallenged single assumption of Right PC. No Republican or Democratic official has raised the question of whether the United States engages in terrorism, nor has it ever become a subject in a presidential debate, in a speech of any member of Congress, or in mainstream mass media. Significant challenges to the way in which the war on terrorism is executed are permitted within the Right PC regime. But a debate about whether the United States is itself a terrorist state is out of bounds and is never part of the discussion between Republicans and Democrats, nor is it an accepted issue in mainstream academic or policy circles.

Yet in much of the world, scholars address this question routinely, with many European and Third World scholars and journalists suggesting that the United States is a leading terrorist nation, a view that gets considerable support as well in the public opinion polls of other nations. One criterion of a terrorist state is a nation carrying out regime changes that installs puppet regimes and then arms them to systematically kill thousands of their own citizens, often by death squads. The United States has carried out many such regime changes—from Iran to Guatemala to Chile to Vietnam—and would be vulnerable to serious consideration as a terrorist state by this one global standard. Yet in the United States, only Leftist scholars such as Noam Chomsky[7] and Edward Herman,[8] who have carried out detailed scholarship of such U.S. state terrorism, are forthright in describing it as such. When they do so, they are marginalized from respectable discourse by reigning elites.

The exclusion of this issue from debate is a serious form of immoral morality. If the question of the United States as a terrorist state were even to be admitted into the mainstream discourse, it would threaten all aspects of Right PC. It would allow Americans to participate in the global conversation about American terror from which they are excluded, something that would break wide open the ideological bubble in which most Americans now live. It would lead to an entirely different self-reflective discussion of the war on terrorism, and it would require a new assessment of all U.S. foreign policy, using universalistic criteria of terrorism that are currently not applied to the United States. It would lead to far closer attention in classes, textbooks, and the mass media of the long history of U.S. support for repressive dictatorships during the Cold War and today. It would ultimately lead to a more honest examination of the two other premises of Right PC about (1) whether patriotism is moral in a U.S. hegemon and (2) whether the United States is a benevolent nation.

Right PC 2: Capitalism = Democracy = Morality

Right PC is not restricted to patriotism. It also operates with ferocious power as a thought control system about capitalism. While it leaves space for debates about most specific economic policy measures—from regulation to welfare to economic monopolies—it silences conversations about the fundamental goodness of the economic system itself. Most important, Right PC silences debate about the central issue of the morality of capitalism.

The economic core of Right PC is that capitalism creates freedom and is an unchallengeable moral order. This PC comes in a variety of strains, one of which is that God has ordained capitalism; another is that free markets are part of nature; another is that there are no viable economic or moral alternatives. These different strains of Right PC all recognize that there may be unfair byproducts or corruptions of capitalism that reduce opportunity or mobility or meritocracy. But they discredit the possibility that capitalism is irretrievably flawed or systemically immoral. Economic Right PC leads to a political culture in which no mainstream politician or respectable intellectual can credibly challenge capitalism as evil. One can propose reforms to soften the imperfections but cannot propose dismantling capitalism as a system of exploitation and domination.

This is closely tied to the idea that capitalism creates freedom and that all other systems are unfree. Right PC creates this unchallengeable proposition partly by linguistic devices that describe capitalism as a "free market" system. A free market appears, by definition, to promote freedom. Right PC makes it impossible to question whether "free markets" are free, or, equally important, whether free markets exist as a part of American capitalism, or indeed, are even theoretically possible. In Orwellian terms, the concept of "free market" is a form of Newspeak, language designed to make the question of whether capitalism truly promotes freedom a nonsensical issue.

American capitalism is, in fact, a system of highly managed markets, which are anything but free. Both governments and big corporations create, shape, and partly determine the limits and outcomes of market competition. The theory of free markets in Economics 101 textbooks bears very little relation to an economy of huge global corporations vying to control largely oligopolistic fiefdoms with generous help from their political patrons. The United States is really a form of state capitalism—characterized by a marriage of big government and big business—which bears little relation to classic definitions of capitalism and raises serious moral questions about both its theoretical and real world forms. But Right PC dismisses this reality as "market imperfections" or political corruption that in no way undermine the fundamental fairness and democracy of a capitalist market economy. Right PC has succeeded in unequivocally equating democracy and American capitalism.

The faith in capitalism as a moral order has not always existed in America. In the late nineteenth century, the agrarian populists challenged capitalism as an immoral plutocracy. They created a third "People's Party" in 1892 to overthrow large parts of the capitalist system as morally bankrupt and proposed detailed platforms for a cooperative economy, with banks and other vital industries publicly owned and controlled. In the 1960s, many of the new radical movements also challenged the morality of capitalism, and proposed a noncapitalist system. Its details were not packaged in a party platform like those of the nineteenth-century populists, but the principles of the post-capitalist economy were clear: public accountability of corporations and the state, participatory democratic decision-making in firms and other large organizations, equality of results as well as opportunity that would vastly shrink the gap between rich and poor, and sustainable production and consumption that would limit environmental destruction.

During the Cold War, the very existence of the Soviet Bloc kept open the idea that alternatives to capitalism existed. The clumsy, inefficient Soviet bureaucratic planning system itself was hardly a viable or moral economic alternative. But many European nations had socialist tendencies, especially in Scandinavia, which were seen as both more efficient and fair than U.S. capitalism. The same was true of socialist or social democratic or populist development models being proposed in Latin America and Africa in the 1960s and 1970s, before globalization had taken root and socialism was discredited. All over the world, the debate about the morality of capitalism was at the center of the political conversation.

Globalization essentially ushered in the new PC regime, where it became impossible for a respectable analyst to question the equation that capitalism = democracy = morality. Globalization essentially globalized the U.S. model of capitalism as inevitable, democratic, and moral: a system with no viable alternatives. As Thomas Friedman, one of the most prominent theorists of Right PC on the subject of globalization wrote, there is now only one way to move forward: "So, ideologically speaking, there is no more mint chocolate chip, there is no more strawberry swirl, and there is no more lemon-lime. Today there is only free-market vanilla and North Korea."[9]

Friedman sets forth several key Right PC propositions in *The Lexus and the Olive Tree*[10] and *The World Is Flat*,[11] his two major best-selling books on globalization. One is that "free market vanilla" is the only flavor in the global economy because it alone can deliver the goods, that is, efficiency, prosperity, and growth. Right PC essentially proclaims the end of economic history, with free market capitalism being the last and best system standing. Second, this is a welcome development because free market capitalism equals capitalist democracy, which is likewise conceived as the only viable democratic system. Third, because it promotes prosperity and democracy, it is a moral order. Fourth, central to capitalism and its morality is the whole system of private property as codified in the eighteenth-century seminal philosophies of John Locke and Adam Smith. Right PC makes private property sacred, rooting itself in revered ancient traditions of Anglo-American law and the American Constitution, which is the official creed of enterprise, freedom, and morality itself. To question private property or any of the "free market vanilla" propositions is outside the boundaries of Right PC.

Friedman is a centrist Democratic, and he recognizes that "free market vanilla" and corporate globalization create winners and losers and that the losers deserve help. Right PC is effective as thought control precisely because it makes it legitimate to debate a wide range of policy prescriptions to soften the harsh effects of the markets. And the debate about such reformist policies—both domestic and global—are often vibrant and heated. In much of the rest of the world, such as Latin America after Argentina had its financial meltdown, the debate has boiled over. But all the partisan divide about trade rules and globalization in the United States itself only serves to mask the underlying Right PC to which both major parties and all respectable members of the Ideological Apparatus subscribe, that is, that capitalism itself is the only democratic and moral order consistent with the values of the American people.

Right PC remains invisible and powerful not only because it permits debate about many reforms, but because even those who challenge its core tenets are not usually killed or jailed. Many Leftist members of the Ideological Apparatus teach or publish ideas that challenge and contradict Right PC. Often, they are able to keep their jobs and make a respectable living. The same is true of activists and protestors on the streets who oppose core Right PC ideas. In periods of war or national crisis, this can change: the vast peace movement against U.S. involvement in World War I was brutally repressed; the same was true of liberals and Leftists in the McCarthy era, and today there is evidence of a new crackdown on anyone who strays outside Right PC thought parameters on matters of patriotism, U.S. hegemony, and the war on terrorism.

Nonetheless, the Right PC regime, unlike many other hegemonic thought control systems, tolerates significant dissent. This is a secret of its great success. By pointing to the dissenters and celebrating their "right to disagree," as President Bush often says of his critics on the Iraqi war, Right PC only intensifies its hold on the nation. Necessary illusions of freedom are sustained, while at the same time the core Right PC ideas and morality of patriotism and capitalism are sustained. Dissent simply reinforces the power of Right PC, while discrediting the dissenters. This more flexible system of PC can be more effective in controlling ideas and values than Orwell's Big Brother.

8

Left Political Correctness
When Free Thinkers Become Dogmatists

While Right PC dominates America, most PC critics are conservatives who view Left PC as the moral trash bringing down America. They include the Republicans' moral czar William Bennett, Fox's raucous pundits Bill O'Reilly and Sean Hannity, the flamboyant right-wing columnist Ann Coulter, and the Leftist-turned-crusading-Rightist David Horowitz. All reject the very concept of Right PC. Instead, they define PC as the Left's way of using its elite positions in the Ideological Apparatus to impose its views about race, sex, religion, and America on the rest of the population. As a result, many on the Left have argued that PC is a myth created to discredit the Left itself. British Left-leaning journalist Will Hutton writes: "Political correctness is one of the brilliant tools that the American Right developed in the mid-1980s as part of its demolition of American liberalism.... What the sharpest thinkers on the American Right saw quickly was that by declaring war on the cultural manifestations of liberalism—by leveling the charge of political correctness against its exponents—they could discredit the whole political project."[1]

Hutton is on to something. PC has been a devastating instrument used by the Right to conceal its own PC as well as to debunk Leftist thinking. Critiquing PC has become something of a right-wing cultural industry in itself: a standardized way to make fun of and demonize the Left and then dismiss the whole liberal and Leftist enterprise. To a large degree, it has worked.

But while Hutton is correct that the Right uses PC as a merciless weapon to take down the Left, the Left's propensity toward PC has long been one of its own most suicidal tendencies. While many Leftists are reluctant to discuss the subject since it is so mercilessly exploited by the Right, the risks of not discussing it are even greater, since Left PC has played a historic role in undermining the Left itself. As authors who have had long personal experience with the Left, we try to understand in this chapter why Left PC—a form of immoral morality of the opposition—has been so persistent and how the Left can change. When we criticize Left PC, we speak as insiders hoping to make the Left more effective.

One often sees left-wingers wearing protest buttons saying "Question Authority." This slogan sums up a main Leftist theme: the need for critical thinking in all areas. It makes Left PC more surprising than Right PC. Since the Right is devoted to preserving order and traditional authority, it easily slides into PC. If you accept tradition, you accept prevailing thought and try to prevent questioning of long-standing notions of truth or morality.

The Left in the United States has always been an opposition movement, seeking to question all dogma and existing power. Since it is theoretically subversive of all authority, it seems almost by definition a contradiction to be both Leftist and PC. To be Leftist is to be committed to the idea that no idea is sacred. But PC silences people who try to challenge sacred ideas. Despite this contradiction, Left PC has long been a serious problem globally, most brutally exemplified during the Stalinist and Maoist eras, in which deviation from Communist Truth and opposition to the regime meant death to millions. In the United States today, Left PC takes a very different form and does not lead to Leftists killing people, but involves a persistent tendency to censor or silence those who disagree with Left Truths.

In describing Left PC, we need to distinguish between a Left in power and one that has never ruled. The first we call the *hegemonic Left* and the second the *oppositional Left*. PC in a hegemonic Left—such as in the Stalinist Soviet state or Maoist China—can become the form of ruinous immoral morality found on the Right. In these regimes, the Left can use official police, military, and legal powers to enforce its PC and sometimes jail or kill millions in the process. Moreover, when the Left gains state power, its interests change from opposition to control. This can poison Leftist ideology, greasing a path toward immoral morality and violent PC, and raising the question of whether a Left in power can actually still be a "Left."

The most important purpose of the state is to preserve order, making it an inherently conservative institution. If the Left controls the state, it becomes the authority rather than the challenger of authority. However, although the state ultimately promotes social stability, it can advance a more or less equitable distribution of resources, greater or lesser freedom of expression, and increase or decrease people's control over their everyday life. In those cases when the Left did take state power, it usually faced enemies who it had to either suppress or overthrow, increasing any tendencies toward violence and immoral morality. In this chapter, we use the term hegemonic Left to emphasize that assuming state power transforms Leftist interests and ideology, and that the tragedies described in this chapter are a function of both structural and ideological Leftist deformation.

Where Leftists do not rule, as in the United States, they lack the coercive powers to inflict the hegemonic Left's horrific and widespread damage. Nonetheless, in opposition, the Left can still develop its own PC and seek to silence others without using state police powers. Such nonofficial ideological intimidation in the name of Leftist truth we call *"embryonic immoral morality,"* since it can evolve into the real thing if such a Left gains power.

When we speak of the Left, we are not speaking of liberals, such as mainstream members of the Democratic Party. Conservatives tend to confuse liberals with the Left. By the Left, we mean those who tend to operate outside of the Left of the Democratic Party. The U.S. Left is those in popular movements who seek radical democratization, transformation of the capitalist system, and the end of the American Empire. The Left sees the Democrats and liberals as embracing the basic framework of American capitalism and global hegemony.

In describing the pathologies of the Left, we do not mean to exonerate liberals and Democrats, who are guilty of their own very serious immoral morality, since leaders from Woodrow Wilson to Hillary and Bill Clinton have gained state power and, in fact, built the American Empire. In Part I, we showed that both Republican and Democratic presidents were imperial leaders who draped American Empire in high principles. The Left's future is, nonetheless, tied to that of the Democrats, since they must form a united front to prevent continued disasters of rule by the Right.

Although the Left should ally with liberals for the foreseeable future, liberals arguably have more in common in ideology with the Right than they do with the Left. That is because both liberals and the Right consider American inherent goodness and global leadership beyond the pale of questioning, an assumption rejected by the Left. At this time, the primary function of the Left, at least within the United States, should be to create an opposition that liberals must answer to and thus push debate among liberals and Democrats leftward.

The Democratic Party, then, should not be confused with the Left, even if they need to engage in tactical alliances. Their moral orders are fundamentally different. And since the American Left has never had state power, its embryonic immoral morality is on a different scale than that of either the ruling Republican or Democratic parties. In other countries, though, a Left in power has sometimes demonstrated immoral morality on the same scale as the Right or governing liberals.

While this chapter is devoted to exposing the history and current problems of the Left, two caveats need to be emphasized. Despite the story we tell here, the Left has been the indispensable vehicle for a more just society, from the abolitionists to the populists to the feminists, and peace and environmental activists of today. It remains critical to the creation of a better world. And, second, while a major sector of the Left has been poisoned by PC, many Left groups have not succumbed. Today, groups such as MoveOn.org, the American Friends Service Committee, the National Labor Committee, Global Exchange, Code Pink, and thousands of other groups in the peace, justice, and environmental movements, prove that the Left can thrive without descending into PC or any form of immoral morality. Moreover, we are not trying to offer a full description of why Leftist movements or revolutions fail, since this would require its own book on both structural and ideological forces. We are interested in describing the ideological poisons that have recurrently emerged to undermine Left-inspired visions of liberation.

A Brief History of Left PC and the Left in Power: The Jacobins and Stalinists

The Left in the West was born in the seventeenth and eighteenth centuries, as part of the reaction against Church authority that had dominated Europe since the Middle Ages. The Enlightenment—of which the Left was one offshoot—included a wide range of philosophers, scientists, and literary figures such as Rene Descartes, John Locke, François Voltaire, and Jean Jacques Rousseau. All these thinkers helped create a revolution against the Church. They championed reason, science, and natural rights as the foundation of a new way of thinking. In the eyes of Enlightenment thinkers, the Church increasingly stood for the dogma of faith and unquestioned obedience to the Church. This translated into a broader conservative philosophy that religious and secular authority was sacred and should not be questioned, even when both Church and State were increasingly corrupt.

Enlightenment thinkers were not antireligious, but most believed in Deism—a view that God created the universe but then stood aside from history. Nature was governed by its own laws that were to be discovered by science. Faith remained possible, but people had to use reason to understand the world and guide their own lives. This meant a sharp break from the Church and its emphasis on faith and obedience. The Enlightenment meant each individual had to look skeptically at the views of anyone in authority and rely on rationality and experience to determine the truth and make their own decisions.

The Western Left was born from the Enlightenment. The Enlightenment concept of critical thinking was inherently radical, requiring both an intellectual and political revolution against not only the Church but all the conservative powers that had dominated Europe for centuries: the state, the landed aristocracy, and even the new capitalist merchants. It is hardly surprising that the Right attacked many Enlightenment thinkers, even political moderates such as Voltaire. An ultra-Right group broke into Voltaire's tomb and stole his remains, including his heart and brain, a revenge for the trouble he had kicked up, which led ultimately to the French Revolution.

Enlightenment thinkers, such as Locke and Rousseau, planted the earliest seeds both of the Left and Left PC. While he was a liberal defender of property, Locke pioneered ideas of natural rights. Far to Locke's Left, Rousseau openly challenged the conservative aristocracy and had radical views about everything from government to parenting. Rousseau argued that citizens had the right to revolt and create a government of popular sovereignty, and he helped inspire the French Revolution's manifesto, called the Declaration of the Rights of Man, which in turn helped inspire popular revolutions against colonialism around the world.

But if Rousseau helped inspire radical ideas of freedom and human rights, his views of the social contract and the "general will" carried also the early seeds of Left PC. Rousseau saw the social compact as a union based on shared community interests (the "general will") of all members, and States were formed to protect and enforce the general will. But despite his radical emphasis on rebellion and rights, Rousseau gave the State a power that carried the danger of authoritarianism and PC: "As nature gives each man absolute power over all his members, the social compact gives the body politic absolute power over all its members also ... and when the prince says to him [the citizen]: 'It is expedient for the State that you should die,' he ought to die, because it is only on that condition that he has been living in security up to the present, and because his life is no longer a mere bounty of nature, but a gift made conditionally by the State."[2]

Rousseau goes on to argue that we become citizens with rights only as long as we abide by the authority of the State. If we violate its dictates, reflecting the general will and decision by courts, then we lose any moral authority or rights. Rousseau sees this only as the fate of "the outlaw" rejecting society itself, but his willingness to vest absolute authority in the State and to deny rights to the rebel are dangerous precedents for Left PC. Although Rousseau was careful to claim that the State could not silence or kill those who conformed to the general will, his absolutism contradicted his belief in rights and rebellion—and was a recipe for potential abuse of power and thought control. This danger was proved in the French Revolution, when Maximillien Robespierre, Jean-Paul Marat, and their Jacobin colleagues, inspired by thinkers like Rousseau, became Leftist authoritarians who enforced a ruthless dogma and used the guillotine to dispose of their enemies.

In 1792, the Jacobins, led by Robespierre, became the first Leftists in the West to gain state power and soon proved that their PC could become a form of hegemonic morality as deadly as that of the Right. Robespierre argued for the killing of the king, Louis XVI of France, on moral grounds: "Louis ought to perish rather than a hundred thousand virtuous citizens; Louis must die, so that the country may live."[3] Louis was guillotined in early 1793, and shortly thereafter, on September 17, 1793, the Jacobins passed the "Law of Suspects," which set up tribunals to enforce the Revolution's PC. The tribunals identified "internal enemies" who showed insufficient faithfulness to Revolutionary values and who might "subvert the General Will." Its provisions, reminiscent of today's Patriot Act, stated that "Immediately after the publication of the present decree, all suspects within the territory of the Republic and still at large, shall be placed in custody." It goes on to say that suspects for surveillance and detention include "those to whom certificates of patriotism have been refused."[4]

This is an early Left in power, putting at mortal risk anyone opposing the Jacobins' PC. By late 1793, the Terror was in full swing; the French Revolutionaries imprisoned and killed thousands whose class background was suspect or whose zeal for fraternity and justice they deemed insufficiently weak. Under the Terror, the many designated "heretics" were to lose their heads in the guillotine, the victims of a Left PC that degenerated into terror and mass murder.

Robespierre, who had advocated a "Republic of Virtue," helped lead the Terror *in the name of morality*: "If virtue be the spring of a popular government in times of peace, the spring of that government during a revolution is virtue combined with terror: virtue, without which terror is destructive; terror, without which virtue is impotent. Terror is only justice prompt, severe, and inflexible; it is then an emanation of virtue."[5]

The Terror was full-blown immoral morality by a new hegemonic Left. The Revolution—which overthrew the aristocracy and established the great democratic principles of liberty and fraternity—was destroyed in a few years by its own suicidal tendencies toward ideological purity. In the end, a new monarchy emerged under Napoleon.

The modern form of "hegemonic Left" PC emerged more than a century later when the Bolsheviks took power in Russia. Karl Marx was a child of the Enlightenment and the father of the modern Left. Left PC developed most clearly from within the Marxist tradition, and a large part of Marxism degenerated into a Leftist dogmatic religion. Leninism became the pure embodiment of Left PC, consolidating a period in which Marxism evolved from an Enlightenment philosophy into a Communist dogma. That dogma would create a new model of an absolutist Leftist party and state based on the Leninist concepts of the "vanguard party" and "democratic centralism."

The Communist Party claimed it had discovered a scientific theory of materialism and that it constituted a vanguard whose politically correct truths needed to be respected by all good Leftists. Lenin wrote, "The role of a vanguard fighter can be fulfilled only by a party that is guided by the most advanced theory."[6] Lenin continued that "it will be the duty of the leaders to gain an ever clearer insight into all theoretical questions" and that everyone must obey the vanguard party because of its mastery of Marxist scientific materialism. The notion of a Marxist scientific truth would quickly evolve into a prescription for Left PC. The vanguard who knew the truth would enforce the principle of democratic centralism: the idea that once party leaders enunciated a doctrinal truth, everybody was required to accept it unquestionably. The freedom to criticize or dissent, Lenin wrote, became unacceptable heresy:

> It will be clear that "freedom of criticism" means freedom for an opportunist trend in Social Democracy, freedom to convert Social Democracy into a democratic party of reform, freedom to introduce bourgeois ideas and bourgeois elements into socialism.
>
> "Freedom" is a grand word, but under the banner of freedom for industry the most predatory wars were waged, under the banner of freedom of labor, the working people were robbed. The modern use of the term "freedom of criticism" contains the same inherent falsehood.[7]

This is an astonishing attack on "freedom of criticism" from a Left whose existence is based on critical thinking. When Lenin continues that believers in science would "not demand freedom" for dissenters to the new scientific truths, he demonstrated how doctrinaire Communists had turned science into a new dogmatic Church. The Enlightenment revolution against the Church spawned a pseudo-scientific Left Church enforcing its own thought control.

When the Bolsheviks came to power, Lenin did not hesitate to use the state's coercive powers to crush dissenters to his power. In December 1917, he established the "Cheka," a secret police force investigating "counterrevolutionaries." This happened when the white Russian army, with American and British support, tried to restore the czar. However, the Cheka soon began to execute its own justice against ideological heretics, terrorizing and killing the propertied bourgeoisie and anyone opposing Lenin's rule or truth, all allegedly to protect the brightest ideals of the Left. Lenin was a "true believer" and laid the foundation for a Bolshevik system that would torture and kill in the name of revolutionary moral purity.

Stalin succeeded Lenin and pushed Leninist PC to its limits, creating a murderous dictatorship and a new Left terror. While Leftists today tend to see Stalinism as the antithesis of Leftism, a form of radical Left degeneration or brutal centralized "state capitalism," Leftists at the time saw it as a moral inspiration. Communist Parties and Leftists in the United States and around the world, as we show later, looked to the Soviet Union and to Stalin for political and ethical guidance. It is simply dishonest to deny that Soviet Communism, including both Leninism and Stalinism, represent a recurrent upsurge of one major form of Left in power, one governed by an authoritarian PC and a vanguard vision that has been all too deeply embedded in the entire Leftist tradition.

Stalin ruled in the name of Communist truth, and set himself as the sole arbiter of Communist morality, dispensing "heretics" to their death literally by the millions in the name of prescribing the new moral order. Orwell modeled Big Brother, in *1984*, after Stalin, who resurrected Lenin's Cheka in 1932 and turned it into a vast terrorist police system. The Cheka became the NKVD, Stalin's secret police who executed hundreds of thousands and then purged many of their own members under Stalin's orders.

Stalin's enemies included famous rival leaders such as Leon Trotsky who "deviated" from the Stalinist gospel and threatened his monopoly of truth (and was later killed in Mexico with an axe blow to his head by a Stalinist agent). But anyone, in or out of the party, was at risk. These included people whose moral crime was that they had been clergy, merchants, or employers before the Revolution, even if they supported the Bolsheviks now. Indeed, Stalin ended up killing virtually all the original Bolsheviks and most of the later ones, simply to consolidate his power, although always in the name of Communist high moral ideals.

Much as in *1984*, the entire population, in fear for their lives, became informers to prove their loyalty and faith in the regime. They raced to denounce "enemies of the people," Stalin's famous phrase for heretics and precisely the phrase earlier used by the Jacobins during the French Terror. Frank Smitha, a scholar of the Stalinist purges, describes them in terms reminiscent of Orwell and of the French Terror: "Denunciations became common. Neighbors denounced neighbors. Denunciations were a good way of striking against people one did not like, including one's parents, a way of eliminating people blocking one's promotion, and ... a means of proving one's patriotism."[8] This, Smitha adds, was all done in the name of Communist idealism: "A society that is intense in its struggle for change has a flip side to its idealism: intolerance. People saw enemies everywhere, enemies who wanted to destroy the revolution and diminish the results of their hard work and accomplishments, enemies who wanted to restore capitalism for selfish reasons against the collective interests of the nation."[9]

The most famous chronicler of Stalin's horrific immoral morality was political scientist Robert Conquest, who called it "The Great Terror."[10] Conquest estimated that the combination of Stalin's genocidal war in the 1920s against the Kulak peasants—in the name of a moral cleansing of capitalist rural landholders—with the terrorist purges of the 1930s combined to create as many as 20 million deaths. He showed that the incessant killing was so vast that it undermined the Soviet economy, thereby creating the need for Stalin to stoke fear of ever more enemies of the people in defense of the Revolution's sacred ideals.

In various official addresses, Stalin intensified his war on heretics like Trotsky and other Leftist leaders, party members, and managers or bureaucrats who opposed his party line. He thundered against "deviations" by those from the Left and Right who were "sworn enemies of Leninism." Stalin is often described as the "pragmatist" in contrast to Lenin's "true believer," but Stalin ruled by turning the regime into a Communist theocracy. At Lenin's funeral, Stalin had signaled this tendency when, in his elegy, he spoke of his life commitment to defend Lenin's revolutionary and unchallengeable truth.

That Stalin murdered millions is widely known, although it was denied by many Leftist fellow travelers around the world before Stalin's death and the revelations of 1956 and the gulag. What is less well appreciated is the immoral morality involved, the fact that this evil was all done in the name of the highest egalitarian Communist values.

The American Left:
Embryonic Immoral Morality

The American Left never seized state power. This meant it could not use the state to enforce its PC and was incapable of turning into the killing machine of the Jacobins, Stalin, or later Mao in the Cultural Revolution. Nonetheless, disturbing and harmful PC tendencies emerged in sectors of the Left from the Communist Old Left of the 1930s to the feminist, minority, and other Leftist movements of today. And there certainly were tendencies within the Old and New Left that suggest they could be just as destructive to life and freedom if they ever seized power. For the good of their cause, committed Leftists need to recognize and resist these tendencies.

As noted earlier, we call the PC of a Left out of power "embryonic immoral morality." The harm it inflicts is on a totally different scale and does not involve mass violence or murder. But the American Left's PC carries its own dangers both to its own members and to the larger culture because it contradicts the Left's own principled commitment to free speech and critical thinking and has scary intimations of the full-blown ideological repression seen in the French and Soviet Revolutions.

The Communist Party and the New Left

While many on the American Left ultimately repudiated Stalinism as a nightmare antithetical to Leftist principles, Soviet Communism was a prime force on the global Left for many decades. In the United States, the American Communist Party saw itself as a vanguard party faithful to the Soviet leadership. It became the leading Leftist group in the United States from the Great Depression until the late 1950s, and it helped organize the new labor unions of the CIO, fought racism in factories and prisons, and pushed the New Deal to promote truly meaningful social change. But despite these accomplishments—and resistance from many of its own grass-roots partisans who harbored far more democratic inclinations—it operated through its own repressive model of democratic centralism, repressing unorthodox ideas in the name of Leftist solidarity and morality. For decades, members of the American Left overlooked the horrifically brutal crimes of Stalinism and either kept silent or supported Stalinism as superior to the capitalist alternative.

The Leninist and Stalinist tendencies were evident from the very beginning of the American Party. In 1919, C. E. Ruthenberg, the new party's executive secretary, described top CPUSA leaders as "agents of Lenin in

America." Ruthenberg distributed letters from Russian Communists, such as Nikolai Bukharin and Ian Berzin, instructing the American Communists how to operate. He approvingly notes that the American Communist must create "FIGHTING ORGANIZATIONS FOR SEIZING CONTROL OF THE STATE, for overthrow of the government, and the establishment of the workers' dictatorship."[11]

Leftist historian Richard Flacks wrote that the CPUSA demanded from its "members total fidelity to policies and lines promulgated by a top-down centralized leadership."[12] It essentially cloned the Stalinist model in a Left that was antihegemonic to capitalism, but hegemonic in its own internal authoritarian structure. As a "red diaper baby" whose parents were Communists, Flacks was in a position to know and—while he retains great respect for the community and social justice ideals of the members—had this to say about the party:

> Its organizational doctrine implied ... that "correct ideas" were held by those who were masters in their knowledge of Marxist-Leninist theory, and that such mastery could be claimed only by those at the top of party leadership ... the true test of revolutionary courage was readiness to accept and implement the Party line in the face of private doubts, to recognize the superior validity and reality of the leadership's positions compared with one's own immediate perceptions and judgments.[13]

What Flacks describes is accurate—and it is pure Left PC. The CP in the United States cloned the Soviet concept of a vanguard party based on scientific Marxism. Anyone opposing the leadership was a heretic who refused to accept the "correct ideas." The American Communists were creating their own Church, with leaders wielding the power of excommunication to silence dissenters and maintain their power in the name of preserving the highest moral truths. The grass-roots activists were subjugated both to the U.S. and Soviet popes. This not only weakened the party internally, driving many activists out of the movement and contradicting the Left's own core values, but made it easy for Senator Joseph McCarthy and other right-wing fanatics to attack the Left as Soviet stooges and traitors.

PC in the New Left and the Wild Sixties

The New Left rose up in the early 1960s as a movement blissfully free of Left PC. It stressed personal authenticity, freedom of thought, the vision of "letting a thousand flowers bloom," and the theory of pure participatory democracy. These themes were enshrined in the 1962 Port Huron statement, the founding document of Students for a Democratic Society (SDS), the main white New Left organization of the 1960s.[14] Tom Hayden, who wrote the Port Huron statement, expressed a new, genuinely free spirit that was very different from the centralized dogma of the Old Left. In the early 1960s, the New Left was what a Left should be: largely free of PC and democratic both in its talk and walk.

How was the New Left able at first to transcend the long tendency toward Left PC? The fever of the McCarthy witch-hunt had left Americans weary of fanatical zealotry and dogma from any side of the political spectrum. In the late 1950s, the Beats, including Jack Kerouac and Allen Ginsberg, had begun a cultural revolution against the stultifying corporate conformity and dullness of the new postwar suburban American culture. The New Left would find inspiration in all the forms of youth revolt—from rock and roll and Elvis to James Dean to the Beats—that shared a passion for a life free of bourgeois conventions.

The growth of postwar affluence created a new sense of security, alienation, and rebelliousness among white middle-class youth. They came to college in the early 1960s with unprecedented opportunities as the economy boomed; jobs for graduates seemed available to everyone, even those who dropped out for a while or didn't do so well in classes. The new prosperity created a space for experimentation and freedom to revolt against parental expectations and societal values. The era bloomed with free spirits who nobody could silence. The New Leftists lived the philosophy that the great revolutionary Rosa Luxemburg had unsuccessfully preached to dogmatic Bolsheviks half a century earlier: "Freedom is always and exclusively freedom for the one who thinks differently."[15]

This new "free space" was born in a new liberal political era, sparked by the election of President John F. Kennedy and the rise of the civil rights movement. Kennedy and then President Lyndon Johnson were not Leftists, but Kennedy symbolized an idealism that encouraged the free thinking of the new generation. Johnson's "Great Society" would also converge with the civil rights movement, and both catalyzed new ideals of freedom for white students. The courage and radicalism of the black civil rights activists, who were risking their lives to desegregate the South, helped white students break out of the "cultural prison" of white suburban life and imagine revolutionary changes in their personal lives, as well as in an increasingly corporatized and militarized America.

Affluence, idealism, models of radical activism among the black and poor, and a drab new corporate suburbanism all combined to create conditions for a new free-thinking and free-spirited revolt. The sense that all things were possible and the huge premiums put on personal authenticity and free expression made PC distinctly unattractive. Moreover, the New Left was young enough that it had not yet had the time to develop an orthodoxy or hierarchy that could enforce PC. New Leftists who knew the history of the Old Left, including people like Flacks, who was very close to Hayden and part of a key New Left circle at the University of Michigan in Ann Arbor, were determined not to repeat the mistakes of history. They wanted a new movement without dogma or a "party line."

SDS blossomed as a free-spirited movement for several years, proving that the Left is not always dominated by PC or immoral morality. It organized on hundreds of campuses, catalyzing activism across the country that helped to end segregation and the war. There was a small national organization, but the real action was on the campus and in the community. No national party was formed and there was no serious effort to impose a party line. Lenin was dead and participatory democracy ruled the day. The students enjoyed Groucho Marx as much as Karl Marx and they buried Lenin for the more free-spirited revolutionary, Emma Goldman, who famously said, "If I can't dance, it's not my revolution."[16]

But things changed dramatically by the end of the sixties, when SDS disintegrated. The costs of the long Vietnam War sapped the economy and the job market tightened, making students feel they had to toe the line. The war itself sparked a huge growth in the ranks of the New Left, but the government's political repression of the antiwar movement bred a new cult of discipline and control within the New Left itself. SDS was beginning to develop a hierarchal PC structure dominated by young white male students. An ultra-left splinter group of Leftist leaders, the Weathermen, formed their own revolutionary group and embraced violence, bombing campus buildings tied to the military. They romanticized as the Left "Vanguard" the Black Panthers (a more radical and sometimes violent black civil rights group) that urged true revolutionaries to "pick up a gun." We recall one Panther leader coming to a campus Left meeting and instructing white students in the Panther PC of revolutionary commitment: "When I come back here next year, I don't want to see a beautiful campus. I want to see rubble."[17] "You White students have shown you can march, but can you kill? I want to see if you can kill." "Go left! Go Right! Go pick up the gun."

The Panthers exemplified the most extreme form of Left PC—and violence—that could move embryonic immoral morality to the real thing. Its statement of the party's basic rules read as follows:

Every member of the Black Panther Party throughout this country of racist America must abide by these rules as functional members of this party. Central Committee members, Central Staffs, and Local Staffs, including all captains subordinated to either national, state, and local leadership of the Black Panther Party will enforce these rules.... Every member of the party must know these verbatim by heart. And apply them daily. Each member must report any violation of these rules to their leadership or they are counterrevolutionary and are also subjected to suspension by the Black Panther Party.[18]

This has more than the whiff of Leninism or Stalinism. Among the rules were: "All chapters must adhere to the policy and the ideology laid down by the Central Committee of the Black Panther Party."[19] Another rule was that "All Panthers must learn to operate and service weapons correctly."[20] The beginnings of a new scary Left PC were stirring, one that suggested a commitment to dogma and violence that could move embryonic immoral morality into the full-blown form.

Many small, white, splinter Marxist groups—such as the Progressive Labor Party (PL)—began to emerge, including Old Left vanguard parties with strong PC tendencies not unlike the Weathermen or Panthers. SDS had worked hard to create an open, participatory, and nondogmatic spirit. But the very openness of the SDS organization, which allowed anyone to join and participate fully, made it easy for groups like PL to infiltrate and dramatically change SDS culture. The PL activists came to meetings early, stayed late, and fought fiercely to superimpose their own vanguard model on the New Lefties. They succeeded in turning meetings into confrontational struggles about who was ideologically most "correct" and who was truly radical or pure. One of us (Magrass) experienced this debilitating dynamic personally in a community-based New Left organization that evolved into a Leninist PC nightmare after consolidating with a more traditional "Old Left" Marxist coalition. This authoritarian degeneration of the New Left did not carry out mass violence and can hardly be compared to the Jacobins or Stalinists in the scale of harm they created. Because they exercised no societal power and were a small radical opposition, they had no capacity to become that sort of monstrous killing machine. Nonetheless, from their own position of marginality, they tried to impose a form of Leninist "democratic centralism" on their own members that imitated many aspects of the Stalinist approach to power and PC.

This could do serious harm, mostly to the members of the group—and the broader Left itself. Magrass did a field study as he participated in the group and wrote about its fevered ideological campaigns to ensure ideological purity, which they called "Sharp Ideological Struggle (SIS)":

> "Sharp Ideological Struggle" entailed confronting each other and examining the minutest details of one's behavior, attitudes, vocabulary, ideas, and emotions with the goal of purging all racist and petit bourgeois elements from your consciousness....Those who deny having such faults, or who for any other reason refuse to engage in SIS are satisfied with themselves, acquiescing to their own weaknesses, and are in effect being racist and petit bourgeois, the argument is entirely circular. Once anyone is accused, if s/he denies the charge, s/he is guilty by definition.

Magrass shows that the groups pursued ideological correctness in Orwellian style. The leaders felt they had the right to scrutinize anyone's intimate personal affairs in the name of protecting the group's morality and truth. The group denied any distinction between individual and community interests. Therefore, no one was entitled to a sanctuary into which the vanguard could not intrude, including the home. In fact, the group's leaders knocked on doors late at night and refused to leave when not invited in.

By the group's logic, there was but one scientifically correct position. In effect, the group operated as a self-certified coterie of psychoanalysts, most of whose clients did not solicit their services. Their primary goal was not the health of their patient but of the party. Because they recognized no right of privacy, they need not maintain confidence. They could feel perfectly justified because the long-term interests of the individual can be realized only after the vanguard party has seized power with its moral vision intact. The party will assume responsibility for individual well-being, and therefore individuals will have little need for formal mechanism to protect them from the leadership.

In the spirit of the Jacobins and Stalinists, the group believed that class background determined almost everything you think, feel, and do. Hence, the revolutionary credentials of anyone with a background other than the industrial working class is suspect. No white person is exempt from "white chauvinism." Because their intentions are seldom conscious, all must undergo sharp ideological struggle to unveil how their background corrupted their revolutionary commitment. This applied both to the group members and to outsiders whom they deemed must be struggled with. Since the past can never be changed, a suspicious background is a fault that can never be corrected no matter what you do. If you are accused of having racist or anti–working class "tendencies," the charge must hold because a tendency is a potentiality, not an actuality.

What occurred in this organization was typical of many New Left groups, including the Weathermen and the Panthers. In their attempt to morally purify themselves, often driven by the leader's own ego and power needs, they drove away most of their membership and support. They reduced the Left to a shell. For the moment, its residues are primarily found among liberalism and identity politics.

Many on the Left would argue this all represented extremist "aberrations," rather than the true New Left. And it is fair to say (1) that most New Leftists were nonviolent and not as PC as this group or the Weathermen and Panthers, (2) that the Right greatly exaggerated the spread of ultra-Left PC and morally justified violence in the New Left, and (3) that police repression provoked much of New Left's PC and violence. Nonetheless, less extreme forms of the same tendencies were rampant in most New Left groups, and the tiny number of extremists were able to drive away many activists from the movement and destroy the most important, more free-thinking New Left organizations, including SDS.

But the PC extremism did not destroy the radical impulses that had bubbled up in the sixties. As SDS fell apart, many of the female members, who had felt suppressed by the white male student leaders, began to form consciousness-raising groups that evolved into a new wave of the feminist movement. Other radical students went to work in poor slums of Newark or in Chicago factories and helped to create a new generation of community and labor activists. The environmental movement also began to rise up in the 1970s, as did a new gay rights movement. A post–New Left politics was exploding on the scene.

Identity Politics Today: PC in the Feminist, Gay, and Race Movements

The new movements fragmented the Left, since they had no unifying ideology or organization. But they had spectacular energy and creativity. Operating as independent, decentralized grass-roots movements, they helped to transform the nation's consciousness about sexism, homophobia, environmental degradation, and consumerist individualism. This would turn into a cultural revolution, dramatically changing views about gender, sexual orientation, race, and lifestyle. The new politics—which linked the personal in the kitchen or bedroom to the political in the boardroom and the White House—turned the Left from Marxism to identity politics. It built pride among groups long subordinated in America and successfully eroded generations of deep and often invisible discrimination, not just on the basis of class but of race, gender, sexual orientation, ethnicity, and other cultural differences.

The new identity politics emerging in the 1970s was free-spirited, existential, and relatively free of dogma. The ethos was emotional and expressive, and the organizational structure was localized and anarchistic. Identity politics seemed the opposite of Leninism; there was no vanguard party and no official party line. As in the early New Left, "identity Leftists" seemed to have transcended the old suicidal impulses toward dogma and immoral morality. They celebrated difference, spontaneity, diversity, and authentic personal free expression.

But once again, something like an iron law of Left PC reasserted itself in the 1980s and continues to plague the new movements today. While they did not create a national party or official party line, the identity movements each began to develop some of their own high priests and new types of PC. They operated in a different way than earlier Left PC since the Left itself had splintered and almost disappeared as a recognizable "Left." The new PC did not enforce a single Leftist way of thinking, the views of a national Left vanguard party, or a unified Left doctrine of scientific orthodoxy. It did not display the violent tendencies of parts of the New Left. Nor did it crush the creativity of activists and their growing influence in the culture.

Nonetheless, various "correct ideas" began to become entrenched in the identity movements, and it became increasingly difficult for activists in the movements and ordinary citizens to question them. In what follows, we describe this new form of Left PC, but we need to emphasize again that since the identity movements do not control the police, military, or White House, they practice a form of *embryonic* immoral morality that is very different than either Stalinism and Jacobinism (and, of course, very different from Right PC that operates with the power of the State behind it). Such embryonic immoral morality does not kill, physically assault, or physically silence people inside the movements or outside in the larger society. And it opposes the immoral morality or the ruling elites we have described throughout this book.

Yet it does involve efforts to control and often censor or silence the speech or conduct of people in the name of justice and truth. While counterhegemonic to the larger capitalist and patriarchal order, it breeds hegemonic authority within its own ranks—and seeks to extend forms of censorship or silencing of alternative viewpoints—in universities, churches, communities, and, as conservatives have emphasized, the courts. Conservatives warring against Left PC note correctly that both liberals and some Leftists occupy positions in the Ideological Apparatus, especially in the judiciary. Conservatives thus argue that Left PC can use state power, especially in the legal system, to enforce its ideology. This manifests itself in everything from hate laws to coercive speech codes to more informal means of silencing debate about the truths they embrace. Conservatives overstate the argument since (1) the liberals are not the Left, (2) most of the state apparatus has been controlled by the Right during the period of the culture wars, and (3) the Left in the United States never controls the coercive branches of government—the military, police, and executive branch—that backs Right PC and has supported the full-blown immoral morality of the Lefts in power: Jacobins and Stalinists.

Nonetheless, there is no denying the tendencies toward PC within the identity movements that manifest most strongly in the universities and cultural sphere. They are largely not embodied in official rules but in everyday life and cultural presses both within and outside the movements themselves. We have observed this from our positions as professors in the university, where it can be very difficult to get honest discussions of race or gender because students are so afraid of asserting politically incorrect positions.

Feminism is one of the most liberating movements in history, and, along with the civil rights movement, it has created more strides toward equality and justice than any other contemporary movement. But PC has begun to plague both movements. Within the feminist movement, just raising the following questions for discussion—or defending the rights of others to ask them—can besmirch your reputation as a good feminist, even if your own position is consistent with the feminist orthodoxy:

1. Is it wrong to have abortions in the third trimester or even earlier?
2. Do fetuses have any rights?
3. Should the rights of the pregnant woman always take precedence over those of her partner or fetus?

All three of these questions relate to abortion, the hottest topic in the culture wars. While there are differences among feminists, there is an orthodoxy in the feminist movement that proclaims (1) women should always have a constitutional right to have an abortion at any stage of pregnancy, including the rare third term, (2) fetuses are not persons and do not have rights, and (3) women's rights trump those of the partner or fetus, neither of which has clear rights within established feminist thinking. While these are eminently defensible positions, those with other views should not be silenced or viewed as antifeminist. Abortion is a complex and personal decision, and the nuances that millions feel have been lost in the culture wars' bitter divisions. The most obvious case is abortions in the third trimester; the absolutist defense by feminists on this issue may have actually weakened feminist positions and expanded the broader public support for antiabortion laws. It reflects the fact that almost everyone feels some discomfort in thinking about abortion of a highly developed fetus, and even though the third-trimester abortion is a tiny fraction of the abortions carried out, a point ignored and manipulated by antiabortion forces, feminist absolutism may have damaged the pro-choice position. A feminist movement that shuts down debate about such issues among its members—or makes people inside or outside the movement uncomfortable about expressing their honest doubts or views—is involved in a serious form of Left PC. Since it silences people, stifles debate, and sets a small group up as arbiters of a complex issue, it represents embryonic immoral morality. It does social harm in the name of good, even though not remotely on the scale of those groups, such as Jacobins or Stalinists, that could use the state to jail or kill those who disagreed with them.

Here are other questions that the new PC of identity politics has made "unrespectable" or incorrect:

4. Within the walls of the family, do many women wield more power than men?
5. Have the power advantages men once enjoyed over women now diminished radically?
6. Are fathers discriminated against in marriage laws or divorce courts?

These questions all relate to the power relations between men and women. A feminist orthodoxy on these issues proclaims (4) men still exercise far more power than women inside as well as outside the family, (5) women have gained more power but are still radically, socially disempowered compared to men, and (6) men are not discriminated against in marriage laws or divorce courts, where patriarchy still rules. In our view, women are still disempowered in many spheres, but we believe, particularly in the family, that power relations are complex and highly variable, something that any viewer of the sitcom *Everyone Loves Raymond* would immediately recognize. Raymond, while empowered as the breadwinner who indulges his own narcissistic self-absorption, is terrorized by his wife's anger and defers to her out of emotional intimidation while constantly trying to appease her. Even some feminists have dared to talk about the "powers of the weak" and the control that women may exercise at home over their spouse or children that partly reflects their disempowerment in the public sphere, a notion that would be obvious to many Italians or Jews who grew up in families where women dominated the household.[21]

Any honest examination of marriage or family should permit people to ask any questions they feel and speak freely, both about their personal situations and wider societal norms about patriarchy or matriarchy in the American family. While patriarchy remains deep-seated, people who believe otherwise should have their say in and out of the movement, including on such charged issues as custody rights. A feminist movement that shuts down such conversation—within or outside the movement—is, again, practicing Left PC that will only weaken feminism itself. It is embryonic immoral morality in the sense that, in the name of truth and morality, it silences debate, sustains the power of ideologues, and does social harm to families, students, and everyone trying to deal honestly with these problems in their own life (although, again, it is very different from the full-blown immoral morality of a Left in power that uses the state to jail or murder dissenters.)

7. Do feminist speech codes on such subjects as pornography violate free speech?
8. Has feminism made it impossible to have honest discussions—in classrooms, workplaces, or any social settings—about what people really think and feel about what is going on between men and women?

These additional "unrespectable" or incorrect questions relate to the core of PC itself, the issue of freedom of speech and thought. On these questions, too, we believe a feminist orthodoxy exists, which states (7) banning of pornography is not a violation of free speech but a protection of women's dignity, safety, and rights,[22] and (8) feminism has opened up rather than shut down honest discussions of male-female relations, and any feminist restraints on those discussions are a valid means of repressing sexist language or thought. But it only damages the social order and weakens the feminist movement to impose moralistic dogma on complex, vital questions. The tension between free speech and bans on pornography is real, and the question of when essential respect for women turns into dangerous disrespect for free speech is not subject to formulaic rules. It can only hurt feminists and the broader Left if they become a force for censorship that contributes to the Right's ongoing repression of free expression and thought in the larger society. This does not mean that violent pornographic images should not be banned, but rather that the feminist movement should defend free speech with the same fervor it has for the well-being and safety of women and resist blanket bans on pornography that do not take account of both free speech and women's rights and safety.

Regarding the larger issue of whether feminism has opened or shut down honest conversation about and between men and women, we think both are true. Feminism has opened up crucial areas of insight, speech, and inquiry, and, to reemphasize our own values, it is one of the major liberating forces of modern culture all over the world. At the same time, it is vulnerable to the debilitating PC that has historically plagued and often fatally weakened the Left, with uncomfortable similarities to the PC of Jacobonists, Stalinists, and Maoists. We know how powerful this new form of PC is because when we decided to write about it, this was the scariest issue to approach. Some colleagues advised us not to touch the subject. Many students and colleagues acknowledged to us that they do not personally feel free to say or write what they feel about feminist issues—and that honest and open classroom conversations can be very difficult because of feminist dogma. We realized that writing this section could threaten our "feminist credentials" and worried about the consequences, an almost sure sign of Left PC and at all immoral morality.

The newest stage of race and civil rights movements also may now be mired in Left PC. The questions here have similarities to those about feminist or gay PC and suggest that there are special issues of PC in identity politics that are somewhat different than the earlier PC crises of the Marxist Left. Here are some of the questions that suggest the possibility of PC in race and ethnic movements for equal rights:

1. Should racial affirmative action be replaced by class affirmative action?
2. Has pushing racial affirmative action undermined the possibility of class politics that can change the larger balance of power in the country?
3. Are there a substantial number of "welfare cheaters"?
4. Has welfare produced a serious culture of dependency among many African Americans?

The first two questions focus on affirmative action, another of the hot button topics in the culture wars. In our view, the Left race-based movements have largely signed on to an orthodoxy that insists (1) race-based affirmative action must be maintained, and (2) class politics will not be seriously undermined in the long term by such affirmative action and, even if it were, it should still be retained.[23] Again, we find these positions utterly defensible but think it unacceptable that those arguing for a shift to class-based affirmative action should be silenced in the name of antiracism. In fact, those arguing against any form of affirmative action should be heard and respected within the movement if Left PC is to be avoided.

PC on affirmative action silences a very important conversation about the relation between class and race in America. Virtually all on the Left want to reduce and ultimately eliminate class and race privileges. Racial division has been one of the worst obstacles to a viable Left, and the need to build a cross-racial movement is critically important. But that does not translate into any particular strategy such as race-based affirmative action. Squashing debate about affirmative action on the grounds of privileging either race or class is counterproductive and hurts both minorities and the larger Left.

The second two questions revolve around welfare. The Right has used welfare and "welfare cheats" as a wedge issue to win mainstream support, much in the same way that it has used abortion and gay marriage. The Left only helps the Right when it embraces Left PC on any wedge issue. When the Right uses vicious stereotypes about the poor or African Americans to exploit white prejudices, the Left should obviously strike back hard with truth. But the Left tendency is sometimes to hit back with the same arrogant moral rigidity that the Right displays. So while the Right may wildly exaggerate the number of "welfare cheats," the Left may deny that freeloaders exist at all. This not only weakens the ability of the Left to think clearly about the problems of poverty and welfare, but it creates an almost unbridgeable communication problem with many white workers. Many of these workers may have racist stereotypes but also have more immediate experience with welfare and "welfare cheats" than middle-class white Leftists, whose knowledge comes mainly from books or Left biases. When Leftists with such "book knowledge" use PC to denigrate or silence those disagreeing with them, especially workers with more direct experience of the issues, this only widens the gap that separates the middle-class white Left from the white working class. PC on race-based affirmative action has already weakened class politics and the Left's ability to succeed. It also suggests some of the reasons why Left PC has emerged so repeatedly and tragically over the history of the Left, the final subject to which we now turn.

Root Causes of Left PC

The Left needs to understand why it has been so prone to PC if it is to kick the habit. This requires first that Leftists admit it. Many Leftists, as shown earlier, dismiss Left PC as an invention of the Right. To acknowledge it would be to simply empower the Right's use of it as a weapon. Other Leftists believe it exists but see it as inevitable and a minor distraction. Yet others interpret it as a virtue—simply a way of speaking truth to power and remaining authentic or "pure." Others do not want to discuss it at all because they use it to gain or keep power, the classic reason for PC on both sides of the political spectrum and a driving force behind all embryonic or full-blown immoral morality.

Since PC violates the founding principle of the Left—to apply critical and free thinking to all issues—Left PC makes the whole Left enterprise seem contradictory and inauthentic. Historically, the evidence is also in. Left PC has "burned out" many Leftists who quit the movement because of disenchantment with PC. PC has proved a suicidal factor in Leftist politics from the French Revolutionaries to the Soviet Bolsheviks to the Old and New Lefts in America.

The Left is always a product partly of the system that it is fighting. Leftists grow up and are socialized in the cultures that they try to change. In France and the Soviet Union, and also in America, the ruling system was authoritarian and its culture highly controlled by the Ideological Apparatus. Leftist activists inevitably absorb the authoritarianism of their society's schools, workplaces, and governments. When they wake up and reject moral dogma or thought control, they cannot shed their own socialization overnight. They are always vulnerable to fighting authority with the authoritarian style virtually everyone has been taught. Left PC is always partly a mirror of Right PC and the reigning system of thought control and immoral morality.

Moreover, free thinking in an authoritarian culture can seem weak or immoral, since everyone has been socialized to some degree into authoritarian moral codes. Much of the populace sees critical thinking as subversive, deviant, and a license for lawlessness or anarchy. Moreover, tolerant free thinkers can be easy prey for adversaries who don't believe in tolerance. It is similar to the dilemma faced by nonviolent dissenters facing a Hitler.

They can win in rare circumstances, but there is an enormous cost and a great temptation to adopt the strategy of the enemy.

The tolerant and often anarchistic style of Leftist organizations contributes strongly to Left PC. During the 1960s, as noted earlier, radical students formed nonhierarchal, participatory groups open to all comers, including Old Left types who did not share their anarchistic style. In the spirit of participatory democracy, SDS believed not in shutting down discussion but in letting people talk late into the night until a consensus emerged. Open membership, rotating leadership, and a resistance to hierarchy and to formal voting rules made New Left organizations vulnerable to infiltration and takeover by authoritarian groups. These groups exploited the open space and superdemocratic ethos to grab power. By staying longer, never straying from their own party line, and seeking to impose their own Leninist style of "democratic centralism," they slowly subverted the participative ethos in the name of moral truth, driving away the tolerant majority and ultimately destroying the movement.

Left PC reflects partly the "Iron Law of Oligarchy" pronounced by the European social theorist, Robert Michels.[24] Open and participatory organizations are likely to evolve toward more authoritarian structures and ideologies—indeed, Michels argued all organizations suffered this fate. On the Left, authoritarians find an easy organizational target lacking the means to resist their oligarchic incursions. Free thinkers often leave in desperation to try to form new organizations, which are vulnerable to the Iron Law again. Or they stay and get absorbed into the "purity" of the new PC system.

The Left seems particularly vulnerable to radicals who are "holier than thou." The holiest radicals denigrate those less pure as cowardly or bourgeois or reformist. PC then becomes synonymous with being truly radical, a catastrophe for the Left.

Why would Leftists so frequently be vulnerable to such ideological manipulation around "purity"? Ultimately, we suspect that in the United States this is caused by the political weakness of the Left. While liberalism ruled during the New Deal, the radical Left has never been in power in the United States. Both Republicans and Democrats have become parties of business, and third parties have always been marginal. This means that the prospects for the Left actually taking power are slim to nil, even if the Democrats capture the White House.

This does not mean that the Left movements do not influence America; they have been one of the nation's greatest forces in helping end slavery, building civil rights, and ending hegemonic wars. The Left has helped transform the country in critical eras and is responsible for most of America's most important advances in democracy and human rights. But the Left has always been outside the formal power structure and is not likely to get inside. This creates an enduring structural position of Leftist marginality.

This, in turn, creates a perpetual sense of weakness among activists that can lead to Left PC in several ways. Since you are not a serious contender for power, you have the freedom to be as radical as you want. For liberals or mainstream Democrats who might actually get power, there are costs to purity: the prospects of losing mass support. If you compromise and build a big open tent, you have a chance of taking over the country.

But if you are permanently on the margins, there is little incentive to compromise and strong psychological inducements to stay pure and be "more radical than thou." Your purity makes you feel empowered—by the sense that you are better than others who are not as willing to stick their neck out and fight for what they really believe. Purity makes you better than the liberals who have "sold out" in the mainstream political process. It is a way of recouping self-esteem for those who have to constantly cope with the agony of defeat.

Weakness and marginality create status anxiety. Leftists cannot gain the status that comes with political power. They are also not rewarded or admired by those outside the movement for their vision or dedication. More often, they are mocked, ignored, or hated. PC can be a shield against such disparagement from the outside. If others attack you as unpatriotic, immoral, or foolishly radical, you can sustain your own sense of status by the purity of your own radical values. Your values become the key to your feeling that you are worthwhile. If you compromise your values, you erode that self-worth. You are giving up the one thing—your radicalness—that allows you to feel that you are better than those who are attacking you or "selling out."

Status anxiety creates a vicious spiral. Leftists gain status by having the truth and they create PC that makes them appear smarter than everyone else. But this creates the sense of arrogance and elitism that Right PC exaggerates and hypes to make the populace feel that the Left is nothing but a bunch of effete stuffed shirts out of touch with ordinary people. The Left sets itself up as a target by embracing a PC that invests the Left with the Truth and appears to make everyone else feel stupid. The Left can add fuel to the fire with the idea that the masses who don't support them have "false consciousness," a Marxist concept that ordinary people can't see their own interests because they are easily manipulated or propagandized by those in power.

Leftists tend to have more formal education than the rest of the population, and many people on the Left spend considerable time in the university as professors or students. Higher education can contribute to the sense of knowing more and being better than those who haven't gone to college. For people with higher education who tend not to make a lot of money—a characteristic of many on the Left—status is closely tied to a sense of having knowledge and truth. Left PC becomes part of a wider social pattern in which educational elites boost their sense of esteem by claims of truth and expertise.

Left PC also becomes part of a power and status struggle among members inside the movement. Leftists often try to prove their worth by showing that they are more truly radical or pure than fellow radicals. This sets up the basis for ongoing PC struggles inside the Left about who has the truth. These competitive ideological struggles mask status struggles and the need of activists to affirm their worth in ways that are contrary to the cooperative values that the Left itself prizes.

The internal competition is also about power. As with all forms of immoral morality, PC is ultimately an instrument for gaining power. Since Leftists face limits on their external power in the larger society, their power drives often turn inward. Competitions over who is more "correct" is the most acceptable kind of power struggle that Leftists can engage in, since, as radical democrats, they are not supposed to seek or wield hierarchical, organizational power over others. But since Leftists value truth, struggle over "correct ideas" appears to be consistent with the most basic aims of the Left, and power struggles thus become masked and legitimated as a fight about truth. Ideological and sectarian rifts have long tragically burdened the Left; too often, these are actually covert contests through which Leftists meet their very human needs for both status and power. The winners get to impose their own PC, but both the truth and the Left itself are the losers.

The Left needs to confront and transcend its own PC for its own moral integrity and to succeed in its social justice agenda. This is difficult but not impossible and is likely to happen in stages. As in most addictions, the first step is to recognize and admit the problem; the second is to make small steps, day to day. The aim is to create a new virtuous spiral slowly eroding PC. Each small step—to be discussed more in the conclusion—will help build the Left's moral integrity, status, and power, which in turn will slowly reduce the unmet psychological needs for status and power that create Left PC in the first place.

PART IV

Morality Wars in the Obama Era

9

When Losers Are Winners
How Americans Are Finding a New Moral Compass

The fact that immoral morality runs rampant in our culture—and is doing great harm to many Americans and the world itself—does not mean conditions will improve. Leaders or followers addicted to a self-destructive culture can be like lemmings running off a cliff. In his celebrated book about America's "Heartland" values—*What's the Matter with Kansas?*—Thomas Frank offers little hope: "Kansas is ready to lead us singing into the apocalypse. It invites us all to join in, to lay down our lives so that others might cash out at the top; to renounce forever our middle-American prosperity in pursuit of a crimson fantasy of middle-American righteousness."[1]

Frank's pessimism anticipates few changes in the kind of hegemonic and born-again morality discussed in this book. These values get traction because (1) the elites rely on them to keep power, (2) the elites also have great control over the media and other elements of the Ideological Apparatus to spread these values and distract the public from its own economic self-interests, and (3) the values themselves have historical resonance in the Bible Belt and heartland America. Frank puts it succinctly: "Why shouldn't our culture just get worse, if making it worse will only cause the people who worsen it to grow wealthier and wealthier?"[2]

Values of any kind change slowly. And deeply embedded values often do not change for centuries. But Frank is correctly showing that hegemonic morality has strong economic and political foundations that make change even more difficult. Political elites in America are deeply invested in hegemonic morality since it is necessary to maintain control of wealth and power—and they use every means at their disposal to perpetuate existing codes of immoral morality. In any discussion of immoral morality, it is critical to remember the old Sicilian adage that "A fish rots from the head first." The entire system of immoral morality is carried mainly by economic, political, ideological, and religious elites, who differ in their interests from ordinary citizens. The majority of the U.S. public, as we discuss below, has long been more progressive than elites on virtually all issues. Nonetheless, the hegemonic morality promoted by the leaders of both parties still resonates among a significant sector of the public, especially in the South, West, and exurban and rural areas. If the kinds of morality discussed in this book were to change, it would be revolutionary, subverting the empire at home and abroad.

The election of Barack Obama amidst the most severe economic crisis since the Great Depression could bring a transformative change in U.S. politics and morality. The moral compass of President Obama and Obama Nation, a country in deep economic crisis, is the subject of the next chapter. In this chapter we focus on trends mainly before Obama's election. We show that for at least a generation, U.S. economic and military hegemony have been eroding and that new posthegemonic values have been spreading through much of the population since the 1960s.

The obvious needs to be repeated first: People resist change in their values. Elites hold on to immoral values because it cements their power. Ordinary people hold on to their moral code because they have been indoctrinated since childhood by the Ideological Apparatus, and their moral values are part of their identity. And identity change is always threatening and breeds resistance.

Moreover, both personal and national identity are at stake. A country changing its values is shedding its national solidarity. Trying to get major value change quickly—either among elites or ordinary people—is nearly impossible, although, as Jared Diamond has shown in his book, *Collapse*,[3] people become more open to such change after catastrophes that affect them personally and threaten their civilization. Moreover, there are contemporary examples of transformations in moral values; for example, we have seen an unprecedented shift away from hegemonic morality in Europe in the late twentieth century.

For most of the last five hundred years, nations such as Britain, France, Germany, the Netherlands, and Spain ran the world with their own empires. To do so, the elites in these nations created hegemonic moralities that helped define European culture. But in the last half-century, as European empires crumbled after two World Wars, their prevailing hegemonic morality also began to crumble. At the beginning of the twenty first century, change in Europe has accelerated, with polls showing huge shifts in European moral values and the actual behavior of European nations moving dramatically away from their ancient hegemonic ideologies.

This is a moral revolution in the making. The most obvious signs during the George W. Bush years were the sharp division between Europe and the United States on Iraq policy and the broader growing rift in European and American views regarding U.S. hegemony, the UN, international law, preemption and unilateralism, diplomacy, and peace as collective security. The European move toward a posthegemonic morality has been documented and widely bemoaned by neoconservatives such as Robert Kagan,[4] while also widely discussed and applauded by American liberals such as Jeremy Rifkin.[5] According to many pundits, European hegemonic decline has turned Europe into "Venus" while the United States, as number one, has turned into "Mars." The morals of Venus and Mars are literally different planets—with Mars hegemonic and Venus counterhegemonic.

The new European morality, still a work in progress, has obviously been driven by the catastrophic collapse of European empires. World Wars I and II destroyed European hegemony and forced European peoples to rebuild their basic worldviews. This did not happen spontaneously or without effort, *and the rise of Fascism in Europe among the losers of the first world war suggests that hegemonic change can create reactionary rather than progressive moral transformation.* Hegemonic decline occurs over phases, and it took several phases before the Europeans rejected the Far Right reactionary turn and committed to the progressive one. It required a long generational struggle in which young Europeans after World War II had to painfully question all the values their parents had taught them. Even now neofascist movements are showing a resurgence in Europe, although they are unlikely to seize power.

In a recent trip to Germany, I (Derber) talked with some of this new generation about the revolution against the old European morality of their parents and grandparents. I talked especially to students, writers, musicians, journalists, union members, and political activists. What I heard from them suggested this was an existential identity struggle that engulfed the nation and the entire continent. It played out in the lifelong efforts by individuals to reject the culture of their ancestors: to be less aggressive in conduct and speech; to create less authoritarian families; to build a new communitarian, environmental, and peace-oriented global outlook; and to create a new kind of democratic politics that emphasized interdependency, dialogue, and collective security while rejecting centuries of old codes of warrior morality. Specifically, it meant rejecting the ancient European view of a world organized around hegemonic powers and values. Europeans want to shift toward a world beyond empire.

This sounds utopian in the American context, but it is becoming common sense in Europe. It reflects the disaster that nearly every European family suffered after World War II. In the twentieth century, Europe moved toward the ultimate conclusion of hegemonic morality. In the name of spreading civilization and democracy, Europeans ravaged most of their colonies and then committed something like collective suicide, destroying the lives of their own people.

Europe's moral revolution shows that hegemonic morality may not be sustained when the Empire is broken. Hegemonic morality is the clothing that Empires have to wear to sustain their dominant power; after all, hegemony reinforces the view that the hegemonic nation is a winner and its social system and moral values the best. But when Empires collapse, the European experience suggests that hegemonic culture will weaken and eventually collapse into the dust. The fall of their empire suggests that the people in the imperial nation will only face greater suffering if they try to retain their dominance, a view incompatible with the messianic and arrogant nature of hegemonic morality.

The European experience tells us that moral values deeply inscribed in a nation's soul can transform, especially after catastrophe. But does this have any lessons for the United States? The United States is not facing complete collapse like Europe after World War II. But we believe that it is already in the process of hegemonic decline and facing long-term catastrophes such as global warming and nuclear terrorism that threaten the survival of all civilizations and will profoundly alter America's world power and morality.

We have argued throughout this book that America has been flawed both by its Empire and its immoral morality. From its very beginning, the United States was rising as a hegemonic power. By the end of World War II, it had become the world's strongest hegemonic power, and after the collapse of the Soviet Union, it became the world's only hegemon—and the most powerful nation the world has ever known.

But by the early twenty-first century, it had become clear to many observers that the United States had reached the limits of its powers. This partly reflected the rise of other nations and regions—including China, India, and the European Union—whose level of economic growth overtook that of the United States. After World War II, the United States owned 50 percent of the world's wealth.[6] Today, that figure has fallen to about 25 percent.[7]

Over the last fifty years, a relative decline in U.S. global economic dominance has unfolded in fits and starts. Vietnam produced a sea of red ink and forced the United States off the gold standard. In the early 1970s, the oil crisis, with its long gas lines, signaled a crippling U.S. dependency on foreign oil. U.S. productivity fell in the mid- and late-1970s. By the late 1970s and early 1980s, a severe recession involving stagflation, a second oil shock, 12 percent unemployment,[8] and prime interest rates over 20 percent in December 1980,[9] helped lead to the end of the New Deal, raised questions about U.S. global power, and led to the Reagan Revolution.

Reagan claimed that America was back, speaking of "morning in America."[10] But his "military Keynesian" policies of massive Pentagon spending to destroy the "Evil Empire,"[11] along with huge tax cuts for the rich, created new huge deficits. His globalization policies and attacks on labor weakened the middle class and helped hollow out the U.S. manufacturing core. Reagan's deregulation also led to the savings and loan banking crisis and to widespread financial fraud on Wall Street, weakening the U.S. further economically. Deregulation laid the foundation for the speculative run-up of stocks in the 1990s, the high-tech crash of 1999, and ultimately to the 2007–2009 Great Recession.

All of this reflected deeper stagnation in the real economy and the shift of capital toward Wall Street and a more "financialized" capitalism where real productivity was replaced by making money from money, mainly highly speculative and leveraged financial trades involving risky credit, mortgage loans and debt. Fast profits through risky financial transactions trumped the longer and harder work of investing in productive goods and services. As globalization eroded workers' real wages, a crisis of consumer demand threatened the productive sector, discouraging further business investment. Capital flowed into the financial sector because (1) it offered quick, easy profits, and (2) it lubricated the larger economy with easy credit and debt, thus allowing beleaguered workers to spend and consume beyond their means, temporarily buoying up the entire economy. But the economy was all based on unsustainable debt—as well as smoke-and-mirrors on Wall Street—and that led to the 2008 financial meltdown. The broader collapse on Main Street followed quickly, leading to the greatest crisis since the 1930s Depression.

In the next chapter, we focus on the implications of the economy's meltdown for U.S. moral values and hegemony. But we need to stress here that the crisis represents the most serious blow to U.S. economic hegemony since World War II. While the entire world economy moved into serious recession, the meltdown had special implications for U.S. dominance—and this in turn has revolutionary implications for the U.S. immoral morality that we have explored throughout this book.

The Great Recession may be a fatal blow to U.S. global economic hegemony. America's economic policies and its huge public and private debt helped create the crisis. Solutions require that China, the Saudis, and other countries buy trillions more of U.S. Treasury Bills and other debt. America's overwhelming dependence on foreign creditors for years to come signals the end of its economic hegemony.

As the United States struggles to revive its economy, stabilize its banks, and pay off new debt, global confidence in the U.S. economy and dollar will waver. U.S. economic hegemony is based on confidence in the dollar as a reserve currency, a likely casualty of the crisis over time. In March 2009, China and other countries were openly calling for a new reserve currency, or other currencies supplementing the dollar.[12] We are also seeing the emergence of new economic blocs in Latin America, Southeast Asia, and Southwest Asia, another sign of declining faith in U.S. economic stability and leadership.

Hegemons depend not just on guns but moral legitimacy. Countries all over the world blame the United States for triggering the global meltdown and spreading bad money and bad "free market" policy. The collateralized U.S. mortgage securities circulated in banks from Iceland to England to Japan; as the U.S. housing bubble popped, the toxic mortgage securities brought down banks and created major crises in entire countries everywhere in a severe global recession. Countries that had looked to the United States for sober fiscal policies and a model of stable global capitalism now saw U.S. capitalism as reckless and even "savage." When French President Nicolas Sarkozy proclaimed in 2008 that the U.S. "age of free markets"[13] was over—and even *Newsweek* ran a headline that "We Are All Socialists Now"[14]—the damage to U.S. hegemony was becoming palpable. In March 2009 at the G20 meeting in London to "fix" the global economy, countries came to the conference with statements from their ministers and media already blaming the United States and its "free market" model for causing the catastrophe. No longer, they said, would the United States have any moral legitimacy— or the clout—to preach solutions to other nations, who would pioneer their own path.

Loss of economic hegemony always has implications for military and political hegemony—and ultimately for the immoral morality that hegemony brings. Military hegemony requires a secure grip on economic power and resources. As U.S. economic hegemony weakens, the United States is undercutting its stature as military hegemon, the fate that Yale historian Paul Kennedy ascribed to all "overstretched" imperial powers.[15]

As U.S. economic hegemony declined, a series of military defeats over the last few decades also eroded U.S. military hegemony. Vietnam raised major questions about how long U.S. hegemony could survive. After Vietnam, America power lost its Teflon coating, and the credibility of U.S. military strength and political commitments was shattered. Disastrous military interventions in Nicaragua and El Salvador during the 1980s intensified global questions about the moral legitimacy of U.S. foreign policy. The collapse of the Soviet Union, though, and the "irrational exuberance" of the U.S. markets in the 1990s temporarily resurrected the view of permanent American hegemony.

September 11 had the opposite effect. It was a huge symbolic event, marking a global recognition of the vulnerability of the United States in a new age of technology and terrorism. Suddenly, American hegemony was decisively uncoupled from any sense of American invincibility. Even small bands of armed groups, such as al-Qaeda, seemed capable of beheading the behemoth.

The war in Iraq was another catastrophic military event, arguably a tipping point in American hegemonic decline. It galvanized world opinion against the United States, leading to a globalized critique of U.S. hegemony and a globalized perception of declining U.S. power. It undermined America's hegemonic capacity in the most strategically important part of the world, raising questions about its ability to secure global energy and oil supplies in the petroleum-dependent world that its own hegemony had created. And it severely weakened American's economy and military at the very moment that challenges to its hegemony were expanding regionally in the Muslim world and throughout Latin America, Africa, East Asia, and even Europe.

Even complete defeat in the Iraqi War would not imply collapse in American hegemony. David Brooks, the conservative *New York Times* columnist, argues quite the opposite. In the wake of the Iraqi debacle, Brooks noted that "many in the world predict than an exhausted America will turn inward again. Some see a nation in permanent decline and an end to American hegemony. At Davos, some Europeans apparently envisioned a post-American world."[16] Brooks argues this is nonsense:

> Forget about it. Americans are having a debate about how to proceed in Iraq, but we are not having a strategic debate about retracting American power and influence. What's most important about this debate is what doesn't need to be said. No major American leader doubts that America must remain, as Dean Acheson put it, the locomotive of the world.[17]

Brooks goes on to argue that "the U.S. military still has no serious rivals, even after the strain of Iraq" and "no cultural need to retrench.... Many Americans have lost faith in the Bush administration and in this particular venture, but there has been no generalized loss of faith in the American system or in American goodness."[18]

The notion that there has been *"no generalized loss of faith in the American system or in American goodness"* is the critical argument. If Brooks is correct, and he may well be at least in regard to American elites in both major political parties, it weakens the argument that the European moral revolution after World War II and the loss of European empire has relevance for America. But on the very same page that columnist Brooks mounts this argument, the *New York Times* prints the lyrics of a song by the popular song-writer Randy Newman with a different message. The last verse goes:

> The end of an empire is messy at best
> And this empire is ending
> Like all the rest
> Like the Spanish Armada adrift on the sea
> We're adrift in the land of the brave
> And in the home of the free
> Goodbye, Goodbye, Goodbye[19]

The contrast in these two messages is hard to miss, and it parallels the contradictory view of America's future at home and abroad. Among American leaders, the hegemonic agenda remains intact—even, as we discuss shortly, with the election of President Barack Obama and his new foreign policy rhetoric. Brooks is correct that no future American president and neither the Democratic nor Republican Party is willing to acknowledge that the era of American hegemony is past. Democrats and Republicans simply have different views of how to exercise that hegemonic power—diplomatically or militarily, unilaterally or multilaterally.

But in many parts of the world, there was anti-American rage during the George W. Bush years, documented by polls on every continent that challenged the legitimacy of American hegemony. This view was explicitly argued by Venezuelan President Hugo Chavez, who famously raised and waved Noam Chomsky's book *Hegemony or Survival*[20] at his 2006 speech at the United Nations to announce the end of American hegemony and his own commitment to hastening the decline. More than a few scholars of every political stripe agreed that at the end of the Bush Jr. era (1) U.S.

hegemony was widely hated in most sectors of the world and (2) historical conditions were changing to weaken U.S. economic power and eventually end the American era.

Many analysts argue that the change is yet more fundamental: we are entering not only a world no longer dominated by America, but one that is *posthegemonic*. America, it is suggested, is the last global hegemon, and we should all be grateful. The posthegemonic world is the only one compatible with the survival of the planet. Hegemony leads inevitably toward global wars and global warming. Both will eventually start the slide toward civilizational collapse that Jared Diamond argues may lead to moral revolution.

In our view, American power has reached its limits and has already begun its decline. This is the key factor that makes a moral transformation possible in the United States. It is new because, until now, America has always—through its entire history—been increasing its power and moving toward ever greater hegemony. This uninterrupted rising ascendancy has been the key underpinning of America's messianic vision of itself as the "shining city on the hill" for two centuries.

The decline in U.S. hegemony is caused by at least four factors: (1) the decline of U.S. economic dominance and the rise of European and Asian competitors who can play on the same field as the Americans; (2) the tendency of U.S. hegemony, now linked to the war on terrorism, to promote unwinnable and catastrophic global wars (as in Vietnam and Iraq) as well as nuclear terrorism; (3) the many links between U.S. hegemony and global warming and broader environmental unsustainability; and (4) the U.S. economic collapse of 2008 that triggered a global meltdown and became a measure of deep stagnation in the U.S. model of capitalism and deeply flawed U.S. economic leadership and policies since at least the Reagan years. These catastrophes cannot be remedied without a shift from U.S. hegemony to a more fair and democratic world. As economic crises and military debacles take their cost in money and blood, American citizens may, as Europeans did after World War II, begin to question their hegemonic and messianic moral values.

Public opinion data, hint that this moral revolt in the United States is already beginning. But first keep in mind a sports metaphor that we used in an earlier chapter. Hegemonic nations are "winners" who believe in their superiority as a civilization because of the supreme power of their nation. The fact that the United States in the second half of the twentieth century accumulated far more wealth and global power than any country in history made this winning mindset easy to sustain, particularly because it resonated with the Shining City and Manifest Destiny visions dating from the earliest days of the nation.

But as U.S. power slides—in Iraq, the Middle East, and the world economy—the idea of America as a winning nation becomes harder to swallow. When your team starts to slow down or lose, you can continue to support the view of it as "number one" for only so long. If the evidence becomes clear that the team is becoming a loser, whether in the economy or in world affairs, you may begin to feel like a loser yourself, although there is also the possibility of becoming even more aggressive to make sure "no one ever messes with you again." Decline is a new prospect for Americans, and we cannot be sure how it will affect their vision of Team America or of their personal and moral identities. But one would certainly expect that a nation whose power is declining is almost certain to feel less like a winner. The new historical conditions for survival suggest that the morality of winning may itself come into question. While this remains speculative, we have the evidence of Europe to suggest that it can lead to moral transformation, in which hegemonic winning is traded in for cooperation and collective security.

These trends have not shaken the faith in America's goodness—and in the unquestioned acceptance of U.S. hegemony—among the nation's elites. Political leaders, corporate CEOs, the mass media, and many of the nation's think tanks and intelligentsia hold on to the view that the United States remains the "leader of the free world" and should stay in that "winning" role. The more liberal sectors of the elite, including President Obama and many on his foreign policy team, have expressed opposition to the Bush administration and the Iraq war, but they have not challenged U.S. global dominance. Indeed, their argument against the war has been that it undermines U.S. ability to remain hegemonic in other areas or conflicts, such as Afghanistan, or in the larger war on terrorism.

The faith in American goodness and U.S. hegemony also remains strong among large sectors of the population, but the trends are suggestive of a deeper malaise. Public opinion polls over recent years suggest that large numbers of Americans not only rejected the Iraq war and the Bush administration but—contrary to David Brooks's assertion—have for some time begun to question the assumptions of hegemony itself. The 2006 Pew poll of U.S. attitudes on politics and foreign policy, for example, reports that 49 percent of Americans said that the United States should "focus on problems at home" while only 44 percent said the United States should "be active in world affairs."[21] A hegemon does not have the luxury to focus on domestic issues; it requires fervent moral commitment to managing the world's affairs.

Other questions in the Pew Poll reinforced the notion of a populace increasingly doubtful about U.S. hegemony. According to the poll, 59 percent of Americans had a "favorable" view of the United Nations while only 32 percent had an "unfavorable" view, a position suggesting at minimum that the United States must show at least symbolic deference to world government, contrary to the spirit of hegemony. Only 37 percent of Americans said that the United States should "follow national interests even when allies disagree," with 53 percent saying the United States should "account for allies' interests, even if it means compromises." This hints at a more humble foreign policy approach, even if it does not explicitly reject hegemony. Only 30 percent of Americans say the "best way to ensure peace is through military strength," while 55 percent say "good diplomacy" is better, another hint at modest antihegemonic sentiment. And only 39 percent say "military force is the best way to defeat terrorism," while 51 percent say "relying too much on force creates hatred and more terrorism." At minimum, this suggests a shift away from the traditional reliance of Empires on guns and a more diplomatic and cooperative basis for U.S. foreign policy.

All these questions indicate that, while American elites may repudiate European visions of the world, the American public is closer to the European antihegemonic perspective. In terms of the red/blue political map, hegemony sells more in the red states but Americans are moving "blue" on hegemonic morality in all states, contributing to the defeat of John McCain and the election of President Obama in 2008. This blue mood is associated with a shift toward the European vision of peace through cooperation, diplomacy, and international law rather than exercise of hegemony, a shift that Obama's campaign speeches—with their emphasis on diplomacy and talking to all sides—appeared to promote.

The blue shift in moral values is happening across the issue map, not just on foreign policy but on economics and social issues. Despite the long reign of immoral morality among American elites, the public has always been more progressive in its values—on virtually all economic and social issues ranging from health care to the environment to corporate power. Although U.S. leaders still pursued hegemony over recent decades, the public mood is now strikingly "blue" and growing bluer.

Public opinion polls, with the Pew polls again especially useful and detailed, have been documenting the public's increasing "blue mood" through most of the last decade, a shift that accelerated during the Bush years. Two-thirds of the public consistently support universal health care. Almost 90 percent support an increase in minimum wage. Three-fourths support much stronger environmental protection and far more aggressive action to prevent global warming; 60 percent of the public supports building labor rights and environmental rights into the heart of trade treaties, and 75 percent of the public believes that big business has too much power over our politics and is undermining our democracy.[22]

The same progressivism is evident on hot-button culture issues. A huge majority of the American public now supports equal rights for minorities and women, with unequivocal rejection of segregation and glass ceilings that were morally embraced by the public before the 1960s. A moral shift on abortion is also evident, since abortions were legally criminal and morally rejected until the *Roe v. Wade* decision in the early 1970s. Today, a majority of Americans now support abortion under certain conditions. The majority of the American public now also support gay civil unions—an even more striking change. A growing percentage question the death penalty, and a majority, while professing faith in God, believes in the clear separation of church and state.

This progressivism of the public is a reflection of the sustained success of the moral revolution that began with the civil rights and antiwar movements of the 1960s and continued in the following decades with the growth of the feminist, gay, and environmental movements. The immoral morality that elites propagate is, as we have argued at some length, a function not just of American hegemony but of the elites' continuing fear of the "sixties revolt." They are right to be afraid; the "question authority" buttons worn by sixties activists have created a questioning mentality widespread now in the general public. Polls show very low trust (typically below 40 percent) of leaders in virtually all institutions, from the mass media to the church, to big business. the government, and political parties themselves. Indeed, this goes beyond distrust of the leaders to a more systemic distrust of the institutions themselves.

Immoral morality in its current form—led by the nation's elites from Reagan to George W. Bush—is thus increasingly a backlash against a remarkable moral change and enlightenment in the general populace. While broadly vilified, the sixties catalyzed an enduring and irreversible progressive shift in the moral values of the people. The decline in American global hegemony is paralleled by the rise in counterhegemonic morality that the sixties activists first advanced. This has spread slowly in the general public but enough to create a decline in the credibility of our leaders at home—and of the institutions they represent. The majority of the U.S. public as it went to vote in 2008 saw an American political system and immoral morality out of whack with its own people. This was a decisive factor in the election of President Obama, whose values seemed closer to the public's.

The public's progressive morality is a powerful basis for hope. Whether or not American's global hegemony continues to decline, the new and blue morality of the public will increase the chances of a broader transformation in American culture and politics. Declining global hegemony at a time of economic collapse and increasingly progressive public morality among the U.S. public could meld into a strong force for systemic change. But such change requires a political vehicle to carry the new counterhegemonic morality and advance a new American vision.

The natural candidate to do this is the Democratic Party, now led by a new inspiring President. But for most of its history, with the possible exception of the New Deal era, the Democratic leadership has strongly embraced hegemonic morality. The party as a whole has failed to advance a systemic change, either in domestic or global moral vision. Since 1980, the party has become more closely tied to the large corporations, a co-champion of globalization and global hegemony, and more rejecting of any residues of counterhegemonic morality among the New Dealers. Prior to Obama, over the last thirty years, including the Clinton administration, the mainstream Democratic elites have moved, despite its opposition to the Iraqi war and the Bush administration's extremes, in a moral direction opposite to that of their own base and the progressive moral base of the nation.

This is not a stable situation. The strongest counterhegemonic morality in the nation lies among the Left social movements and the activist and net-root base of the Democratic Party. The party cannot survive if it does not begin to reflect and act on this new moral base and vision. It may create election victories, as in Obama's case, if only because of the public disgust with the legacy of the Republican Party's extreme immoral morality, the "free market" economic policies leading to the Wall Street meltdown, and a willingness to support "anybody but Bush." But if the Democrats, led by Obama, do not change in a more-proactive and meaningful way, they will find themselves without an activist base and will lose elections in the future.

The coming dance between the hegemonic Democratic Party led by President Obama and its activist counterhegemonic base will define the future of America. The Democratic Party under Obama could slowly relinquish its hegemonic morality, but this remains uncertain, as we show in the next chapter.

The lesson of Europe is to show the potential moral virtues of decline. Put differently, losing can create moral winners. The Europeans lost their Empires but were thereby forced to reject an immoral morality of indiscriminate winning. Decline put in place the conditions for a moral change that rejected winning at all costs.

The European model shows hope for the most difficult question: whether elites can abandon their ancient hegemonic values. Hegemonic decline has finally struck home, most deeply among the European publics, but increasingly with European elites. This is one of the few modern morality lessons of immense importance: that elites steeped in hegemonic morality can slowly embrace a new higher ground morality in the face of hegemonic decline.

The question the larger world is asking is whether the United States in the twenty-first century—and particularly its elites led by President Obama—might also begin to change its hegemonic moral values. Beginning to lose can be the start of a journey toward a new and better morality, one already visibly emerging in the American public. One must hope that American leaders will come to recognize that hegemonic winners are moral losers, mired in immoral morality, a lesson displayed throughout the history of civilization.

America—both its peoples and its leaders—will have to learn this lesson quickly before catastrophes strike. America has always prided itself on being a winner. But surviving as a nation and keeping peace in the world now require the rejection of Manifest Destiny, the White Man's Burden, and all the other moralities of winning to remain King of the Mountain. Americans must learn the lesson that hegemonic winners are today's losers. When we do, we will move beyond our immoral morality toward a higher moral ground. The world's survival depends on it.

10

My Brother's Keeper, My Sister's Keeper

Morality Wars in the Age of Obama

In his August 29, 2008, acceptance speech to the Democratic National Convention, Barack Obama proclaimed this:

> That's the promise of America, the idea that we are responsible for ourselves, but that we also rise or fall as one nation; the fundamental belief that *I am my brother's keeper; I am my sister's keeper.*[1]

Obama contrasted his moral philosophy with that of President Bush Jr. and the Republican Party. The "Republican philosophy," Obama said, gives

> more and more to those with the most and hope that prosperity trickles down to everyone else. *In Washington, they call this the Ownership society, but what it really means is, you're on your own.* Out of work? Tough luck. No health care? The market will fix it. Born into poverty? Pull yourself up by your own bootstraps, even if you don't have boots. *You're on your own.*[2]

Obama contrasts two starkly different visions of American morality. One emphasizes competition, the other community. One is "unilateralist" and isolating; the other based on interdependence and cooperation (pillars of Obama's global vision). The "on your own" competitive morality has long been a foundation of U.S. capitalist and hegemonic morality. "My brother's keeper" is tied to different values challenging "free markets" and hegemony.

The American people elected Obama in 2008 on a mandate of change. Obama ran as a "values" candidate. He expressed a new unifying morality leading the nation in a new direction—starting with ending the war in Iraq that he never supported. While Obama did not run on radical policies, he presented himself as somebody who would partner with the people to create a new America that would not start unjust U.S. wars, such as Iraq.

Cynics had reason to wonder whether Obama was for real. They had seen other Presidents, such as Bill Clinton, make similar promises and express similar values. Clinton had proclaimed "We need a new spirit of community, a sense that we are all in this together.... Our destiny is bound up with the destiny of every other American."[3] Clinton also called for a "peace dividend" after the Soviet Union collapsed, hinting at a less militarized America. Yet Clinton ended up promoting much of the "free market" and the wars of Presidents Reagan, Bush Sr., and Nixon himself.

Many Americans, though, sensed things might be different this time. Obama's words soared high and his values seemed to come from deep within him. He spoke of community at home and abroad, and he spoke as a man who had spent several formative years of his life as a community organizer, more concerned with fighting poverty than fighting wars.

Moreover, the crash of Wall Street and the broader meltdown of the economy in 2009 as Obama began his presidency put everything into a different context. The economic collapse meant the role of the United States in the world would also have to change. As discussed in the previous chapter, the economic crisis may be a tipping point in the long erosion of U.S. hegemony. If Obama wanted to solve the U.S. economic crisis and bring a new era of global peace, he would have to reassess not just the Iraq war but the U.S. role in the world. All the corporate and state structures promoting hegemony are intact, but the price of hegemony is becoming painfully high and unsustainable.

In the last chapter, we saw that Europe shifted away from its centuries-old imperial morality after the collapse of its Empires and its economies in World War II.[4] As Obama was elected, the United States confronted an economic debacle bringing the United States and much of the world's economies to their knees. While this crisis was different than the situation faced by Europe after World War II, the election of Obama during an economic meltdown makes possible a "regime change" in America itself. Opinion polls show the majority of the U.S. public supports "my brother's keeper" philosophy and seeks a drastically different U.S. direction, including a quick end to the Iraqi war and a new, more peaceful U.S. global role.

In this chapter, we look at the prospects for changes in morality and in the U.S. global role in the Obama era. Even presidents have trouble changing the direction of the ship of state, since many other corporate, political, and military hands are on the steering wheel. Elections themselves lead only very rarely to dramatic shifts in fundamental values, particularly when it comes to sacred doctrines like America's global power and goodness.[5]

Obama is also a complex politician facing huge political constraints. His own moral and political philosophy is multifaceted, often contradictory, and still a work in progress. His advisors are centrist or liberal technocrats. They are versed in the ways of the hegemonic global American system and less visionary than Obama himself. Contradiction may well be the operative word in the Obama years, with a step toward posthegemonic morals (e.g., drawing down troops in Iraq) followed by a step back (e.g., escalation in Afghanistan). It is a path whose ending lies shrouded in danger, promise, and mystery.

Obama's Morality and the Meltdown: A Perfect Storm for a Posthegemonic America?

As we pointed out in the previous chapter, historian Paul Kennedy[6] has argued that Empires fall on their own swords. He meant that hegemonic powers overextend themselves economically and politically in the process he calls "imperial overstretch." Hegemonic expansion ultimately leads to unsustainable costs that led to the collapse of Empires from Rome to Britain.

The Great Collapse of 2008 may represent the last phase of an overstretched U.S. hegemon. As discussed in the previous chapter, the economic meltdown of 2008 reflects an underlying stagnation in the real economy of U.S. capitalism, partly linked to globalization and U.S. military hegemony.[7] The turn toward financial services and speculation as the dominant economic enterprise has long marked the decline of hegemonic empires—and the current crisis is a different phenomenon than that seen in normal business cycles.[8] The structural roots of crisis in the U.S. capitalist model and the colossal magnitude of the economic collapse necessitate a regime change in U.S. economics and foreign policy. It will be the main driver of any major shift in U.S. foreign policy.

From his first days in office, President Obama set forth an ambitious commitment to renew the U.S. economy by bringing a new ethos of "my brother's keeper" to all aspects of our society. That requires fundamental shifts in domestic and foreign policy priorities, from hegemonic warfighting to rebuilding America and a peaceful world. But Obama and his advisors do not seem to understand the depth of the crisis and the policies required for fundamental transformation in a stagnant and failed U.S. capitalist model.

In most of this chapter, we shall be looking at the prospects for a more peaceful U.S. global role and morality. But we need to begin by considering America's problems at home since they are intertwined with any chance of a change in U.S. morality wars abroad. Like FDR,[9] Obama is approaching the U.S. economic crisis pragmatically and ambitiously. He aims to renew not just the economy but the health care system, the environment, the energy infrastructure, and the educational system.

It is far less clear, however, that he sees the true systemic roots of the crisis. He has not recognized the structural stagnation of the underlying economic system, the downward pressure on wages fueled by globalization, and the unsustainable costs of global military dominance.[10] This raises serious questions about his ability to bring about the changes we need, a matter we explore in detail shortly.

Obama's strength is that, rhetorically, he proposes to solve an interrelated set of economic, environmental, health care, and education crises based on his morality of "my brother's keeper." The phrase comes up over and over again in Obama's books and speeches:

> **Alone we are weak, but united we are strong. That is the essence of what America is all about.** That is why we're called the United States of America. And that's why we call it the *union* movement.
>
> That spirit of looking out for one another, that core value that says "**I am my brother's keeper, I am my sister's keeper,**" that spirit is most evident during times of great tragedy … it's most evident during times of great hardship, it's most when natural disasters strike.… We all understand that **we have to come together.**[11]

Obama strikes this same moral chord repeatedly:

> A belief that we are connected as one people. If there's a child on the south side of Chicago who can't read, that matters to me, even if it's not my child. If there's a senior citizen somewhere who can't pay for her prescription and has to choose between medicine and the rent, that makes my life poorer, even if it's not my grandmother. If there's an Arab American family being rounded up without benefit of an attorney or due process, that threatens my civil liberties. It's that fundamental belief—I am my brother's keeper, I am my sister's keeper—that makes this country work.[12]

In his first hundred days, Obama laid out a legislative agenda, suggesting that this might be more than moral rhetoric. Obama proposed to spend trillions to remake America. Obama committed $650 billion as a down payment to make sure that everyone can see a doctor and pay for their medical prescriptions. He committed more than $150 billion[13] to ensure that every child can read, learn, and go on to higher education. He proposed $50 billion[14] for building a new clean energy economy. He proposed billions more for reconstruction of the larger physical infrastructure and even more to stabilize and re-regulate the banks and larger financial system. All of these were part of a stimulus program to remake the economy and sustain it for the long term.

Critics claimed Obama was trying to do too much. But like FDR, Obama recognized that renewing and remaking the economy meant tackling many issues together to reform the Darwinian capitalism of Reagan and Bush. Obama called for a "paradigm shift"[15] in economics and made clear in his August 29, 2008, acceptance speech to the Democratic convention that his values led to a different measure of economic success:

> We measure the strength of our economy not by the number of billionaires we have or the profits of the Fortune 500, but by whether someone with a good idea can take a risk and start a new business, or whether the waitress who lives on tips can take a day off to look after a sick kid without losing her job, an economy that honors the dignity of work.

He added that "We measure progress by how many people can find a job that pays the mortgage; whether you can put a little extra money away at the end of each month so you can someday watch your child receive her college diploma."[16] When you factor in his emphasis on clean energy, Obama seemed to be proposing something like a Green New Deal. FDR had also proposed new values for a major economic "paradigm shift." FDR was not trying to overthrow capitalism; he was seeking to save capitalism from itself. But he changed core priorities and tilted the government toward a "brother's keeper" role rather than protecting the rich. For example, FDR supported important changes in mortgage agreements to protect people facing foreclosure.[17] This may have cost the banks money and weakened property contracts, but it gave the brother and sister on the street a better chance to stay in their homes.

Obama's agenda is less ambitious but has some similarities. It is hardly socialist, but it seeks to undo some of the damage of the last few decades and restore some New Deal social protections. Obama sees the economy and society itself as rooted in interdependence and mutual support; we need to be responsible to ourselves but just as much to our brothers and sisters. It is these bonds of community and mutual obligation that make or break us as individuals, a nation, and the world as a whole.

Obama clearly believes that the economic collapse reflects a collapse of these moral ties, a consequence of "you are on your own" policies of Reagan and Bush. His agenda is designed not just to revive the economy but also to remake parts of the social order based on reality of our interdependence and the morality of "my brother's keeper."

Obama's agenda, though, is still far too modest to solve the economic crisis and build a systemic morally grounded alternative. This is evident in his approach to the Wall Street bailouts. He and his team have poured trillions into rescuing AIG and other financial firms deemed "too big to fail."[18] But he has been unwilling to take the true control that the government's investment of taxpayer funds requires—and that remaking the economy demands. By pouring vast taxpayer rescue money into AIG, Citigroup, and other giant financial firms—more money than they are actually worth on the market—the government becomes the real owner of these companies and must protect the public. But when it comes to Wall Street, Obama's morality of "my brother's keeper" extends only to the financiers themselves. The bailouts represent solidarity with the financial class at the expense of workers and homeowners, with public monies rewarding the very financial elites who created the economic disaster.

Obama has not offered similar bailouts to workers losing their jobs and homeowners being foreclosed. His brother's keeper morality is being invoked selectively, a kind of socialism for the rich while failing to shelter the economically battered public at large. This helps to explain the public outrage at the infamous AIG bonuses, coming out of taxpayer money, and the growing public opposition to further bailouts of the biggest banks. Understandably, workers feel abandoned as the rich are rescued. Americans increasingly understand that risks are being socialized—that is, paid for by the workers—but that the profits are still privatized, gobbled up by the banks and CEOs. Nobel laureate economist Joseph Stiglitz calls this "ersatz capitalism";[19] others call it "lemon socialism."[20] Either way, it represents Obama's betrayal of his own moral philosophy of my "brother's keeper," and it could spell disaster for any hopes to remake the economy on new moral principles.

By passing the $787 billion stimulus plan in the first weeks of his administration, Obama made clear that he would not only bail out the biggest banks but also spend money to create green jobs for millions of workers, to provide expanded health care, and improve public education. This is a reflection that his brother's keeper philosophy may be more than just rhetoric—and that his Wall Street tilt in the bailouts does not define his entire domestic agenda. Meanwhile, grass roots social movements, on the Internet and on the ground, are working hard to make his brother's keeper agenda more socially transformative in the face of opposition from the financial and corporate oligarchy. Despite the firestorm of resistance in Washington, the key political reality is that the public supports the president and shares his "brother's keeper" values, as documented in the previous chapter.

Obama's costly domestic agenda may restrict what America can do in the world. Global hegemony requires huge military expenses that will only further balloon the deficits. Moreover, Obama's moral philosophy, extended to the world as a whole, sits in uneasy tension with American hegemony, which Obama has never renounced. In the rest of the chapter, we look at the contradictory prospects for a new U.S. moral approach in world affairs and a less hegemonic global role for America in the Obama era.

The Future of Hegemony: Obama, Global Interdependence, and American Morality Wars

The American public elected Obama as an antiwar candidate. His first and most important promise in the 2008 campaign was his opposition to the war in Iraq. Obama called the war "wrong" and "misguided." He distinguished himself from Hillary Clinton by saying that she voted to authorize the war while he opposed it from the beginning. However, his opposition to war was fundamentally tactical. It did not question the core assumptions underlying it.

His focus on opposition to the Iraq war was one of several factors leading many opponents of U.S. militarism to believe that Obama was on their side. Obama was harshly critical of more than just the war in Iraq. He denounced the following: torture; Bush's cowboy rhetoric of "you are either with me or the terrorists";[21] the hyper-moralistic neoconservative visions of war to spread democracy around the world; Bush's failure to talk to adversaries such as Iran and Syria; unilateralism; preemption, disregard for the UN, and international law; and the failure to build and sign international agreements on arms control, nuclear proliferation, an international criminal court, and global climate change.

Obama is clearly not a neoconservative. He will not use the same rhetoric to fight wars that we have heard in recent decades. He may continue to wage a war against al-Qaeda; he is continuing the Bush policy on executive power and domestic surveillance; and he is escalating U.S. involvement in Afghanistan and Pakistan, a very serious matter that we discuss more below. But his language is different; it abandons much neoconservative morality and appears to fall into a Democratic Party "realist" camp.[22] That position draws back from the hyper-moralism of the neoconservatives and their aggressive agenda to dominate the world militarily. American realists continue to assert U.S. leadership and the need to create a stable global balance of power through both military and diplomatic means. The realists use less lofty hyper-moralism, abandoning the rhetoric of U.S. Manifest Destiny and of a providential mission to spread freedom and democracy everywhere on the planet.

But none of this means the abandonment of U.S. hegemony. Democratic Party realists, including Obama's secretary of state Hillary Clinton and most of Obama's top advisors shaping U.S. policy in the Middle East, the Gulf, and Afghanistan and Pakistan, are well within the mainstream of U.S. hegemonic globalism. They bring a less strident and polarizing moral rhetoric. They offer a greater emphasis on diplomacy and "soft power" than the Bush neoconservatives. But they are not challenging U.S. hegemony, only embracing a more nuanced form of the morality wars—from Iran to Afghanistan and the war on terrorism—that we have described throughout this book.

Obama, himself, is less easy to characterize. He is still clearly evolving in his views of the U.S. role in the world. Just as he is not a captive of his technocratic economic team, he has a broader foreign policy vision and constituency than most of his foreign policy advisors. He has to answer to the anti-war community at home that helped elect him and to the world community that looks to him for a new U.S. direction.

Moreover, Obama's values do not fit neatly into traditional U.S. realism. He brings his brother's keeper philosophy to the world as a whole. Of course, there is a risk that a brother's keeper mentality could become precisely the rhetoric that requires bringing freedom and democracy to the rest of the world at the point of a sword, the hegemonic morality that justified American foreign policy throughout the empire's history. As seen throughout this book, Americans have often supported intervention in the name of helping their less fortunate global brothers and sisters facing tyranny, as in the case of Iraq. A brother's keeper morality, then, is an elastic moral rhetoric that could become a justification of hegemony in the Obama or successive eras.

However, Obama, at this writing, tends to use the language of "brother's keeper" as an expression of values opposite to competition, dominance, and hegemony. He means cooperation, community, and dialogue—on a world scale, not just in the United States. In the name of my "brother's keeper," he advocates for international law and the UN. His view of the common good extends to humanity as a whole, not just to America.

None of this, of course, implies Obama is abandoning U.S. hegemony. He is not. It does, though, imply the possibility of a new direction that might ultimately lead the nation toward a posthegemony world order.

Many forces—including Obama's rhetoric and the financial constraints of the Great Recession—lead Obama on a tentative new path away from hegemony, but many lead toward staying the hegemonic course. Two sources of evidence suggest that Obama will continue to pursue U.S. hegemony. We can look at (1) his speeches and (2) his policies, especially in Afghanistan and Pakistan. Many parts of his speeches can be jarring and even militaristic.

In his acceptance speech at the August 2008 Presidential Convention, the President said "I stood up and opposed this war (Iraq), knowing that it would distract us from the real threats we face." And then he immediately talked in tough terms about those "real threats":

> When John McCain said we could just "muddle through" in Afghanistan, I argued for more resources and more troops to finish the fight against the terrorists who actually attacked us on 9/11 and made clear that we must take out Osama bin Laden and his lieutenants if we have them in our sights. John McCain likes to say that he'll follow bin Laden to the Gates of Hell, but he won't even go to the cave where he lives.[23]

Obama was really saying he was tougher than McCain where it counted. He was the guy who would chase Bin Laden to the "Gates of Hell." He has shown he was serious by launching preemptive attacks into Pakistan from Afghanistan against Taliban and al-Qaeda operatives, a more provocative step than George W. Bush was willing to take. Obama went on to say further that "I will finish the fight against al Qaeda and the Taliban in Afghanistan. I will rebuild our military to meet future conflicts." Obama's plans at this writing are to increase U.S. troops in Afghanistan from 38,000 to 68,000.[24] U.S. and Afghan officials have announced that they seek hundreds of thousands more NATO and Afghan boots on the ground, increasing Afghan security forces alone from 130,000 in early 2009 to 350,000 as rapidly as possible. In a crucial meeting in early March

2009, Vice President Joe Biden argued for a limited Afghan mission to focus on fighting terrorism by weakening al-Qaeda and depriving it of an Afghan sanctuary, but General David Petraeus and Secretary of State Hillary Clinton argued for a broader, more ambitious agenda of "nation building." The same division, with Secretary of Defense Robert Gates siding with Clinton, split Obama's team throughout 2009. By doubling the number of troops and declaring that leaving Afghanistan is not an option, Obama appears to be closer to the hawkish, hegemonic positions of Clinton, Petraeus, and Gates.

In rhetoric that comes close to classic Manifest Destiny, candidate Obama proclaimed that in his foreign policy "America is once again that last best hope for all who are called to the cause of freedom...."[25] Now this can be dismissed as political rhetoric that a presidential candidate has to declare to get elected. This is undoubtedly a factor. But Obama has backed up this hegemonic war moralism with policies to fit. In his budget, he proposed a serious overall global buildup of the U.S. military. The rapid buildup in Afghanistan and the intensification of U.S. attacks into Pakistan from Afghanistan are just two components of a larger hegemonic policy that suggests, as military analyst Andrew Bacevich[26] has argued, more continuity than break from the Bush era. Bacevich, a former military officer and leading scholar of U.S. empire, believes that Obama is structurally restrained from any prospects of ending the hegemonic policy that has been at the core of U.S. foreign policy almost since the founding of the nation.

Many progressives rightly fear that Afghanistan—and the intensification of conflict within Pakistan due to the Afghan occupation and preemptive strikes into Pakistan itself—will be Obama's Vietnam.[27] It could destroy his hopes of rebuilding America and ruin his Presidency, just as Vietnam ended Lyndon Johnson's dream of building a Great Society at home. The political fragility of Pakistan and Obama's repeated strikes inside Pakistan to take out radical Taliban and al-Qaeda forces are reminiscent of Nixon's incursions into Cambodia and Laos. But since Pakistan has nuclear weapons and the entire Southwest Asian region is far more strategically important than were Cambodia or Laos—Obama is truly playing with fire. And no Great Power over centuries has gotten out of Afghanistan with hegemonic success or "victory," suggesting that Obama could crash and burn in Afghanistan, something that might lead to even greater military interventionism and disaster in Pakistan.

Moreover, Obama has fudged on his 16-month pullout of U.S. troops in Iraq, extending the drawdown of combat troops to 19 months[28] and leaving uncertain how many residual troops would remain long-term either in Iraq or just offshore on naval carriers in the Gulf. Obama is also talking tough about Iran and its potential for nuclear weapons, and he has not significantly realigned the U.S. tilt toward Israel in the Palestinian conflict, nor brought peace closer in that endless conflict, despite his appointment of George Mitchell as his special negotiator, a man known as more balanced than earlier U.S. envoys. He promises to continue a global battle against terrorism and to hunt down and destroy al-Qaeda. There is no talk about closing bases or drawing down U.S. forces around the world.

Despite all this hegemonic posturing, though, contradictions prevail—and it is the contradictions that make Obama interesting and offer at least modest hope of change. In his morality wars rhetoric about America as "that last best hope for all who are called to the cause of freedom,"[29] the context suggests something new. The morality rhetoric is used to legitimate different kinds of wars that are not military in nature. Yes, he says, "I will finish the fight against al-Qaeda and the Taliban in Afghanistan. I will rebuild our military to meet future conflicts."[30] His acceptance speech then moves abruptly to suggest a totally different global vision:

> I will build new partnerships to defeat the threats of the twenty-first century: terrorism and nuclear proliferation; poverty and genocide; climate change and disease. And I will restore our moral standing, so that America is once again that last, best hope for all who are called to the cause of freedom, who long for lives of peace, and who yearn for a better future.[31]

Here, Obama says that America's standing in the battle for freedom will not come in traditional military interventions for U.S. military dominance. Rather, his wars will be against nuclear proliferation, poverty, genocide, climate change, and disease. These are the true "threats of the twenty-first century."

This is a new view of threats and aims—and it is quite different than hegemonic morality. Wars against poverty, climate change, and disease are entirely different than wars of conquest. They are serious threats and ambitious goals but not those at the heart of a militarized hegemon's mission.

It is this new language that the Nobel Prize Committee recognized when they awarded Obama the 2009 Nobel Peace Prize. He was not being rewarded for his accomplishments but for a new American moral vision. The Nobel Committee almost certainly hoped that awarding the Peace Prize to Obama might increase the chances that he would walk the talk.

Looking more closely at Afghanistan creates a contradictory picture. We have noted above Obama's tough rhetoric about al-Qaeda and the

Taliban—and the worrisome expansion of the U.S. military footprint in Afghanistan. But while Obama wants to pursue bin Laden even to the "Gates of Hell" and is sending more troops to Afghanistan, he does not describe this as a mission of Manifest Destiny or Providence—or even democracy, despite a growing commitment to the language of "nation-building." The high-flying neoconservative morality rhetoric, at least, is gone. In its place is the morality of self-defense. To a lesser but important degree, Obama also speaks of stability and U.S. vital interests, as well as some form of nation-building agenda, but there is no moralistic vision of remaking Afghanistan into something that it is not. The troops are there to take out al-Qaeda and the most violent Taliban. Everything else is up for discussion and negotiation. By dialing down the rhetoric and aims, Obama is leaving himself the space to withdraw troops within a year or two, fulfilling his campaign promises and maintaining his political "credibility" but then getting out.

At this writing, we can't be sure which Obama will prevail. The hegemonic Obama has the upper hand. Every new president inherits centuries of U.S. militarism and Manifest Destiny—and is a virtual captive of the foreign policy establishment. Moreover, the powerful corporate, political, and military forces that created modern U.S. hegemony remain overwhelmingly dominant in Washington and still shape U.S. foreign policy by virtue of their financial clout, lobbying influence, and ideological power. U.S. dependency on foreign oil is just one of many structural conditions that will make it extremely difficult for Obama to withdraw forces from the Islamic Crescent or the world as a whole. The historic ideological pressures for sustaining hegemony are so great that even in the 1960s, Lyndon Johnson escalated forces in Vietnam, a war he thought the U.S. could not win, because he feared being branded "soft on Communism," and that he would be impeached. Such folly has not changed today, and it remains plausible at this writing that Obama will further rachet up military involvement in Afghanistan to counter Republican charges of weakness and to try to ensure his own re-election.[32]

The counterhegemonic Obama—more rhetoric than policy at this writing—embraces the dream of the peace movement in the U.S. and of peoples all over the world as symbolized by the Nobel Peace Prize award. But the hegemonic Obama will likely dominate his counterhegemonic alter-ego, the Obama recognized by the Nobel committee, unless the rest of us move quickly to support and pressure Obama to walk his more progressive talk. Obama has long claimed that "this moment is not about me. It's about you."[33] Nowhere is this more true than in the future of America's hegemony and morality wars. If the peace movement and the American progressive public stand up forcefully for their values and hold Obama and the nation to the "better angels of our nature"—a phrase from Lincoln's first Inaugural Address which many people associate with Obama[34]—we will see the beginning of a new genuinely moral world free of U.S. morality wars. We could begin the journey away from hegemony. It's up to us.

Notes

Notes to Introduction

1. "The Ministry of Reshelving," *Boston Globe* editorial page. August 21, 2005, E3.

2. Mark Silk, "The GOP Gets Religion," *Religion in the News* 6 (Spring 2003).

3. E. Neville Isdell, "Things Go Better with Social Justice," *Wall Street Journal*, February 3, 2007, A10, 21.

4. George Orwell, *1984* (New York: Signet, 1977), 35.

5. Ibid.

6. Trevor B. McCrisken, "Exceptionalism," in Frank Longevall et al. *Encyclopedia of American Foreign Policy* (New York: Simon & Schuster, 2001), 77.

7. George Fitzhugh, *The Failure of Free Society* (Ithaca, NY: Cornell University Press, 1854), 248.

8. David Christy, *The Kingdom of Cotton* (Augusta, GA: Abbot & Loomis, 1860), 335.

9. Antonio Gramsci, *Prison Notebooks* (New York: Columbia University Press, 1992).

10. Cited in Robert Minehart, *Information Warfare Tutorial* (Carlisle, PA: U.S. Army War College, 1999), Module 8.

11. Megan Rice, "I'm Tearing Up My Boston College Diploma," *Agape Community Christian Nonviolence*, June 2, 2006.

Notes to Chapter 1

1. Winston Churchill, *The River Wars: An Account of the Reconquest of the Sudan* (Chapel Hill, North Carolina: Project Gutenberg, 2004), 8.

2. Beck Sanderson, *Ethics of Civilization V. 5 Roman Empire 30 BC to 610* (Goleta, CA: World Peace Communication, 2004), Chap. 4.

3. Virgil, *Aeneid,* translated by John Dryden (New York: Penquin Classics, 1997), lines 283–294.

4. Wilfred McClay, "Founding of Nations," *First Things* (March 2006): 161.

5. Walter Oppelo and Stephen Rosow, *The Nation State and the Global Order* (Boulder, CO: Lynne Reiner Publishers, 2004), Chap. 1.

6. John Chuchiak, "The Imperial City of Rome" (Springfield, MO: Missouri

State University Press, 2001). http://history.missouristate.edu/jchuchiak/HST%
20101—Theme%2010—Imperial_city.htm.

7. Paul Halsall, *Library of Nicene and Post Nicene Fathers*, 2nd series (New York: Christian Literature Co., 1990), Vol 1, Chap. 28, 489–491.

8. Ibid., Chap. 31.

9. Cited in Lee Shelton, "The American Empire: An Unholy Alliance between Church and State," *Sierra Times*, Sept. 7, 2007.

10. Rudyard Kipling, "The White Man's Burden," *McClure's Magazine*, February 1899.

11. Cited in Robert Slater, "Black Rhodes Scholars in Academia," *The Journal of Blacks in Higher Education*, No. 2 (Winter 1993–1994): 102–107.

12. Cited in George Courtauld, *The Pocket Book of British Patriotism: The History of Great Britain and the World* (New York: Sterling, 2005), 37.

13. Cited in David Korten, *When Corporations Rule the World* (San Francisco, CA: Berrett-Koehler, 2001), 5.

14. Pratap Bhanu Mehta, "Empire and Moral Identity," *Ethics & International Affairs* 17 (2003): 49–62.

15. Robert Baden-Powell, *Scouting for Boys* (London: C. Arthur Pearson LTD, 1908), 10.

16. Ibid., 39.

17. Ibid., xi–xii.

18. William Garden Blaikie, *The Personal Life of David Livingstone* (Salt Lake City, UT: Gutenberg Literary Foundation, 2004).

19. Niall Ferguson, *Empire* (New York: Basic Books, 2004), 129.

20. Ibid., 101.

21. Ibid.

Notes to Chapter 2

1. Cited in Stout, "Bush Vows Not to Negotiate on Iraq Timetable," *New York Times*, March 28, 2007.

2. Cited in Pratap Bhanu Mehta, "Empire and Moral Identity," *Ethics & International Affairs* 17 (2003): 49–62.

3. Joseph S. Nye, Jr., "Propaganda Isn't the Way: Soft Power," *The International Herald Tribune*, January 10, 2003.

4. Dimitri K. Simes, "The Reluctant Empire," *Foreign Affairs* (Nov/Dec 2003).

5. Stephen Kinzer, *Overthrow: America's Century of Regime Change from Hawaii to Iraq* (New York: Henry Holt, 2006).

6. William Appleman Williams, *Empire as a Way of Life* (New York: Oxford), 43.

7. Alexander Hamilton, John Jay, and James Madison, *The Federalist Papers* (New York: Signet Classics, 2003), Paper 11.

8. Cited in Hezekiah Niles, *Centennial Offering: Republication of the Principles and Acts of the Revolution in America* (New York: A. S. Barnes & Co, 1876), 340.

9. Frank Bond, "Louisiana and the Louisiana Purchase," Government Printing Office, 1912 Map, No. 4.

10. Cited in C. C. Goen, "Jonathan Edwards: A New Departure in Eschatology," *Church History* 28 (March 1959): 25.

11. Williams, 19.

12. Ibid., 17.

13. Ibid., 45.

14. Hamilton, Jay, and Madison, Paper 10.

15. John Taylor, *An Inquiry into the Principles and Policy of the Government of the United States* (Fredericksburg, VA: Green and Cady, 1814).

16. Ibid., 509.

17. Cited in MacDougall, "Empire as American as Apple Pie," *Monthly Review* (May 2005).

18. Thomas Jefferson, *On Politics and Government* (Charlottesville, VA: University of Virginia, 1809).

19. Ibid., 28.

20. Ibid., 30.

21. Andrew Jackson, Address to Congress, December 8, 1830.

22. Andrew Jackson, Address to Congress, December 3, 1833.

23. John L. Sullivan, "The Great Nation of Futurity," *The United States Democratic Review* 6 (1839): 426–430.

24. Stephen Austin, speech in Louisville, Kentucky, March 7, 1836.

25. Sullivan, "The Great Nation of Futurity."

26. Austin, speech in Louisville, Kentucky.

27. Sullivan, "The Great Nation of Futurity."

28. Grover Cleveland, Address to Congress, December 1896.

29. General James Rusling, "Interview with President William McKinley," *The Christian Advocate*, January 22, 1903, 17; reprinted in Daniel Schirmer and Stephen Rosskamm Shalom, eds., *The Philippines Reader* (Boston: South End Press, 1987), 22–23.

30. Brad Bauer, "Continuity of U.S. Imperial Legitimation," 2006.

31. Cited in James MacGregor, *The Three Roosevelts: Patrician Leaders Who Transformed America* (Berkeley, CA: Grove Press, 2002), 45.

32. Theodore Roosevelt, *The Rough Riders* (New York: Charles Scribner's Sons, 1899).

33. Cited in Maurice Lemoine, "Uncle Sam's Manifest Destiny," *Le Monde Diplomatique*, May 2003.

34. Williams, 131.

35. Roosevelt.

36. Cited in Jerome Karabel, *The Chosen* (Boston, MA: Mariner Books, 2006), 43.

37. William McKinley, "The Acquisition of the Philippines," U.S. Department of State, Papers Relating to Foreign Affairs, 1898, 904–908.

38. Quoted in George Marion, *Bases and Empire* (New York: Fairplay Publishers, 1949), 84–85.

39. Quoted by Vince Copeland in "The Republocrats," *Workers World*, No. 17, 1998.

40. Fareed Zakaria, "Annals of Foreign Policy: Our Way, The Trouble with Being the World's Only Superpower," *The New Yorker*, October 14, 2002, 72–81.

41. Woodrow Wilson, Address supporting the League of Nations, Sioux Falls, South Dakota, September 8, 1919.

42. Woodrow Wilson, Address to the United States Senate on essential terms of peace in Europe, January 22, 1917.

43. Williams, 136.

44. Woodrow Wilson, Campaign Address in Jersey City, New Jersey, May 25, 1912.

45. Harry S. Truman, Address before a Joint Session of Congress, March 12, 1947.

46. Ibid.

47. Quoted by Molly Ivins, at http://www.TruthDig.com, March 14, 2006.

48. Quoted by Jack Brubaker, in "Bush Quietly Meets with Amish Here: They Offer Their Prayers," *Lancaster New Era*, July 16, 2004.

49. Ron Suskind, "Faith, Certainty and the Presidency of G. W. Bush," *New York Times*, October 17, 2004.

50. Andrew Bacevich, *The New American Militarism* (New York: Oxford, 2005), 117–118.

51. Samuel Berger, Remarks to the National Press Club, January 7, 2000.

52. Bachevich, 126.

53. Ibid., 127.

54. Ibid.

55. Suskind, 50.

56. George W. Bush, Remarks at a Town Hall Meeting with citizens of Ontario, Ontario Convention Center, California, January 5, 2002.

57. George W. Bush, State of the Union Address, January 2006.

58. George W. Bush, Inaugural Address, January 20, 2001.

59. George W. Bush, Address to Joint Session of Congress, September 21, 2001.

60. George W. Bush, in St. Charles, Missouri, November 2, 2002.

61. Cited in Suskind, 46.

Notes to Chapter 3

1. Quoted in John B. Judis, *The Folly of Empire: What George W. Bush Could Learn from Theodore Roosevelt and Woodrow Wilson* (New York: Simon and Schuster, 2004), 14.

2. Walt Whitman, "The Errand-Bearers," *New York Times*, June 27, 1860.

3. Louis Althusser, "Ideology and the State: Lenin and Philosophy," *Monthly Review Press*, 1970, 127–186.

4. Ann Coulter, *Godless: The Church of Liberalism* (New York: Crown Publishing Group, 2006).

5. Bernard Goldberg, *100 People Who Are Screwing Up America* (New York: Harper-Collins, 2005).

6. Quoted in Goldberg.

7. Quoted in Richard W. Stevenson and Nagourney, "Bush's Campaign Emphasizes Role of Leader in War," *New York Times*, March 17, 2004.

8. Quoted in Maureen Dowd, *New York Times*, August 5, 2006, A26.

9. Emile Durkheim, *The Elementary Forms of the Religious Life*, translated by Karen Fields, (New York: Free Press, 1995).

10. Henry Fountain, "The Lonely American Just Got a Bit Lonelier," *New York Times*, July 2006.

11. Karl Marx, *Marx on Religion*, edited by John Raines (Philadelphia, PA: Temple University Press, 2002).

12. Quoted in *Bringing Watch*, November 15, 2005.

13. Karl Marx, "The Communist Manifesto," in *Karl Marx: Selected Writings*, edited by Lawrence H. Simon (Indianapolis, IN: Hackett, 1994), 161.

14. Thomas Frank, *What's the Matter with Kansas* (New York: Metropolitan Books, 2004).

Notes to Chapter 4

1. Adolph Hitler, *Mein Kampf*, translated by Ralph Manheim (Boston, MA: Houghton Mifflin, 1971).

2. Ibid., 65.

3. Ibid., 534.

4. John Weiss, *The Fascist Tradition: Radical Right-Wing Extremism in Modern Europe* (New York: Harper & Row, 1967), 12.

5. A. James Gregor, *The Ideology of Fascism: The Rationale of Totalitarianism* (New York: Free Press, 1969), 142.

6. Ibid., 143.

7. Ibid., 143.

8. Ibid., 144.

9. Ibid., 155.

10. Ibid., 155.

11. Ibid., 172.

12. Ibid., 12.

13. Roger Griffen, *The Nature of Fascism* (New York: St. Martin's, 1993), 32–33.

14. Ibid., 33.

15. Ibid., 35.

16. 6 Ibid., 37.

17. Ibid., 38.

18. Ibid., 38.

19. Ibid., 39.

20. Konrad Heiden, *Introduction to Mein Kampf* (Boston, MA: Houghton Mifflin, 1998).

21. Hitler, *Mein Kampf*, 290.

22. Ibid., 231.

23. Ibid., 232.

24. Ibid., 257.

25. Aldoph Hitler, first radio address, February 1, 1933.

26. Michael Burleigh and Wolfgang Wipperman, *The Racial State: Germany 1933–1945* (New York: Cambridge University Press, 1991), 188.

27. Ibid., 183.

28. Walter Laquer, *Weimar, A Cultural History 1918—1933* (New York: G. P. Putnam's Sons, 1974), 228.

29. Ibid., 228.

30. Hitler, *Mein Kampf*, 258.

31. Ibid., 258.

32. Ibid., 259.

33. Ibid., 263.

34. Ibid., 267.

35. Ibid., 267.

36. Ibid., 303.

37. Ibid., 303.

38. Ibid., 290.

39. Ibid., 298.

40. Ibid., 299.

41. Ibid., 299

42. Ibid., 299.

43. Ibid., 299.

44. Ibid., 280.

45. Ibid., 170.

46. Ibid., 171.

47. Ibid., 172.

48. Ibid., 172.

49. Adolph Hitler, *The Speeches of Adolph Hitler, 1922–1939, Vol. 1* (London: Oxford University Press, 1969), 369–372.

50. Hitler, *Mein Kampf,* 383–384.

51. George Mosse, *The Crisis of German Ideology* (New York: Grosset & Dunlap, 1964), 4.

52. Ibid., 4.

53. Ibid., 16.

54. Ibid., 17.

55. Ibid., 4–5.

56. Ibid., 17.

57. John Weiss, *The Fascist Tradition* (New York: Harper & Row, 1967), 2.

58. Ibid., 2.

59. Data from Richard Evans, *The Coming of the Third Reich* (London: Penquin, 2003), 209.

60. Ibid., 261.

61. Ibid., 340.

Notes to Chapter 5

1. Quoted by Roger Ebert, *Chicago Sun-Times,* March 30, 2003.

2. Ibid.

3. Alexander Hamilton Stephens, at Savannah, Georgia, March 21, 1861.

4. Jefferson Davis, at Fanueil Hall, Boston, Mass., October 11, 1858. Transcribed from Dunbar Rowland, ed., *Jefferson Davis, Constitutionalist,* Volume 3, 315–332.

5. Susan Lawrence Davis, *The Authentic History of the Ku Klux Klan* (New York: American Library Service, 1924).

6. Stanley F. Horn, *Invisible Empire: Story of the Ku Klux Klan 1866–1871* (Dahlonega, GA: Crown Rights Book Co., 1939).

7. D. W. Griffith, *Birth of a Nation,* DVD (Narbeth, PA: Alpha Video, 2005).

8. Louis Rubin et al., *I'll Take My Stand: The Twelve Southerners* (New York: Harper, 1962), xlii.

9. David O. Selznick, *Gone With The Wind,* DVD (Burbank, CA: Turner Entertainment Co., 1999).

10. Rubin, xliii.

11. Selznick.

12. David Pilgrim, *What Was Jim Crow,* Museum of Racist Memorabilia, Ferris State University, Big Rapids, Michigan, September 2000.

13. Stetson Kennedy, *Jim Crow Guide: The Way It Was* (Boca Raton, FL: Atlantic University Press, 1959/1990), 216–217.

14. Dr. Martin Luther King, Jr., National Historic Site Interpretive Staff, January 5, 1998.

15. R. Gordon Thornton, *The New Rise of the Old South* (Gretna, LA: Pelican Books, 2000).

16. Cited in Thornton, 16.

17. Thornton, 16.

18. Ibid., 17.

19. Ibid., 15.

20. Ibid., 16.

21. George Wallace, Inaugural Address, 1963; Alabama Department of Archives and History, Montgomery, Alabama.

22. Ibid.

23. Ibid.

24. Richard Nixon, Acceptance Speech, Republican National Convention, 1968; recorded at John Woolley and Gerhard Peters; *The American Presidency Project* [http://www.presidency.ucsb.edu]. Santa Barbara, CA: University of California.

Notes to Chapter 6

1. George W. Bush, *A Charge to Keep* (New York: Morrow, 2001), Chapter 10.

2. Andrew Carnegie, *The Gospel of Wealth* (Cambridge, MA: Harvard University Press, 1962).

3. Ibid.

4. Lee Atwood interview by Bob Herbert, *New York Times*, October 6, 2005.

5. Reported by Bob Herbert, "A Platform of Bigotry," *New York Times*, September 28, 2006, A23.

6. Quoted by Ted Olsen, "Dobson Again Calls For Parents To Pull Kids Out," *Christianity Today*, July 24, 2002.

7. Quoted by Chris Hedges, *American Fascists* (New York: Free Press, 2007).

8. Quoted by Linda Kimball, "The Real Evil of Evolutionary Humanism," *Sierra Times*, November 15, 2005.

9. Donald Rumsfeld, speech delivered at the 88th Annual American Legion National Convention, Salt Lake City, Utah, August 29, 2006.

10. Chip Berlet, "The Roots of the Culture War," *The Nizkor Project*, February 18, 1996.

11. Frank Donner, cited in Berlet.

12. Berlet.

13. American Computer Science Association Inc., "Is Kerry a Traitor?" New York, October 11, 2004.

14. Lynn Cheney, *Telling the Truth* (New York: Touchstone, 1996).

15. Ibid.

16. Transcript of the telecast of the "700 Club," September 13, 2001.

17. Ibid.

18. Ibid.

19. Griffin, *The Nature of Fascism*.

20. Gil Troy, *Morning in America: How Ronald Reagan Invented the 1980s* (Princeton, N.J.: Princeton University Press, 2005).

21. George W. Bush Speech, in Grand Rapids, Michigan, January 2003.

22. Chris Hedges, "The Christian Right and the Rise of American Fascism," Center for Religion, Ethics and Social Policy, Cornell University, Ithaca, New York, 2004.

23. Quoted in Frederick Clarkson, "Theocratic Domination Gains Influence," *The Public Eye Magazine* (Somerville, MA: Political Research Association, May/June 1994).

24. Clarkson.

25. *Holy Bible: Standard Edition* (New York: Doubleday, 1999).

26. Stephen McDowell and Mark Bellies, *America's Providential History* (Charlottesville, VA: Providence Foundation, 1989), 19.

27. Ibid., 184.

28. Tim LeHaye and Jerry Jenkins, *Left Behind* (Wheaton, IL: Tyndale House Publishers, 2000).

29. George W. Bush, Address from the Oval Office, September 11, 2006.

30. Glenn Plummer quoted in Chris Hedges, "Soldiers of Christ II: Feeling the Hate with the National Religious Broadcasters," *Harpers,* May 2005.

31. John Hagee, *Jerusalem Countdown* (Lake Mary, FL: Frontline, 2006).

32. Cited in Clarkson, "Theocratic Domination Gains Influence."

33. Gary North, "Capitalism and the Bible," 2006. Accessed at http://goldismoney. info/forums/.

34. Cited in Gordon Bigelow, "Let There Be Markets: The Evangelical Roots of Economics," *Harper's,* May 2005.

35. McDowell and Bellies, 251.

36. Cited in Edd Doerr, "Pat Robertson's Agenda for America," *USA Today,* July 1996.

37. Tom Rose, *Biblical Economics* (Mercer, PA: American Enterprise Publications, 2006).

38. David Van Biema and Jeff Chu, "Does God Want You to Be Rich? A Holy Controversy," *Time,* September 7, 2006.

39. *Holy Bible: Standard Edition.*

40. Joel Osteen, *Your Best Life Now* (New York: Warner Books, 2004).

41. Data from Richard Evans, *The Coming of the Third Reich* (London: Penquin, 2003), 340.

42. The Pew Research Center for the People and the Press, "Many Americans Uneasy with Mix of Religion and Politics," August 24, 2006.

43. Ibid.

44. Ibid.

45. The two best sources of this poll data that pull together a composite of all major polls on political attitudes are, first, PollingReport.com, at www.pollingreport.com. Second, see Media Matters for Americans, "Progressive Majority: Why a Conservative America is a Myth," 2007, at www.mediamatters.org/progmaj/report.

46. Frank, *What's The Matter With Kansas.*

Notes to Chapter 7

1. Anonymous, Center for Computer Intelligence; "Politically Correct Dictionary." Accessed at http://funny2.com/dictionary.htm.

2. Charles Osgood, accessed at http://www.saidwhat.co.uk/quotes/political/ charles_osgood.

3. Robert Louis Stevenson, *An Inland Voyage* (Whitefish, MT: Kessinger Publishing, 2004), Ch. 3.

4. Noam Chomsky, *Necessary Illusions* (Boston: South End Press, 1989).

5. Todd Gitlin, *The Intellectuals and the Flag* (New York: Columbia University Press, 2007).

6. George W. Bush, State of the Union Address, January 29, 2002.

7. Noam Chomsky, *Failed States* (New York: Henry Holt, 2007).

8. Edward Herman, *The Real Terror Network* (Montreal, Canada: Black Rose Books, 1985).

9. Thomas Friedman, *The Lexus and the Olive Tree* (New York: Farrar, Straus and Giroux, 1999), 104.

10. Ibid.

11. Thomas Friedman, *The World Is Flat* (New York: Farrar, Straus and Giroux, 2005).

Notes to Chapter 8

1. Will Hutton, "Race in Britain," *The Observer,* December 16, 2001.

2. Jean-Jacques Rousseau, *The Social Contract,* translated by Maurice Cranston (New York: Penquin Classics, 1983), Book II, Chapter 4, 74.

3. Quoted in Richard Covington, "Marie Antoinette," *Smithsonian,* November 2006.

4. Jean-Baptiste Duvergier, *Collection complète des lois décrets, ordonnances, règlements, avis du conseil d'état ... de 1788 a 1830 ...,* 2nd ed., 110 vols. (Paris, 1834–1906) 6: 172–173.

5. Maximilien Robespierre, "On the Principles of Political Morality," February 1794, translated by Paul Halsall, Fordham University, August 1997.

6. Vladimir Lenin, in "What Is to Be Done?" *Lenin V.I., Collected Works V5,* translated by Nathaniel Knight, Moscow, 1964.

7. Ibid.

8. Frank Smitha, "Purges and Hysteria in the Soviet Union," Macro History, 1998.

9. Ibid.

10. Robert Conquest, *The Great Terror* (New York: Oxford University Press, 1991).

11. Cited by Patricia Cohen, "Communist Party USA Gives Its History to NYU," *New York Times,* March 20, 2007.

12. Richard Flacks, *Making History* (New York: Columbia University Press, 1988).

13. Ibid., 149–150.

14. Tom Hayden, *The Port Huron Statement: The Vision Call of the 1960s Revolution* (New York: Thunder's Mouth Press, 2005).

15. Rosa Luxemburg, "The Problem of Dictatorship," *The Russian Revolution* (Ann Arbor, MI: Ann Arbor Paperbacks for the Study of Communism and Marxism, 1981).

16. Quoted by Judy Gradford, *If I Can't Dance It's Not My Revolution: Music as a Force for Change* (Rochester, NY: Hartland Music, 2007).

17. Brandeis University, 1970. From a personal memory of a speech.

18. The Sixties Project, *Rules of the Black Panther Party* (Charlottesville, VA: Institute for Advanced Technology in the Humanities, 1993).

19. Ibid.

20. Ibid.

21. Elizabeth Janeway, *Powers of the Weak* (New York: Random House, 1988).

22. Catharine A. MacKinnon (with Andrea Dworkin), "The Roar on the Other Side of Silence," *In Harm's Way: The Pornography Civil Rights Hearings* (Cambridge, MA: Harvard University Press, 1997).

23. William Wilson, *The Truly Disadvantaged* (Chicago, IL: University of Chicago Press, 1990).

24. Robert Michels, *Political Parties* (Piscataway, NJ: Transaction Publishers, 1999).

Notes to Chapter 9

1. Thomas Frank; *What's the Matter with Kansas* (New York: Metropolitan Books, 2004), 251.

2. Ibid., 250.

3. Jared Diamond, *Collapse* (New York: Penquin, 2005).

4. Robert Kagan, *Of Paradise and Power* (New York: Vintage, 2004).

5. Jeremy Rifkin, *The European Dream* (New York: Penquin, 2005).

6. Art Preis, "No Classes in U.S.? Myth of 'People's Capitalism,'" *International Socialist Review*, 23 (Winter 1962): 3–9.

7. International Monetary Fund, 2005.

8. U.S. Bureau of Labor Statistics.

9. Board of Governors of the Federal Reserve System.

10. Gil Troy, *Morning in America: How Reagan Invented the 1980s* (Princeton, NJ: Princeton University Press, 2007).

11. Ronald Reagan, Remarks at the Annual Convention of the National Association of Evangelicals, Orlando, Florida; March 8, 1983.

12. Tania Branigan, "China Calls for End to Dollar's Reign as Global Reserve Currency," *The Guardian*, March 24, 2009.

13. *Syndey Morning Herald*, September 26, 2008.

14. Jon Meacham and Even Thomas, "We Are All Socialists Now," *Newsweek*, February 16, 2009, p. 23.

15. Paul Kennedy, *The Rise and Fall of Great Powers* (New York: Vantage, 1989).

16. David Brooks, *New York Times*; February 1, 2007, p.A23.

17. Ibid.

18. Ibid.

19. Randy Newman, "A Few Worlds in Defense of Our Country," *New York Times*, February 1, 2007, p. A23.

20. Noam Chomsky, *Hegemony or Survival* (New York: Metropolitan Books, 2003).

21. The Pew Research Center for the People and The Press.

22. Ibid.

Notes to Chapter 10

1. Barack Obama, Acceptance Speech, Democratic National Convention, Denver, Colorado, August 29, 2008.

2. Ibid.

3. William Clinton, Little Rock, Arkansas; October 3, 1991.

4. Jeremy Rikin, *The European Dream* (New York: Jeremy P. Tarcher, 2004).

5. Charles Derber, *Regime Change Begins at Home* (San Francisco, CA: Berrett-Koehler, 2004); *Hidden Powers* (San Francisco, CA: Berrett-Koehler, 2005).

6. Paul Kennedy, *The Rise and Fall of Great Powers* (New York: Vantage, 1989).

7. John Bellany Foster and Fred Magdoff, *The Great Financial Crisis* (New York: Monthly Review Press, 2009), 41–42.

8. Kevin Philips, *Bad Money* (New York; Penquin, 2009).

9. Yale Magrass, *Thus Spake the Moguls* (Cambridge, MA: Schenkman, 1981); William Leuchtenburg, *Franklin D. Roosevelt and the New Deal* (New York: Harper, 1963).

10. Seymour Melman, *Pentagon Capitalism* (New York: McGraw-Hill, 1970), 22.

11. Barack Obama, Speech, Milwaukee, Wisconsin, September 2, 2008.

12. Barach Obama, Videotaped Message to the Iranian People; March 20, 2009.

13. Sam Dillon, "Stimulus Plan Would Provide Flood of Aid to Education," *New York Times*; January 27, 2009.

14. David Herszenhorn, "Congress Moves on Stimulus Bill and Bailout Money;" *New York Times*; January 15, 2009.

15. "The Stimulus Debate," *New York Times* Editorial, January 10, 2009.

16. Barack Obama, Acceptance Speech, Democratic National Convention.

17. Yale Magrass, *Thus Spake the Moguls*; Leuchtenburg, *Franklin D. Roosevelt and the New Deal.*

18. Bill Saporito, "How AIG Became Too Big to Fail;" *Time*, March 19, 2009.

19. Joseph Stiglitz, "Obama's Ersatz Capitalism," *New York Times*; March 31, 2009.

20. Robert Reich, "How America Embraced Lemon Socialism," January 23, 2009. http://robertreich.blogspot.com/2009/01/how-america-has-embraced-lemon.html.

21. George W. Bush, quoted in *Chicago Sun-Times*, September 21, 2001.

22. Andrew Bacevich, *Limits of Power* (New York: Holt, 2009).

23. Barack Obama, Acceptance Speech, Democratic National Convention.

24. CNN, February 18, 2009.

25. Barack Obama, Acceptance Speech, Democratic National Convention.

26. Bacevich, *Limits of Power.*

27. John Barry and Thomas Evans, "Obama's Vietnam," *Newsweek*, February 9, 2009.

28. Peter Baker and Thom Shanker, "Obama's Iraq Plan Has December Elections as Turning Point for Pullout;" *New York Times*, February 25, 2009.

29. Barack Obama, Acceptance Speech, Democratic National Convention.

30. Ibid.

31. Ibid.

32. Kennedy almost annihilated the planet rather than appear weak by accepting Soviet missiles in Cuba, which he knew posed little real threat to the United States. Roosevelt knew he would not survive a fourth term and whoever he named vice president would soon be president. His third-term Vice President, Henry Wallace, would almost certainly continue his policy of cooperating with the ally who bore most of the burden for defeating Nazi Germany, the Soviet Union. Wallace's program would have prevented an arms escalation that could have erupted into a third world war and did cost 100,000 American lives in Korea and Vietnam. The money that was spent on weapons would

have been freed to build a peaceful domestic economy. Instead, Roosevelt succumbed to pressure from anticommunist Republicans and Southerners within his own party to replace Wallace with Harry Truman, protégé of the corrupt Pendergast machine of Missouri. Under Truman, the cold war bloomed.

33. Barack Obama, Acceptance Speech, Democratic National Convention.

34. John Nichols, "The Better Angels of Our Nature," *The Nation*, November 4, 2008; John Ellis, "The Better Angels Side with Obama," *Los Angeles Times*, January 19, 2009.

Index

About the Authors

Charles Derber, a noted social critic, is professor of sociology at Boston College. He is the author of thirteen internationally acclaimed books, including *Corporation Nation, Hidden Power,* and *The Wilding of America.* His books have been translated into multiple languages, and he speaks on and writes for the mass media. He is a longtime social activist working for democracy and social justice.

Yale R. Magrass is a chancellor professor of sociology at the University of Massachusetts–Dartmouth, where he teaches social theory, political sociology, and the social impact of science and technology. He is the author of three other books and more than thirty articles, including encyclopedia entries; has served on the board of six journals; has been a recipient of several grants; and has participated in numerous international forums.